Ordinary WONDERS

Stories of Unexpected Grace

OLESIA NIKOLAEVA

Translated by
ALEXANDRA WEBER

T0164204

HOLY TRINITY PUBLICATIONS
THE PRINTSHOP OF ST JOB OF POCHAEV
Holy Trinity Monastery
Jordanville, New York
2018

Printed with the blessing of His Eminence,
Metropolitan Hilarion, First Hierarch
of the Russian Orthodox Church Outside of Russia

Ordinary Wonders: Stories of Unexpected Grace
© 2018 Holy Trinity Monastery

PRINTSHOP OF
SAINT JOB OF POCHAEV

An imprint of

 HOLY TRINITY PUBLICATIONS
Holy Trinity Monastery
Jordanville, New York 13361-0036
www.holytrinitypublications.com

Cover Design: James Bozeman
Cover Art: Watercolor by Archimandrite Cyprian (Pyzhov)

Originally published in Russian by
Sretensky Monastery Publications, Moscow, 2015

ISBN: 978-0-88465-423-0 (Paperback)
ISBN: 978-0-88465-466-7 (ePub)
ISBN: 978-0-88465-467-4 (Mobipocket)

Library of Congress Control Number: 2018933774

The publication was effected under the auspices of the
Mikhail Prokhorov Foundation TRANSCRIPT Programme
to Support Translations of Russian Literature.

Scripture passages taken from the New King James Version.
Copyright © 1982 by Thomas Nelson, Inc. Used by permission.
Deuterocanonical passages taken from the Orthodox Study Bible.
Copyright © 2008 by Thomas Nelson, Inc. Used by permission.
Psalms taken from A Psalter for Prayer, trans. David James
(Jordanville, N.Y.: Holy Trinity Publications, 2011).

Contents

In Lieu of an Introduction

I understand that it may be considered indelicate, if not impertinent or even a sign of spiritual delusion, to relate miraculous stories of events that happened to you or your friends . . . I know many wonderful people who lead spiritually rich lives and who are wary of speaking about miracles that occurred in their own lives, considering this a very personal and intimate subject.

Nevertheless, having weighed the "pros and cons," I will take that risk, for any stories that witness to the workings of providence in the world and in the human soul, to the mercy of our God and Saviour, to the fact that "where God wills, the order of nature is overruled" are comforting, joyful, and spiritually uplifting.

Such moments are revealed to an individual within the Church, which keeps and manifests the "mysteries of the heavenly kingdom" in the form of its sacraments, services, and prayers. But occasionally, this also occurs in love, in the sense of approaching death, in the moment of making a moral choice, in rejoicing, in sorrow; it happens especially when the individual, turning to God, begins to see with believing eyes, if only a little, if only nearsightedly, if only "in a mirror, dimly" (1 Cor 13:12), feeling their inviolable connection to the Creator of all, asking divine providence for help and answers, and receiving them in the end. In this manner, the entire life of a believing person becomes a continuously unfolding miracle, the reading of astonishing works, of which, of course, they understand far from everything, only partly, a little bit, only just . . .

Each time, even in the seemingly least significant instance, this is a manifestation of the glory of God. Sometimes it's impossible to express this in human language, for it is indescribable. Sometimes it's directed at you individually, and if you attempt to relate it to someone in fear, wonder, and trembling, your confidant may not understand you: what is really so miraculous about that?

Thus, I once arrived at the Lavra[1] to see the elder Archimandrite Kirill. I was afflicted with a terrible problem—insomnia. At night I would fall asleep, at best for an hour and a half, when suddenly I would be woken as if by an internal shock, after which, in spite of my overwhelming fatigue, I couldn't close my eyes any more. This continued for almost two years. In addition, I also stopped eating.

Emaciated and distraught in my infirmity, I finally presented myself to Fr Kirill. He listened to me attentively—gentle, loving, and compassionate as always—gave me a box of candy, and said:

"You need rest . . ."

"Father, what rest? How am I supposed to get it? I have a large family, and so many cares, fears, passions, things to do, all the hustle and bustle . . ."

"You need rest," repeated Fr Kirill. "Go right now and venerate St Sergius . . ."

I left his cell in disbelief.

"Rest, indeed," I thought, "easy for him to say! And how am I supposed to get it? Lord, I'm perishing!"

With these thoughts I went inside the Church of the Holy Trinity.

At that very moment, the priest had begun to read the Gospel—an excerpt with which I was, of course, not only familiar, but which I also knew by heart. I froze in my tracks in the entryway.

"Come to Me, all you who labor and are heavy laden, and I will give you rest" (Mt 11:28).

The word "rest" struck me in the heart and filled it with rest. A word that I had heard many times suddenly became a living word, having as it were its own existence, containing reality, a word of healing, a word addressed personally to me.

It would be ungrateful of me to forget this word or to pay it no attention.

"If I forget you, O Jerusalem, may my right hand forget its skill."

But there are also stories from church life that are amusing, awkward, even humorous. These are sometimes told by monks, priests, or parishioners to one another . . . And why not smile in response to hearing them?

There is a story in an old patericon[2] about a father—an ascetic who led a holy life—who occasionally joked or laughed about something with his students.

People asked him, "How can you do that?"

And he replied, "If you tighten a bowstring too much, it can snap from the pressure. So you must loosen it from time to time."

Many names and titles in theses stories are true, but others have been changed: in such cases the names are of no consequence to the reader, while the true heroes of the stories are thus protected from curious eyes.

To everything that has taken place and been recorded here, there is nothing to add except: O Lord, glory to Thee!

The Conjurer of Rain

The following story is often told about Archimandrite Seraphim (Tiapochkin).

Archimandrite Seraphim served in the village of Rakitnoe, Belgorod Region. The Church authorities had sent him there after many years spent in concentration camps, which changed him so much that he was unrecognizable in appearance. When he returned home to his native Dnepropetrovsk, his own mother didn't recognize him.

When he arrived there, the church in Rakitnoe was in deplorable condition: suffice it to say that there was an enormous hole in the dome, and the snow fell onto the altar and table of oblation when Fr Seraphim performed the Liturgy.

However, through his ascetic labors, his prayers, and God's help, church life in the village began to revive, and soon the repaired and restored church was filled with parishioners and pilgrims from all ends of the earth, who came because of their respect for Fr Seraphim as an elder.

There are many stories of the miraculous power of his prayers, of his sanctity, prophetic second sight, compassion, and love. He healed incurable diseases, comforted the despairing, converted the unbelieving to faith in God, banished demons . . .

His service took place during the times of the godless authorities, who, upon seeing how the monastery flourished with multitudes of people, placed all sorts of obstacles between him, his clergy, and the people visiting them: sometimes the police would detain them, or train local hoodlums to frighten them where it was deemed necessary.

He was persecuted by both local agents and authorities, who barraged him with all the strength of their ideological forces; the attacks of the secretary of the Regional Committee, however, were especially zealous. All this Fr Seraphim bore good-naturedly. When one of his parishioners would begin to talk to him about the godless Soviet authorities, the elder would softly reply:

"God allows it to be so. Let's talk about spiritual things instead . . ."

And so, in the summer of 1972, I think it was, the country was seized by a long and terrible heat wave and drought. There was no rain for more than a month, everything was burning, and the crops were perishing. The secretary of the Regional Committee faced not only a strict reprimand, but a complete removal from his position, which he greatly feared.

And so, one stiflingly hot night, Fr Seraphim heard someone knocking on the door of his priestly abode. He opened the door, and there stood the secretary of the Regional Committee, trembling, holding his finger to his lips, as if to urge him to keep quiet, "Sh!"

"Comrade Fr Seraphim, I'm here in secret on a highly important government matter."

Fr Seraphim let him in and the secretary of the Regional Committee continued to speak, so haltingly and beseechingly!

"Holy father, the drought, our crops are perishing! Pray for the rain to come!" He even clumsily bowed low in front of the priest.

The following morning after Liturgy, Fr Seraphim arranged a large procession to the fields, where he served a moleben (a service of intercession) and blessing of the waters, asking the Lord not to destroy the crops and to preserve the harvest.

He had only just crossed the threshold of his little house when clouds began to gather in the sky and large raindrops starting pouring down.

The rain fell all day and all night, then another day and night, then one week, then two. The husks began to grow black from the water, but the rain never stopped. It kept knocking on the roofs the whole night through. At this rate, the entire harvest could rot, and for that the secretary of the Regional Committee would surely be driven from his place with a filthy broom.

And so, once more, one night there came a knock at Fr Seraphim's door.

Once again, there stood the figure of the secretary, drenched and wretched.

"Fr Seraphim, thank you, of course, for your efforts, for the rain, but how do you think we can stop it now, eh? I mean, it's enough, so to speak, thank

God! Maybe you can send another signal up there, for the sun to shine out, so that we could have time to gather the harvest, cut the grass, dry out the husks? Put in a good word for us!"

The next morning after Liturgy, Fr Seraphim served a moleben, and the sun came out in the sky, the puddles dried up, and bright, temperate weather came to stay.

～ *The New Nicodemus* ～

All those licensed officials in religious affairs who were given such power during the Soviet times warrant their own separate story. Sometimes the fate of a priest or parish lay entirely in their hands; they had the authority not to give a godly priest his registration papers at all, or to take them away, leaving him without a church, twixt the heavens and the earth, or to merely blackmail him by threatening to do so. Most of the time, the experienced priests, proficient in matters of the human soul, knew how to deal with them: they knew that they were easily swayed by money or drink; they were greedy, materialistic, and as a rule, easy to buy off or to ply with alcohol. Among the church folk they were called "liquored officials"...

Fr Anatolii, however, a village priest with a large family, the spiritual son of Archimandrite Seraphim, who had also suffered much at the hands of his area's licensed official, converted the official to the Faith in the end. This is how it happened.

The licensed official that Fr Anatolii got stuck with was highly dedicated, aggressive, a true thorn in his side: he would constantly go out of his way to play some dirty trick on priests. And so he established the following pattern: as soon as a godly priest, assigned to a new parish, would settle in to his new place and the parishioners would become comfortable with him, as soon as his children would start attending school, as soon as he would finish remodeling his porch or plant his vegetable garden, the official would immediately transfer him to another village in the very opposite corner of the diocese. Officially, he would complain that the priest was conducting anti-Soviet agitation in his church. But for such a serious accusation, claiming the priest's participation in criminal activity, solid evidence was required. And so from the beginning this official would drop by during the sermon, trying to catch the priest saying something compromising, and then, as if he was himself scared of something, he would send in his secret informants with the same aim. Giving them instructions during one of his briefings, he uttered a phrase that took on a life of its own: "You must listen carefully to everything around you, but don't go into the actual church too often or for too long, or it will suck you in!"

In short, having failed to collect any proof against this Fr Anatolii, he still gave him and his nine children their share of troubles, tossing them around from village to village, from one community to another.

Then one day he got another idea: there were new epidemics constantly springing up all over the country—whether of the flu, measles, or cholera. And so he commissioned a local artist to make a descriptive poster depicting an obese priest with a villainous, reddish-purple face standing with the chalice and communing malnourished old women. And on the chalice he ordered the artist to write: "flu epidemic" or "cholera epidemic." The old women, walking away from the priest, all stumble and fall on top of each other dead.

The licensed official hung these posters all over the place—at the train station, at the clinic, in his own office—and summoned Fr Anatolii to him.

"There, Anatolii Vasilievich, have a look at that," he spoke to him using the secular form of address of name and patronymic. "There's a country-wide epidemic, and you're spreading the disease by putting the same spoon in everyone's mouth. You can't do that. It's not sanitary! I should forbid you to give communion at this time! I should alert the Sanitary Epidemiological Services!"

"But we give communion for the healing of soul and body," Fr Anatolii began, but the licensed official repeated:

"Forbid it!"

Fr Anatolii looked at that vulgar scribble of a poster, sighed, examined the miserable-looking figure of the licensed official and that rotten little face of his, and said sympathetically:

"I think that way sometimes too—I have all sorts come to me for communion. They have tuberculosis, cancer, hepatitis, who knows what else. And when they've all communed, I consume whatever is left in the chalice. Then I lick the spoon clean after them. And so all that—the tuberculosis bacilli, the viruses, the infections—I guess they all end up inside me . . ."

The licensed official happily nodded his head:

"There you go! You are a spreader of infection!"

"All of this is inside me," mused Fr Anatolii, "and yet look at me!"

With these words he drew himself up to his full height before the licensed official. And what a figure—over six feet tall, his shoulders a full fathom wide, his face smooth, tight, and rosy—the picture of health and beauty. Teeth straight and white like sugar, and his hair—next to the bald licensed official—like a magnificent mane, with large curls waving, and his eyes piercing bright like two falcons . . . In short, Fr Anatolii was a very handsome man! A noble warrior!

The official representative looked and looked at him from the bottom up, and completely lost heart.

Fr Anatolii left him and busied himself with his affairs: service to God, his flock, his children, his *matushka*[1] . . .

Half a year later, the licensed official appeared at his doorstep, all yellow, shriveled, dried up, like grass in the field. He looked at the blooming priest—healthy and attractive—with dull eyes:

"Cancer," he said, "I've been diagnosed. Tumors. Bless me, Fr Anatolii, and then let me have a little bit from that miraculous chalice of yours, out of which you yourself commune. Only do it in secret. I'm a Party member. I shouldn't be doing this."

Fr Anatolii blessed him, and the licensed official became a secret Christian, like Nicodemus from the Gospel. Similar to the official, he had been a member of the Sanhedrin. Nicodemus also came to Jesus at night, and when the time came, buried Him with his own hands, wrapping Him in linens soaked with sweet-smelling oils: aloes and myrrh.

❧ *Confusion* ❧

According to the monks, Fr A. was at first a monk at the Holy Trinity Lavra of St Sergius, from where he was sent "out of the public eye" to the Pskov Caves Monastery.

This is why. During Soviet times, he would perform exorcisms on the demonically possessed in the lower church of the Dormition Cathedral, and many people came to him from all over. Yet the Lavra was an official "tourist attraction" during the Brezhnev era [1964–1982]—foreign delegates and official persons would often be taken there. This was of great ideological importance, as it was supposed to serve as a witness to citizens of foreign governments of the lack of persecution of the Church in our country and a complete freedom of conscience.

One day, a group of important bureaucrats, what's more, of a foreign capitalist background, were brought there. And one of our own greatly important officials, a worker with serious responsibility, gave them a tour of the Holy Trinity Lavra.

They admired its magnificence, the unearthly beauty of the monastery churches, the unique, wonderfully fresh air, while the responsible worker, to prevent them from getting carried away by all this opium, began to tell them anecdotes about the monks—about an underground passageway that they supposedly used to crawl out far from the monastery borders and freely walk around the towns at large, about the chemical substance that they added to the water, and then passed it off as holy water—in short, much nonsense. And then he added something "for humor's sake," some obscene inside joke, contorting his face into an ironic grimace, as if to say, "you and I, we know better!"

All this time they stood huddled together in the Dormition Cathedral courtyard, along which Fr A., already vested in his *epitrachelion*[1] and cuffs, was walking to do his "exorcising" in the lower church. And something caught his attention while he was walking by, so that he paused for a minute next to the tourists—some phrase spoken by the responsible worker gnawed at him and put him on his guard: he even stepped a little closer to him to listen. But as soon as he came nearer, that godless orator's appearance changed: he puckered his lips, pressed his hands to his chest, bent them at the wrist like a puppy "begging" on its hind legs, howled like a dog, and finally he even began to bark.

The sightseers exchanged glances, but since the bark sounded very real, they decided that he was playing a joke. And with great talent, one may add—just like a German shepherd. And so they smiled, laughed, and even broke into applause: what an actor!

For a minute or two he continued to yelp. He clutched his throat but couldn't seem to stop. All red in the face, eyes bulging—any minute they would burst out of his sockets—but he kept going—woof-woof-woof-woof-woof, woof . . .

Fr A. stood for a while next to him, stood some more, then covered the man's head with his *epitrachelion*—and that silenced him. The elder then said to him:

"My dear man, you need to seek treatment. You are ill. You have a demon inside you! Come see me, I'll help you."

And with that he went inside the church.

Several days later, this elder was sent away to the distant, rural Pskov Caves Monastery, farther away from observing eyes and crowds. Just in case. Otherwise, who knows what other high-ranking official would visit the Lavra, and who knows what other confusion might arise in Fr Λ.'s presence: what if that official started to bray like a donkey, neigh like a horse, or crow like a rooster, dismaying the people? You never know . . .

◈ *Two or Three Days* ◈

My good friend, the children's author Gennadii Snegirev, often traveled to the Little Hermitage to visit Archimandrite Seraphim (Tiapochkin). The elder loved him very much, and whenever he invited him to a meal in his priestly home, he always seated Gennadii next to himself.

So one time the Snegirevs visited with Elder Seraphim, took confession from him, received holy communion from him, and began to prepare for the journey home. With this aim, Gennadii's wife Tatiana had specially ridden on a rattling bus for fifty kilometers to Belgorod, had stood in line at the ticket office, and had purchased their tickets back to Moscow.

She then returned to Rakitnoe, arranged with a taxi driver in advance to take them to the train station, packed her things, bade farewell to the hostess in whose cabin they were renting a room, gave her whatever money she had left, and the Snegirevs began their journey home.

They stopped by Elder Seraphim's home to ask for his blessing for their return travels. But he only said to them:

"It would better if you didn't leave today!"

"What do you mean?" cried out Tatiana. "Fr Seraphim, we have tickets, and a taxi, and our things are packed—everything is ready!"

"No," the elder shook his head, "you'd better go in two or three days. Stay here a little longer."

"Oh, Fr Seraphim, we don't have any money left, and all our business is waiting in Moscow. Maybe you'd better bless us after all—let us go! We're all set to go already. Everyone at home is waiting for us."

"Two or three—" the elder softly uttered and lifted his hand for a blessing, "days," he repeated, lightly tapping Tatiana's forehead with three fingers, "or maybe even four;" he transferred his fingers to tap her on her chest, "whenever God," touching her right shoulder, "will bless it," he finally lowered his fingers to her left shoulder.

The Snegirevs sighed and sighed, but there was nothing to be done but turn around and go back. The taxi was canceled. Belongings were unloaded and unpacked. Tatiana again went to telegraph for an urgent money order for their trip home. And the next day she again rode on the rattling bus for their tickets.

"Well, that Fr Seraphim," she thought, "he lives in some spiritual world, he doesn't know anything about the real world to which we belong—all our affairs, cares, money. He's already in God's kingdom. And he thinks that we're all there too, but for now we're here, on earth."

With these thoughts she arrived in Belgorod. As soon as she entered the train station she understood that something was wrong: crowds of people were huddling around the ticket offices, storming the train station manager's office, sitting on the windowsills or even sleeping on the bare floor.

"What happened?" Tatiana asked.

"Well, just last night two trains leaving Belgorod crashed into each other—a passenger train and a freight train. Many people died, and the rest are either in intensive care or the hospital. And the road to Moscow is blocked for now—they say that normal traffic will only resume in two or three days."

Tatiana returned to Rakitnoe and spent several wonderful days there, taking in everything around her as if she had been born anew.

∼ *Flowers for the Shroud* ∼

My friend Gennadii Snegirev and his wife, my godmother Tatiana, often visited the elder Archimandrite Seraphim in Rakitnoe and lived in his Little Hermitage for weeks at a time. They returned full of light and joy, and told me such wonderful stories that I, of course, also desired to go see him. But I sensed that something was preventing Tatiana from taking me with her. Perhaps she thought that I would bring along that spirit of the Moscow life that they so desired to escape, or perhaps she was of the opinion that a person must make some sort of effort on their part in order to see the elder. Every time I exclaimed, "Oh, take me with you!" she grew silent and looked aside.

But I still wanted to see the elder very much—even my subconscious shouted this to me in my dreams. I had the same dream several times, in which I was standing on a subway platform: the train arrived, the doors opened, and there, right behind the open doors, stood Fr Seraphim—just like I had seen him in a photograph, with two pectoral crosses on his chest. And I could either remain standing where I was—on that platform—or I could jump onto the train car and ride away with him . . .

I also had dreams of temptation from the evil one. In them, smoothly shaved gentlemen in bowler hats came to me; they seemed to be Protestant pastors. They doffed their hats in greeting me and invited me to join them, and in the dream I knew that they weren't pastors at all but demons. At that moment, I would try to cross myself, but my arm felt as if it was weighted down by lead, and I couldn't raise it to my forehead . . . In short, this was a time of temptations, and I could not of my own will, without help, reach the elder.

Then the Lord helped me.

One day in April of 1982, I was offered the opportunity to go on a writer's trip—to read poetry in the city of Shebekino in Belgorod Region—and I was promised a sum of money if I went. Since we sorely needed the money, I went. I spoke to local schoolchildren, dorm residents, and club workers, and then set off home. I held in my arms an enormous bouquet of wax-white flowers, calla lilies grown in a local greenhouse.

I boarded the bus going to Belgorod, intending to switch there to the Moscow-bound train. But when the bus finally arrived at the bus station, I suddenly heard an announcement: "The bus to Rakitnoe will depart in five minutes from bus stop three."

At that moment, something happened to me. I suddenly understood that I must switch to this bus and go to see the elder. I shouldn't think about the fact that I must really go to Moscow, where my husband and children were waiting for me. I should rather not think about anything at all and just run to the ticket office, buy the ticket, and jump onto the steps of the bus. The voice on the loudspeaker was not merely the voice of the dispatcher, but the voice of my destiny, addressed specifically to me. And so I did just that.

As soon as I got off near the church in Rakitnoe with my enormous bouquet, a woman dressed like a churchgoer—in a long dress and head-scarf—approached me and said:

"Well, thank God, you're finally here. The priest said you were coming and told me to wait for you. We would have had nothing to decorate the shroud with."

She took my flowers and went into the church. It was Holy Friday.

❧ Monk Leonid ❧

When he found out that I was in Rakitnoe, my husband came to join me. The day after Pascha, the elder died, and we remained for the funeral and burial.

Multitudes of Fr Seraphim's spiritual children came together from all over to bury him and bid him farewell: bishops, priests, monks, laypeople. It was as if the elder was as his final action through his death bringing together all the people that he loved and remembered in his prayers. In any case, we left Rakitnoe having met people with whom we forged lifelong relationships. One became our spiritual father; another, our counselor; a third, our teacher; a fourth, our friend.

And since we practically hadn't left the church since Holy Friday—praying, confessing, partaking of holy communion, and listening to the Gospel, from which the priests took turns reading ceaselessly over the elder's body as it lay in the middle of the church—this marked a genuine start to our life in the Church.

It was in that very place, at the elder's graveside, that we met Monk Leonid along with his novice, the old nun Pelageia. Monk Leonid emerged from his mother's womb crippled: he looked like a woman down to his waist—like a nice, sweet, old lady—but his legs and enormous feet were that of a man. Because of this, he always had problems in men's monasteries: at one he had even been given a "thorough examination." He always looked back on this with tears.

He had been a monk at the lovely Glinsk Hermitage until it was disbanded during Khrushchev's time. He had nowhere to go, as his mother had refused to take him and had even tried to burn him in the village *banya* (steam bath), but the Mother of God saved him. And so he had no choice but to stand on the church portico and beg. There he was noticed by Pelageia, a secret nun who took him in, despite the fact that in the barracks where she lived—a communal eight-square-meter apartment—she already had a paralyzed nun living on her couch, the young woman Barbara. Barbara did nothing but pray, and the wall above her couch had become imprinted with a cross. It was even said that various bishops came in secret to stand in the presence of this wonderful young woman and to venerate the uncreated cross . . .

When we became acquainted with Monk Leonid and Pelageia, however, Barbara had already reposed, and the two of them had moved to a one-room Moscow apartment several tramway stops from the Elektrozavodsk stop. Upon discovering that I write poetry, Fr Leonid became very interested and asked me to come see him in order to record his confessions. One would think that poetry is in no way connected to recording confessions, and yet he probably hoped that a person of letters could give shape to his repentant lamentations.

"I am infirm, crippled from my mother's womb, an invalid from childhood, I have paralysis, a nervous disorder, so there's no way I can go to the elder, Archimandrite Kirill, in the Lavra, but I must confess to him. When you come, I will dictate everything to you, and you will take it to him, so that he can read the prayer of absolution."

Well, so be it. I began to visit him.

"Fr Leonid, are you sure this is a sin?" I would often ask him after hearing something innocent and touching and lifting my pen from the notebook. "It's routine, normal! Why do you have to repent of this?"

"You just sit there and write what I say, don't ask me questions," he would reply, turning away and blushing. "And don't look at me," he would add, letting me know that in this situation I must merely become "the pen of a ready writer" (Ps 44:1), and not meddle with my comments and questions.

We would occasionally fill two thin teacher's graphic notebooks, and yet his confession, as I have now come to understand, witnessed to the fact that this was a man who led a holy life.

He would constantly phone my husband, asking him to come, and giving him all sorts of instructions, and once, he even asked him to help him wash.

"I haven't washed in a year!" Fr Leonid sorrowfully said. "My body is all crusty. And without your help I won't be able to climb into the bath or out of it. I have paralysis! And in general, I'm an invalid since childhood!"

So my husband washed him. He helped him into the bathtub, soaped up his hair and body, scrubbed him clean with a brush, doused him with water from the shower . . . Then he saw—how strange! The soap bubbles floated around on the surface of the water, but the water itself was clean!

"Fr Leonid!" my husband exclaimed in disbelief. "You probably had someone wash you just recently, you just forgot about it!"

"Nobody's washed me for a year already," the other grumbled.

"What are you telling me? The water's still clean!"

"Quiet! Don't you tell anyone about that!"

This was a way that the Lord responded to Fr Leonid's holy prayers.

Another time my husband was away visiting the Holy Trinity Lavra of St Sergius, and I was getting the children ready to go to church for the all-night vigil (this was on the feast day of St Nicholas). Before church, we decided to drink some tea. I began to prepare the stove, lit a match, and a piece of flaming sulfur flew right into my left eye—it even sizzled on contact. Right away an enormous leucoma began to form on my eye, right on the iris!

I should add that in a month I was due to give birth to my third child, and my first two were still little. Nobody was home, a bitter frost stood outside, and black ice lay on the ground. In a word, things looked very bad. I even began to imagine living the rest of my life with only one eye. What humble resignation I felt: what could I do, it was all in God's hands!

Suddenly, as if he felt something was wrong, Monk Leonid gave me a call. I immediately told him of my terrible condition: there I was sitting with an enormous belly, tiny children, and a leucoma on my eye.

"Pray for me, Fr Leonid!"

"You just drop a few drops of olive oil in your eye! And don't go anywhere by yourself!" he said and hung up the phone.

By morning the leucoma had cleared up—but my eye was bloodshot, as if I had spent the entire night crying with the one eye. By evening that was gone, too.

My husband returned from the Lavra and took me to see the eye doctor. The doctor examined me, checked my vision, and asked:

"So what are you saying happened?"

"Burning sulfur right in my eye! It sizzled! Leucoma!"

"But everything looks fine! There's nothing there! Not a trace of anything."

And he gave a look betraying how sorry he felt for me that I was such a liar . . .

But two weeks after that, I became gravely ill with acute bronchitis—I was so short of breath that I could only sleep sitting up, and coughed up blood. I also completely lost my voice and could only croak. They didn't want to take me to the hospital, but I was due to give birth any day. But they didn't take me to the birthing clinic either, because I had acute bronchitis. In short, I sensed my approaching death: "O my soul, rise up! Why art thou sleeping? The end draws near ...”[1] Either I would die, or the baby, or both of us together.

Fr Leonid sent a priest to see me and give me holy unction. I had already accepted the possibility that my days were over, my time was up ... After all, I had lived a good twenty-eight years—more than Lermontov or Yesenin, not to mention Rimbaud.[2] Still, I felt unbearably sorry for everything and everyone: sorry for my life, children, husband, my sick and elderly parents ... Then I began to develop Quincke’s disease; I was suffocating: if it lasted much longer my throat would completely close up. Only then did the ambulance take me to the hospital.

“Yes, I’m praying for her, praying!” Fr Leonid told my husband, as if defending himself, as if he had done something wrong. “Let me go read another canon for her.”

Finally, they delivered me to the hospital, but the nurse at check-in didn’t want to take me in:

“Take off your cross immediately! Laboring mothers are not allowed to wear any trinkets!”

With no voice, I could only gesticulate to her like a mute in response:

“I feel so much better with it on! I won’t take it off!”

“Well, then, I can’t admit you. Look—your ambulance already drove off. So you’ll stay here in the waiting room all night, not registered, all by yourself. Go on, take it off!”

And I again:

“I won’t!”

She all but threw herself at me with her fists, trembling, jumping up and down like a possessed person, spitting and sputtering. I even remembered the words of the prophet Habakkuk, something like: man, like chaos, jumps like a goat, inflates like a bubble, rages like a bobcat, seeks to devour like a snake, neighs like a stallion looking on another’s beauty, lies like a demon.

At this point, another nurse appeared, and saw me suffocating and dying there, while the nurse tortured me, and she finally laid me on a hospital bed.

That morning I went into labor. Lying in the labor and delivery section for the plague-ridden and infectious, all on my own, I felt my little child coming out almost completely, raring to come into the light of God’s day, fighting her way into existence, and there I was, with no voice to even call someone—no nurse, no doctor, no one to take care of me, and what's worse, hearing them all next door loudly talking and even laughing about something. This is where my cross saved me. It was large and heavy—a certain hieromonk had brought it back for me from the Holy Land. I took it off my neck, clutched it in my hand, and began to pound my fist against the nightstand with the cross pressed inside it. The noise from my cross echoed throughout the entire delivery ward. The doctors all ran to the alarm:

"What's wrong with you?"

They ran up to me, and my baby fell out right into their hands! Right at noon! All pink, with golden hair, so plump, looking like she was born not from an emaciated mother weighing all of 117 pounds all together with the baby, but from a rosy-cheeked, well-tended child-bearer with legs like marble columns and a neck like an ivory tower.

"Well, little mother, who did you give birth to? Name the sex of the baby!"

"A girl! Anastasia! Resurrection!"

It was Monk Leonid who rejoiced the most. Though he was but a humble monk, he bought her an array of gifts—a satin blanket, all kinds of little jackets, onesies, and swaddling linens.

"Bring Anastasia to me," he kept asking me. "Let me just take one look at her."

And so I would visit him with her.

But he would just glance at her demurely—and turn away, so as not to develop any strong feelings for her. He was, after all, a monk, and any strong feeling is dangerous for a monk—even deadly. And so he would just take one more look—so!—and lower his eyes.

One day Anastasia and I came to see him as usual, when she had already turned eleven months. She sat in my arms and could move around the room holding on tightly to my finger. Fr Leonid, Pelageia, and I sat down to eat. The table was laid with potatoes and sauerkraut . . . it was the Nativity Fast. We were talking about something, not minding the child at all.

Suddenly, Anastasia reached for the plate of cabbage, took a handful of it, climbed to the floor, and, releasing my finger, walked steadily toward Fr Leonid all by herself, holding out her cabbage to him.

"She knows," nodded Pelageia, "Leniushka prayed for her so much, so much!"

Two months later, Monk Leonid died. My husband and I, together with Anastasia, went to his funeral, then to the cemetery, and then to Pelageia's for the funeral banquet.

There were a lot of people there, all people who loved him and had asked for his prayers, including priests and monks. As soon as everyone sat down at the table and took a sip of their wine, Anastasia, then thirteen months, walked up to the icon corner, which was covered from top to bottom with icons large and small. She crossed herself and began to babble away in her baby talk, making prostrations and praying with intonations from the church services and psalms. And so she continued to get up from her little knees, cross herself, and kneel down once more, leaning her head on the floor . . .

Everyone froze, looking at this wonderful sight, this touching scene, which lasted several minutes.

"Lord, have mercy!" One of the old ladies finally stirred. "Pelageia, this must be that girl for whom Leniushka prayed night and day when she was being born? He prayed so much that it almost killed him, too?"

"That's her, that's her," confirmed Pelageia.

And then the old lady told us the story. Pelageia had gone away to a monastery, and had asked this lady to look after Monk Leonid in her stead. This was exactly the time when I was dying, and the hospitals and birthing centers were refusing to admit me, while Fr Leonid unceasingly prayed for my successful delivery. When the ambulance took me away and my husband told him about this, he even began to make full prostrations, which was incredibly difficult for him, since his one side was paralyzed and he would repeatedly fall onto his side, while the old lady had to help him get up. They both wore themselves thin. This continued almost all night and all morning.

She even began to be alarmed that he would suffer a stroke from such prayerful labors, and kept repeating:

"They will be the death of you, Fr Leonid!"

But he didn't listen to her, and again knelt to his knees, and again couldn't get up, forcing her to give him her own shoulder for support.

Finally he collapsed into a chair, leaned back, wiped the sweat from his forehead, and cried out:

"Phew! She's given birth."

This was at noon.

And now it was the turn of the child Anastasia to pray for the newly reposed lowly Monk Leonid.

❦ *Another Source* ❦

In spite of his constant battle with the passions, Monk Leonid still had one: he was passionate about booklets. He especially loved those that were forbidden, all kinds of forbidden booklets: simply anti-Soviet ones, spiritually beneficial ones, and ones "in support of the New Martyrs."

We were constantly taking him new booklets printed in *samizdat*.[1] In this way, he got his hands on a booklet by Hieromonk Seraphim (Rose), the spiritual son of St John, Archbishop of Shanghai and San Francisco, about the end of days. It was called something like *The Future of Russia and the End of the World*. It affected him so much that he sent me to the Lavra to ask for a blessing from the elder Archimandrite Kirill to pass it around. And when this blessing was received, he hired a typist to retype four copies of this book, which he proceeded to hand out as required reading to his many pilgrims and visitors. But he didn't know how to pray for this Hieromonk Seraphim: was he living or reposed?

No matter how many people he asked, no one could tell him. This depressed Fr Leonid very much—he really wanted to pray for Hieromonk Seraphim. And so he convinced my husband and his novice, the old nun Pelageia, to drive him to the Holy Trinity Lavra of St Sergius to see Elder Kirill.

They arrived after the service had already begun, and Monk Leonid went to the altar directly to Fr Kirill.

"Fr Kirill, this Hieromonk Seraphim—is he living or dead? How do I commemorate him?"

Fr Kirill became silent, lifted his gaze upward for a moment, grew still, and then crossed himself and said sorrowfully:

"May he rest with the saints."

The next day, late in the evening, the radio station BBC, to which our radio was tuned, announced that two days ago, the famous Orthodox writer and missionary, Hieromonk Seraphim Rose, had died after a long illness.

Elder Kirill had learned of this from another source altogether.

✎ How I Battled the Gypsies ✎

One day I came home after visiting the Holy Trinity Lavra of St Sergius, and let slip a few choice words to Monk Leonid about the multitudes of Gypsies walking through the commuter train cars and how those Gypsies pestered everyone.

"Behind every one of these fortune-telling Gypsies fly a host of demons," noted Fr Leonid. "You must be careful. Don't ever start a conversation with them. You know what the holy fathers said: 'Do not enter into dialogue with evil.'"

"But I'm not afraid of Gypsies," I waved my hand nonchalantly. "It is they who are afraid of me."

"And what makes you so frightening that they're afraid of you?" grumbled Fr Leonid, displeased.

"I just know how to deal with them," I announced.

"She knows! And what do you know?" the monk squinted at me suspiciously.

"I will tell you a story of how I once met a Gypsy who kept insisting on telling my fortune and grabbing my hands. But I just turned away from her. Then she switched to threats: 'If you don't grease my palm, this and that will happen to you: I will curse you with my evil eye.' This got me very angry. I turned around to face her, looked into her black, passionate eyes, squared my shoulders, and said: 'And shouldn't you be afraid of my eye of light? Shouldn't you be afraid that I with my eye of light could completely penetrate you? I will take away all your power; I will take your good fortune for myself!'

"Oh, that scared her! Her face fell, she turned and fled from my presence! Some experienced people later told me that my threat hit its mark, because Gypsies are superstitious and are themselves afraid of everything. And for them, an eye of light is just as deadly as their evil eye."

Fr Leonid didn't like any of this at all.

"So what, you began to threaten her with witchcraft of your own? You were inviting the demons to come! Go on and make three prostrations before the Mother of God and repent for what you've done, and then I will tell you what to do next."

What could I do? I sighed, knelt three times before the icon of the Mother of God, asking Her for forgiveness, and again sat down before the lowly monk.

"The power of Gypsies is evil: one can only dispel it and chase it away with prayer. So the next time you see Gypsies, you must immediately begin saying the prayer 'Let God Arise'[1] to yourself. And don't say a word to them. Understand?"

"Understood."

What happened next? Soon I went to the Lavra again, took communion there during the early Liturgy, and then returned to Moscow. I boarded an empty commuter train leaving Zagorsk station and sat down by myself on the bench, when suddenly a crowd of Gypsies came rushing onto the train after me, a whole band of them—all covered in their coin necklaces, earrings, and brightly colored scarves and skirts. They immediately approached me, cornering me in my space between two benches, reaching their hands toward me, almost tearing my scarf from my head, clutching at my hair, crying with many voices:

"Give me your hand, dear, I will read your palm and tell you your whole future!"

"Oh no! Government housing is in your future, all your efforts are for nothing, a long road, a king of clubs!"

There was no one around. It was ten o'clock in the morning on a workday, and evidently no one from Zagorsk needed to go to Moscow.

Suddenly, I remembered Fr Leonid's instructions. Submerging myself into my thoughts, I turned off all my external senses and began to pray: "Let God arise!" As soon as I reached "as smoke vanisheth, so let them vanish; as wax melteth before the fire, so let the demons perish . . . ," I looked around me—and there was nobody there, they had truly vanished. The whole tumultuous band! It was like they had been sucked out by a vacuum. The last one, already halfway through the doors, looked back and began to yell something at me, but I continued out loud, ". . . from the presence of them that love God and who sign themselves with the sign of the Cross . . ."[2] And finally, I put the sign of the cross over her, so, so, so, and so! She screamed, cringed, and ran, just as the doors slammed shut with a bang.

I arrived in Moscow, and told the story to Fr Leonid right away.

"You should have seen me put the sign of the cross over her, and how she shriveled up!"

"Well, you did it all wrong," he began again. "No humility, no obedience . . ."

"But I did exactly as you taught me!" I said, my feelings hurt.

"What is it always with your 'I,' 'me,' 'I!' It was the Lord that drove them away—the Lord to Whom you were praying! He raised them up and scattered them! And why did you have to make the sign of the cross over that Gypsy? What are you, a priest?"

"What's wrong with that?" I tried to defend myself.

"You can only put the sign of the cross over yourself like that, that's what . . . or your children. But if you imprint anyone else with the cross, let alone a pagan, then the demon inside can jump out of them out of pure fear of the cross and come right inside you!"

"I didn't know," I stammered, "What do I do now, Fr Leonid?"

"What do I do, what do I do," he grumbled. "Now you know. For now, go and make three prostrations before the Mother of God, and repent."

I did as I was told.

And since then . . . strangely enough . . . many years have passed, and in those years, I met many Gypsies at train stations, city parks, or even right next to Yelokhovo Cathedral, where they would try their best to sell gold or imitation watches and bracelets to the people exiting the church. But nowhere, at any time—not in Moscow, or Crimea, or Paris—did they bother me, or even approach me, sometimes even passing me by completely.

Although I did once approach them. But these were entirely different Gypsies.

I was coming out of church once after the early Liturgy—this was on the feast day of the Transfiguration—and I saw set up in the churchyard tables laden with fruits of rare beauty—scarlet watermelon halves, golden pears, crimson and rose-colored apples, blue and purple plums, burgundy pomegranates, pearl-colored melons cut up into pieces, purple and green grapes, orange mandarins, blushing apricots, reddish-yellow peaches . . . It wasn't just the abundance of this wonderful fruit of the earth that amazed me, but also how festively they were arranged on enormous platters: every combination of shape and color, like a still life intended for the paintbrushes of the Flemish masters!

Four ravishing young Gypsy beauties, looking just like Pushkin's Zemfira,[3] were fussing around the table, fixing a disobedient plum that was attempting to roll off the mountain of fruit, and arranging the clusters of grapes so that every individual fruit displayed its best side in the brightly shining August sunlight. Two Gypsy men in white shirts rushed to them carrying large baskets full of more fruit.

"Are you going to bless those?" I asked stupidly.

"Well yes, today is the Transfiguration of Our Lord! Does that surprise you?"

"So does that mean you're Orthodox?" I asked even more stupidly.

"Of course. We have an entire band here of Orthodox Gypsies."

"And you go to church?"

"And we go to church," the Gypsy who had answered me began to put out the basketfuls of fruit onto empty platters. She worked like an artist, creating harmony and choosing for every fruit its best complementary companion.

The priest came out of the church and generously sprinkled this Gypsy splendor with a prayer.

I wanted to take my meddlesome questions home with me, but a very young Gypsy girl, seeing a mismatch in one of her fruit towers, offered me an enormous, wet, aquamarine plum.

"It's the Transfiguration!" she repeated.

∾ *Non-Komsomol Gingerbread*[1] ∾

Monk Leonid was a man of great fasting and prayer. He loved to say the following words from the Gospel: "He who is faithful in what is least is faithful also in much; and he who is unjust in what is least is unjust also in much" (Lk 16:10). And in order to be trusted not only with very little, but with the very least, he recruited my help in obtaining some textbooks full of charts that are used by students in the Culinary Institute: these he would peruse and work out the ingredients of products which had previously been considered Lenten. The study of these recipes drew from him many a sorrowful sigh, for it came to light that not all breads that we usually ate without a second thought during the fasts were free of dairy additives. The same discovery applied to certain noodles and pastas, to say nothing of waffle cookies!

The range of truly Lenten foods was catastrophically shrinking. All that was left of the carbohydrates was gingerbread and grains.

At that time we received a dear guest from Tula—Mitrofan Dmitrievich, a former colonel who had fought at the front, a servant of God much beloved by Fr Seraphim (Tiapochkin) for his purity of heart. Well, what would he bring us from Tula, especially during Great Lent, but the famous Tula gingerbread, of course—round, glazed, wrapped in a festive box. So Mitrofan Dmitrievich brought us three of these boxes at once.

As soon as he arrived, I received a call from my friend Andriusha—a former classmate and my godson—who said:

"I'm here not far from your house. Can I stop by?"

He didn't want to come empty-handed, so he stepped into a bakery at a hotel near the subway station, then rang our doorbell and handed me a decorative box with Tula gingerbread through the doorway, all nicely glazed and in a festive box.

My husband, hearing that we had guests, also stopped at the same bakery on his way home from work and arrived just in time for tea with the same gingerbread printed with the word "Tula" in his hands. So there we sat, surrounded on all sides by this gingerbread, which had by now grown in quantity to five boxes, and drank our tea, pleasantly keeping the fast, enjoying good conversation on various spiritual themes. And such conversation!

Mitrofan Dmitrievich had at one time been the cell attendant for Elder Seraphim himself, and knew many wonderful stories, while Andriusha, a neophyte, listened to him with bated breath, mouth agape . . .

And suddenly we got a phone call from Monk Leonid:

"I just finished studying the list of ingredients for gingerbread. It turns out that it's all not Lenten! Yes! There's egg powder in it. There is only one kind of gingerbread that is Lenten, the so-called Komsomol gingerbread. The darkish kind. That, you can go ahead and eat without concern during all of Lent."

After this announcement, he hung up. We had already devoured quite a few of the suspicious Tula gingerbread. We had nothing else to offer! Well, I said nothing so as not to dismay my guests.

Then I met a priest acquaintance in church:

"Why are you so sad? You're not depressed, are you?"

"And how! I fasted and fasted, and then ate something not Lenten after all! Broke the fast," I sorrowfully uttered.

He tried to cheer me up.

"Well, maybe you were traveling? Or you were eating dinner in the house of a pagan?"

"No," I replied firmly, "I was at home."

"Well, maybe you were ill?"

"No, I wasn't ill," I said dejectedly. "I was in good health."

"Well, then, what happened? Did you crave some cheese? Some cottage cheese? Or . . . some meat?" he asked sympathetically.

"I ate some gingerbread."

"Gingerbread? But that's Lenten!" the priest joyfully cried out. "It's allowed, that's not a sin!"

"Only the Komsomol kind. You can eat the Komsomol kind," I said knowingly. "But I ate the non-Komsomol gingerbread, that's the problem!"

The priest looked at me in amazement.

"Wh-what did you say? The non-Komsomol gingerbread?"

"Well yes, the non-Komsomol gingerbread. The not-Lenten kind. It has egg powder in it!"

I even felt my eyes fill up with tears of contrition.

The priest sighed heavily.

"So that's what it is . . . egg powder, eh?"

"Egg powder," I repeated in a subdued tone.

"Oh, the devil!" the priest cried out. "How he manipulates people! So we're straining out gnats, are we? And what about camels? The camel of hypocrisy, it turns out we swallow it! The camel of despondency we swallow!"[2]

I came home just in time to receive a phone call from Monk Leonid.

"I just read about zefir and marshmallows . . ."

"Fr Leonid," I said in a steely tone of voice. "I am obliged to take back those textbooks with the recipes. The owner needs them back immediately."

"But I haven't studied everything yet . . . It turns out that marmalade . . ."

"He said immediately! I will come and pick them up right now."

I came and took them away. And as a gift I brought him the three remaining boxes of our gifted Tula gingerbread. I knew that he was always grateful for any offering, repeating the words "every . . . gift is from above."[3]

This time also he cocked his head and said, taking the boxes from me: "May the Lord save you!"

But then again, this was exactly how a humble monk was supposed to act.

❧ At Blessed Xenia's ❧

A long time ago, in 1985, I took my little children to St Petersburg, which was still called Leningrad at the time. We really wanted to visit the grave of Blessed Xenia, and with that aim took the tram to Smolensky Cemetery.

My friend, with whom we were staying, said to us a little strangely:

"Xenia herself will help you find her there!"

It was bitter winter, December, and the metal tram had frozen so much that it seemed to squeal and whimper from the frost.

The cemetery was deserted and dark, and even the church was closed. I helplessly looked around at the snowy drifts covering the graves, and realized that I would never find that precious grave on my own.

And suddenly, a wretched-looking old woman in a shabby coat appeared out of nowhere—all crooked, with a grotesque-looking face: instead of an eye socket, she had a bump the size of an eyeball, and the eye itself was perched on the edge of this protrusion, this bump; but nevertheless her eyes looked gentle and innocent. And strangely, though she should have been hideous because of all this, the old lady was not at all grotesque, but seemed charming and nice, like someone from a fairy tale.

"Well, dear people, is it Blessed Xenia you are looking for?" she asked. "Are you wondering how to get to her?"

"Yes," I said, "and we don't know where her grave is. And it's cold, and getting dark."

She nodded; shivering from the cold and looking at me with her strange eye, she offered:

"I will take you to her right away. But you can't see her actual grave—the chapel where she's buried is surrounded by a high fence. You can only stand next to it and from there you can venerate her and pray to her. Everyone does it that way!" she explained, leading us through the graves. "I can even show you the grave of martyred priests. They were buried in the ground still living, and the earth groaned above them and shook all night. By morning the cemetery guard saw beams of light rising from that frozen earth up to the heavens. And he understood that the Lord was taking their souls to Him, and that their martyrs' crowns were shining in their flight. I can also take you to the shot-up icon of the Saviour. The Bolsheviks fired a round at it and just left it like that. And now, miraculous healings take place there for those who ask with faith."

We walked up to the mosaic icon of the Saviour—His face was indeed riddled with bullet holes, His eyes damaged—the shooters had taken their best shot.

"They probably all died terrible deaths," I said.

"They all died in different ways," the old woman replied. "The Lord Himself prayed from the Cross for those who knew not what they did . . ."[1]

We stood by this icon, prayed, sang the troparion to the martyrs on the spot where the priests had been buried alive, and finally approached the chapel surrounded by the fence, on which were many, many signs and notes: "Blessed Xenia, return my husband to me!" "Blessed Xenia, heal my beloved daughter!" "Dear Xenia, my son is fighting in Afghanistan—save and protect him."

According to tradition, if you stare at the high window under the dome of the chapel for a long time, you can see Blessed Xenia herself looking down on those who come to her. We gazed at this window, bowed, quietly prayed, and I also wrote several notes to Blessed Xenia and stuck them onto the nails in the fence.

We started to walk back until we found ourselves next to the church. It was open, and people were hurrying inside for the evening service. We looked around—our old woman was nowhere to be found! Not a trace of her. She was there, and then she vanished.

"There now," I said, "we didn't even have a chance to give her any money! That old woman was sick and poor . . ."

Inside the church I asked the woman behind the candle stand:

"Who's the woman who leads people here to the grave of Blessed Xenia? The one with the strange-looking eye?"

She shrugged her shoulders, perplexed:

"I don't know of any such woman . . ."

My friend, who was a priest, later explained to me:

"There is a belief that to those who are visiting her for the first time, Blessed Xenia herself comes out and escorts them to her grave. So you can decide for yourself who led you around Smolensky Cemetery."

When we sat down in the tram with the children to return home, I asked them:

"Well, are you completely frozen?"

"No," they said. And as proof they took off their mittens and touched my cheek with their warm hands.

There is a story about the chapel of Blessed Xenia, that the Bolsheviks had wanted to conceal it from the eyes of the faithful behind a fence. They say that inside they completely defaced it and put a sculptor there who fulfilled government orders for tombstones. He also specialized in busts of

Lenin. And so he sat there and sculpted these heads, and then he would take them to different towns, villages, and organizations, where they would be placed on stands. But the Lord evidently took away his gift of judging proportions correctly—how else can one explain the fact that the sculptor suddenly became obsessed with gigantomania, and decided to carve a bust of Lenin of enormous dimensions, the likes of which had never before been seen anywhere, by anyone? But a client was found for that bust, too.

And so the sculptor sat for many months and worked on this bust. Finally, it was done, and the client came with some men to take it away.

But no matter how hard they tried to take it out of the chapel—through the door, through the window—it was all useless: the bust didn't fit. They would have to destroy the chapel in order to get it out. But Blessed Xenia didn't allow that to happen. And so the bust lay there for several years, taking up the entire space of the chapel, until finally the sculptor in his frustration took a hammer and shattered it to pieces and, bit by bit, took it out to the garbage dump.

The Hunger Striker

I knew the grave and dignified acolyte Vasilii when he was just Vaska and had the nickname the "Hunger Striker." This was how he got his nickname.

In the Brezhnev era, he married an American girl. They had a civil ceremony, but he wasn't allowed to emigrate to the United States, as he was an engineer for some company that worked under a level of secrecy. Soon the young wife's visa expired, and she was forced to return to America.

And so Vasia, who had been released from his job as soon as he married a citizen of an 'unfriendly nation,' dedicated himself to fighting for permission to join his wife. He wrote letters, appeals, proclamations—to the Ministry of Foreign Affairs, to the American Embassy, to the Political Bureau, even to Brezhnev himself. He gave interviews to enemy radio stations, and gathered round himself a group of people like him, "those who weren't being released," who were also married to citizens of foreign nations.

He organized a whole political movement "for the reunion of the family": they would stand with signs near the statue of Yuri Dolgorukiy, hold press conferences, and even declare long-lasting hunger strikes.

Of course, not everyone was capable of doing this. There was among them a young lady from Vladimir who had married an Italian. And when all those people who were separated from their "other halves" had gathered at a Moscow apartment and, under supervision of French doctors, had begun their hunger strike, which had already been announced for several days on the "hostile" radio station *Golosa,* she began to whimper pathetically after only half a day: "Oh, how I want a *pirozhok!*"[1] and by four o'clock she was giving in completely: "I'm going to die without some soup!" She began to cry, naming all her favorite dishes. And so she left the protest.

But the others courageously held on—for two or even three weeks. Our Hunger Striker proved to be the most steadfast and unbending. One of his hunger strikes lasted exactly forty days. So if you considered each of those days as a year, you could say that he, like the new Moses, led his fellow fasters for forty years out from the Egyptian yoke.

Well, of course, if he had undergone such hunger strikes on his own, without supervision, he would have died. But the experienced French doctors kept him alive, giving him glucose and vitamins, allowing him to refresh himself with a sip of water, while photographers memorialized his tortured but noble face that appeared on the pages of the *Washington Post,* the *New York Times,* and the *Paris Match* under the bold headline, "Another victim of the bloody regime."

"All we want is to be reunited with our families! It is our right!" Vasia would repeat with a fading smile.

In the end, meetings were organized in support of the Hunger Striker and heads of state became involved. President Reagan even gave Brezhnev an ultimatum: if he didn't release the hunger striker to his wife, America would impose an embargo. Brezhnev didn't release him, and the embargo came into force

In short, Vasia was slowly becoming a significant political figure. He was a desired guest at all the embassies and a friend to all the Western correspondents. He was very busy. Nevertheless, he managed to stop by and see us once. A month had passed since his last hunger strike, but he looked striking—slender and fit. His former belly fat, previously gathering in rolls on his sides, was gone, his complexion was smooth, he looked younger and his gaze clearer. All in all, he was in total euphoria.

I had a friend over at the time, who was very careful of her figure, and who for one day per week, in order to cleanse her system, tried to eat nothing at all. But hearing about the forty-day hunger strikes and examining the radiant face of the hunger striker, she was tempted: maybe she should also try it?

"Tell me, when you are on a hunger strike, do you . . . er . . . experience a lot of movement?" she asked, trying to understand all the conditions accompanying such an extreme hunger strike.

"Of course!" he readily responded and took a pile of papers out of his briefcase. "Here, I've written three petitions, I gave a long interview to the *Voice of America*, I hold press conferences . . ."

"No, I don't mean that, I . . ." Here she looked at him very meaningfully. "I mean . . . movement . . . Do you go a lot?"

"Absolutely. That's the only way I go, there's no time for anything else. Look—I was at a reception held by the French ambassador, I had tea with the American ambassador, I wrote a letter to President Reagan . . ."

"That's not what I mean," she raised her hands in exasperation. Finally, she resolved to be more direct:

"Do you at least go to the bathroom?" And she even demonstrated for her oblivious companion how one sits on the toilet.

Truth be told, we treated this whole affair of Vasia's leaving, his family drama, his languishing for his beloved wife, with a dose of irony, because we knew that Vasia had mostly married to emigrate, and that his wife soon found a boyfriend in America. After all, if our Natasha Rostova couldn't wait one year to be happily married to Prince Andrei, then why, really, would an American stay faithful to Vasia in a separation of many years? More to the point, however, the fact that a Soviet man was obliged to play so many tricks in order to leave the country was very indicative of the nature of the regime: throughout the whole world people went where they willed; only we sat chained to our places, shaking our fetters.

Meanwhile, Vasia began his next hunger strike. And we finally said to him:

"You know, this is not the Christian way. What if you die from this? It would be suicide! You'd better go and ask a priest for a blessing to do this hunger strike."

We convinced him and went to the Lavra all together. He went to confession to Archimandrite Zosima—an old man who had survived many years of Stalin's concentration camps. They talked, the priest covered him with his *epitrachelion*, and Vasia, pleased with himself, announced to us:

"Well, that's it! He gave me his blessing!"

"What do you mean, he gave you his blessing? Did you tell him everything?"

"Of course. I said, 'My wife is in America, and they're not letting us be together.' And he said, 'The Soviet powers are unlimited in their evil doings. Something must be done!' Then I said: 'Well, we are fighting—I write petitions, protests, I just wrote to the American president . . .' And he said, 'That's right! Fight! Go on, expose them, pressure them whenever you can. I suffered from those godless powers myself. At the hospital the nurse tried to take my blood for analysis, but the blood didn't come. The Bolsheviks drank it all. They came close to taking my eyes out.' Then I said, 'Well, Father, I am going on a hunger strike.' He said, 'Good work! It's the Dormition Fast right now, so may the Lord bless you.'"

In the end, they finally let our Vasia go. He came to America, but found he wasn't really needed there. In the beginning, a lecture tour was organized for him at various universities, where he would invariably tell his story and describe the bloody regime back in the USSR, behind the Iron Curtain. But then, this story became weedy and overgrown and stopped being of interest to anyone. His furious activity suddenly ceased, and it turned out that he had nothing to do; his wife divorced him, and he grew depressed.

He became attached to a family of émigrés and for a while even attended church with them on Sundays, but then he decided to move to another city. They gave him a farewell gift of an icon of the Holy Royal Martyrs: in the Church Abroad, they had already been canonized, but not in the Russian Church—that time was still far away.

The icon was in very poor condition—it was obvious that its former owners had wandered significantly throughout the world with it: the paint was peeling off in some places, and in others it was dirty, the faces were darkened, and the wooden frame was falling apart. But the hunger striker put it in a place of honor in his new haven, lit a lamp in front of it . . .

And, the icon began to slowly restore itself and to stream myrrh. One face grew lighter, then another's features came to light, then the clothing grew vivid with color and the patterns on it became clear. In short, this was no ordinary icon! And it began to restore itself not anywhere, but at the home of our Vaska the hunger striker!

Then he began to take this icon to the churches of the Church Abroad—first in America, then in Europe. He even went to Mt Athos. Granted, there are no churches there belonging to the Church Abroad, but there have always been venerators of the Royal Martyrs in the bosom of the Russian Orthodox Church.

Finally, a new era arrived, and Vasia came with his miraculous icon to Moscow. All this time it had continued to slowly restore itself and to stream myrrh—the faces shone with an unearthly light, the clothing was saturated with purple and emerald, every lock of the New Martyrs' hair seemed to have been meticulously redone, and an otherworldly fragrance emanated from the icon. Vasia himself was somehow restored.

Before me stood a man who was no longer young, but who was still youthful and trim, with a noble manner and streaks of grey hair. Nowhere in his features, his manner of speaking, or his movements could one trace the former agitation and unrest: everything about him was even, deliberate, and dignified. At his apartment he received anyone who, having heard of the miraculous icon, desired to venerate it and offer their prayers to the Tsar-Martyr and his family. Priests would also visit him and would serve memorial services before the icon—sometimes there were several in one day, both priests and memorial services. Vasilii was very busy in connection to all of this. And when the Church in Russia did canonize the Royal Passionbearers, he gave the icon to a church for general veneration, and he began to serve in that church as an acolyte.

Evil tongues gossiped about him that just as he had thrown himself into the fight for the reunion of families, so did he now completely dedicate himself to the service of this icon. Those same tongues continued to say that comparably, former Communists, who before stubbornly worshiped Lenin, now vehemently cross themselves.

But in reality it was all completely explainable. The Apostle Paul, also, at first passionately persecuted Christians, until the Lord Himself appeared to him on the road to Damascus. And then he used that same passion and dedication—even up to his martyr's death—to preach the Word of Christ.

St Macarius of Egypt writes that any evil passion must be transfigured to a higher stirring of the soul and directed toward service to God. Fiery zeal may be converted to burning love, salacity to an expectancy of heavenly consolation, jealousy to ardor for God.

And only a cold-hearted person cannot make use of their senseless and vain heart either for the presence of God or for godly work.

❧ "A Little Piece of Wood" ❧

It was the 1960s. The writer Vladimir Soloukhin, who collected icons from all the villages he visited, gave my father one of these, as he called them, "little pieces of wood." The icon was in terrible condition—first of all, it had fallen apart into three pieces, and secondly, it was impossible to tell what was depicted on it. Wrapped in a cloth, this icon was kept by my parents in a safe place for many years.

But the time came for my husband and me to obtain it and take it to a restorer that we knew, Andrei Vitte. A few months later, we received it back in all of its former glory. It was an icon of the Joy of All Who Sorrow—the Mother of God with Her Child surrounded by a host of archangels and saints: the apostles Peter and Paul, Saints Basil, John, and Gregory, St Nicholas, the Martyr Tatiana, and other lesser known holy men and women. The icon itself was special somehow—if you would simply stand before it with a helpless and contrite heart, you would feel your heart slowly become filled—completely saturated—with peace and joy.

"This is an unusual icon," said the restorer. "I finished it a long time ago, but held onto it, because I didn't want to part with it. And then—it's not that old, it's from the nineteenth century, but I saw signs of a previous restoration on it. This is strange if you consider that such icons weren't restored at that time—it was cheaper to paint a new one. It suggests that this icon was very important to someone. And then—all the saints assembled on it seem to be the patron saints of some large family. Well, let them be the patron saints of your family now . . ."

The icon belonged to my parents, but when they moved to their *dacha* [summer cottage] in Peredelkino, my brother and his family moved in to their apartment, and so the icon remained with them. We had almost no access to it, and my brother was not a praying man. I entreated the Mother of God to arrange for the icon to find its way back to my parents, so that I might visit them and pray before Her.

Then my mother called me and said:

"Please bring me my icon, right away. I really need it."

"All right, I'll do it tomorrow . . ."

"No, it has to be today! Immediately!"

If you hadn't known that I had tearfully entreated the Mother of God for access to Her icon, this would have seemed not only strange, but unbelievable—such insistence on the part of my mother, who also, honestly speaking, looked at it as an object of art rather than a living image.

I took the icon from my brother, wrapped it in a large clean towel given to us by a Ukrainian priest, and, pressing it to my chest, went outside to catch a taxi: I didn't have a car then, and it seemed like blasphemy to take the icon onto the subway or commuter train, especially during rush hour. Moreover, it was large, and heavy.

As soon as I left the entryway, I saw a taxicab with a green light driving right in our courtyard. He had a sign on his windshield saying "To the park," and underneath, "Metro Ryzhskaia taxi parking lot," which was one stop from the house, then: "Shift over at 5:00." It was already after five.

Nevertheless, the cab driver immediately stopped:

"Where are you going?"

"To Peredelkino."

"Take a seat."

And so we went. I had the icon in the towel on my lap. While we were driving, the cab driver kept grumbling:

"Why did I pick you up? I don't understand it! It was like someone told me to stop! My shift was already over."

Then we got stuck in traffic. Again he began:

"Why did I pick you up?"

On top of it all, the bridge over the Moscow Ring Road was under construction, and we were forced to make a detour around it on a one-lane road. We dragged along slowly or stood at a complete standstill. By that point, he had begun to hit the steering wheel in despair:

"Why did I pick you up? I was two minutes from my taxi lot. When am I going to get home now?"

"All right," I said. "I will explain to you why you stopped and took me. Here," and I unwrapped the towel, showing him the icon. "It was the Mother of God who put the thought in your head to stop, otherwise I wouldn't have reached my destination with this icon."

He was silent. And then he said:

"I also have a connection to the Church. Yes! I was drafted into the army, and they sent me to war in Afghanistan . . . My mother went to Elder Kirill in the Holy Trinity Lavra of St Sergius and asked him to pray for me. And he told her: 'Don't cry, your son will return alive and unharmed—you just pray for him every day. I will pray, too, but when he returns, he must come and see me.'

"And so my mother prayed for me. I felt that some power was protecting me—everyone in my unit had been killed or wounded, I alone remained unharmed; I even felt guilty about it: not a scratch on me, everything had passed me by."

"I came home, and my mother told me about the elder, saying that I must without fail visit him and thank him. But soon she passed away, and I got caught up in all my worries and cares, in my work, and this Lavra was so far away—how was I supposed to find it? So I never made it, to this day . . ."

"Well, do you know why else the Lord arranged for you to drive me?" I asked him, wrapping the icon back in its towel, as my parents' *dacha* came into view. You picked me up because right there, after the turn in the road, is the Church of the Transfiguration. That Fr Kirill, whom for so many years you couldn't manage to visit, is there now. Go into the church courtyard, he's seeing people to the left in the baptistery, until eight o'clock exactly. You have another half hour."

He let me out and flew down the road, leaving a cloud of dust behind him.

What became of him—only God knows ... But it's possible that if he made it to Elder Kirill, he understood to Whom he must offer prayers of gratitude for his miraculous preservation. It's even possible that he became that hieromonk from a distant monastery of whom some monks that I knew told me recently:

"By God's miraculous providence, our Fr N. came out of the very thick of the Afghan War without a single scratch."

I, in the meantime, brought the icon to my mother, and she greeted it like the living image it was. Later, when my husband was ordained a priest, she gave the icon to us.

∾ *The Gypsy* ∾

My friend's mother died, and he asked me to take his sister Anna, who was my neighbor, to the funeral.

My husband and I picked her up and set off on our sad journey.

His sister and I knew each other from childhood—we were at summer camp together and had been fast friends there: we would run away together and climb into people's *dacha* gardens, stealing unripe apples.

Later, when she matured into a young adult, I heard that she had fallen in love with a famous poet who was much older than she and who lived here in our little writer's town, and whose attention she fought to obtain with all her power. She spied on him at his gate when he would return home late at night, kept watch at his door when he would set off to Moscow in the morning, and once even sneaked into his house in his absence and hid in his closet. He came home, opened his closet, and there she was!

But she—alas—never managed to conquer his heart. Moreover, at the mere mention of her name he would start to yell and curse, remembering how she had frightened him that time. So she fell into a terrible melancholy. It was even suspected that she was ill.

And so we were driving to Moscow, getting stuck in traffic, fretting about being late, and suddenly she said to my husband:

"I remember, Fr Vladimir, how one Gypsy predicted that you would be a priest!"

"What?" My husband said, surprised, "What Gypsy? I don't remember any such thing!"

It's doubtful, I thought: even before he started attending church, he had always preserved a purity in connection with the metaphysical. He was never interested in extraterrestrials, or fortunetelling, or spiritualism; even when someone would tell him excitedly about what a mess the evil spirits had caused . . . And yet, I now began to dimly recollect something . . .

"You told me about it when you were reading my coffee grinds," Anna said humbly. "And it all came true!"

And suddenly I saw it all before my eyes as if I was there, everything that had happened then, many-many years ago, before we were even baptized . . .

Anna had once come to us—acting strange, as if she were in a fog, all melancholy, and spoke to us through her fog, staring with an unfocused gaze, looking straight through us, and we felt very sorry for her. We had already been informed by the famous poet about the closet. I brewed some coffee, and my husband decided to conduct a psychotherapeutic séance with her:

"Anna, do you want me to read your fortune in your coffee grinds?"

Of course, he had no idea how this was done. He just took the cup from which she had been drinking, and began to tell her, borrowing from her situation, what his good sense suggested to him:

"Anna, you suffer much and are wasting too much spiritual strength on this, but it means nothing to the person you are thinking about. You must give away this love to other people who are in need of it—the sick, the lonely, the miserable. You have enough love and compassion for them all. People like you become nurses, comfort the fatally ill who have been abandoned by even their family, or raise orphans . . ."

My husband said some other encouraging and spiritually beneficial words to her then, in order to distract her from her obsession with that useless famous poet.

"Actually," suddenly he started to backtrack, "don't listen to me! I was once told by a Gypsy that I would become a priest!"

"You—a priest?" she laughed.

I laughed too. And my husband laughed. So strange, unlikely, impossible it seemed then . . .

And now Anna, having herself become a nurse in a sisterhood of Orthodox nurses, reminded us of this.

"Yes, yes," she said as we drove up to the church where the funeral was being held, "you told me about that Gypsy yourself! Well, do you remember now?" And she climbed out of the car, slamming the door behind her.

What difference does it make, I thought, if a Gypsy actually told him that or not—he just made it all up at the time. And that means that some mysterious premonition had whispered to him of the impossible, and he had said aloud: "I will become a priest!"

And those words came true! For a priest he truly became.

❧ *Martyr Tryphon* ❧

I had heard many stories about the miraculous aid of the Martyr Tryphon, but some things I can add from my own experience. We had an icon with a piece of his miracle-working relics in our Church of the Mother of God of the Sign, near Ryzhskaia metro, where we had been going for many years with our children until we moved to the other end of Moscow. For all those years, we prayed before that icon of St Tryphon.

In fact, the Martyr Tryphon was a Greek saint. He was famous for healing people, driving out demons, performing many miracles, and suffering terrible torments and death for his missionary work. In Russia, he became especially revered after he had saved one Tryphon, who was Tsar Ivan the Terrible's hawker. This hawker had released the tsar's favorite hawk and couldn't find him, for which offense he faced the tsar's anger and a terrible death. But he saw a vision of his holy protector, Tryphon, on whose shoulder sat that very same imperial hawk . . .

The akathist[1] to the Martyr Tryphon includes his words encouraging people to pray to him for help with cares and illnesses and promising to come to their immediate aid. And in truth, he really does immediately respond to a person's plea.

Usually people pray to him in cases of illness, asking for healing; often they ask him to help a lonely man find a kind wife, or to send a young girl or lonely woman a good husband, but neither does he forsake those who turn to him on regular matters.

They ask him to help with household and life problems, to destroy harmful pests in the crops, and finally, remembering how he found the lost hawk, they ask his help in finding and returning lost items.

I, too, once requested a moleben and akathist to the saint, asking him to help me join a writer's union. My case had already reached the Selections Committee, where I heard I had influential ill-wishers. On the other hand, all official indicators pointed to my acceptance: after all, in spite of my young twenty-five years, I had a book of poems published in the prestigious *Sovetskii pisatel'*, I had publications in *Novyi mir* and *Den' poezii*, I had positive reviews and criticism of my poetry . . . I was almost certain that everything would be all right, but it never hurts to pray . . .

And so I prayed at this moleben on the very day of the meeting of the Selections Committee; I came home, my husband had already bought a little cake to celebrate, my friends came over, it would seem that we were already celebrating my victory . . . and then, the phone rang.

"Olesia, you were voted down."

"What do you mean, voted down?"

"Well, they didn't accept you!"

"Why?"

"Just like that. They didn't take you, and that's that! They said that you were the daughter of a writer . . ."

I was dumbfounded. Honestly speaking, this was a huge shock to me. Being accepted into a writer's union in those days meant roughly the same as receiving a noble title in imperial times. It meant social status. Moreover, for my struggling family, with two children already, it would have given us the chance to emerge from long-lasting poverty. Compensation and fees for lecturing were twice as high for union members as for mere mortals who happened to write something. I could have traveled for free once a year to a boarding house for artists—in Koktebel or Yalta, in Pitsunda or Dubulti, in Maleevka or Peredelkino—and pay close to nothing or nothing at all for a day's stay. Every year, I could have written for the *Writer's Sanitorium*

Bulletin and made good money on this three-month assignment. I could have gone on a writer's business trip wherever I wanted—Georgia, Estonia, Lake Baikal—and not have to answer to anyone for what I did there or if I wrote anything while I was there . . .

In short, the benefits were many, and I had already been mentally preparing to make use of them: the travel, the business trip, the newsletter, the doubled salary . . . and now this shock. I even took my complaints to St Tryphon—not to say that I was upset with him, but I did ask him, what did he mean by it? I had small children, no money, my clothes were shabby, my shoes were old, we had junk for furniture . . .

Then I received a phone call from the Bureau for the Advocacy of Literature and was given an offer to read poetry to the town of Shebekino in Belgorod Region. I, of course, agreed: no doubled salary here, but it was a chance to earn a little money.

It was when I was returning from Shebekino with a bouquet of calla lilies in my arms that I miraculously ended up going to see Elder Seraphim (Tiapochkin). After that, I forgot about the writer's union completely because my life and that of my family took a turn in an entirely different direction—monasteries, monastic sketes, holy springs, elders, miracles, midnight liturgies, fasts and prayers, monks, holy fools and fools-for-Christ . . .

On more than one occasion, I thought about what a good thing Martyr Tryphon did for me, leading me away from a dubious path. For if they had accepted me at that time into the writer's union, I would never have gone to Shebekino, I would not have seen the elder, I wouldn't have met my father confessor or my spiritual father or the miracle-working lowly Monk Leonid. In a word, I wouldn't have known any of those precious people who surrounded the elder and with whom the Lord then gave us such a strong connection; I would have taken on that three-month bulletin, the three-day trips to Koktebel, a business trip to Georgia to my friends. I would have demanded a good apartment for myself and would have acted how a young wife with two children and a husband with the reputation of a doer and a dissident was expected to act: i.e., support their well-being and progress in the world.

I would have continued to go rarely to church, taking my children to communion and thinking that these Church Mysteries[2] were for simpletons, and that for enlightened and creative types like me other mysteries of the spirit existed: the mystery of inspiration and the tabernacle of the spirit. Just like that, I had seen something of that nature in the writings of the Russian religious philosophers Berdyaev, Merezhkovsky, Solovyev ... Who knows where that path would have led me ...

Thus, the Martyr Tryphon did not let me go to the writer's union at that time in my life and did not allow me to make use of all its privileges. When I finally realized that this was a GOOD thing, I began to turn to him often in dubious situations, and I always received his help. Several times, in dramatic and extreme cases, I asked him to find some item of considerable importance. I would like to tell you about one of these instances.

While my husband and I sat in the admitting room of the hospital, waiting for him to be checked in, Nastia called me in tears and told me that she was not being allowed to take her exam because she had forgotten her exam sheet at the *dacha*. This was at the time of day when the commuter trains didn't run, and going to Peredelkino on other forms of public transportation would be a long and uncertain journey. And so I left my husband at the hospital, and rushed off in the car to find her exam sheet on my own.

This was the end of July, and there was terrible traffic leaving Moscow. The cars moved inch by inch. Finally, I reached the house and rushed into Nastia's room, which should rather be called a den—it was so small, low, and dark even in the light of the bright sun, which was blocked by the thick crowns of trees. And to my dismay, the whole community had no working electricity.

Throwing open the door to her room, I froze in the doorway: there were piles of books, notebooks, and papers heaped up high everywhere—on the desk, on the bed, on the chair, even on the floor. It was obvious that my daughter had been seriously involved in a fierce quest for knowledge in this room ... I began to go through the papers with a trembling hand, bringing them up to my eyes and trying in the thickening dusk of her den to identify the document that was so indispensable to her.

I dug through everything on the table, on the chair, on the bed, and finally, on the floor, but there was no trace of it! I helplessly lowered myself onto the doorstep with no idea of what to do next. And at that moment I noticed a small icon of Martyr Tryphon on the shelf above the desk. He stood in his full-length red cloak, and his right shoulder was adorned by the lost hawk of Ivan Vasilevich . . .

And I began to pray! My husband sat in the hospital waiting for a terrible operation, my daughter stood before the doors to the examination room waiting for her forgotten document, I sat in the dark in her vandalized den, where I had looked through and reexamined everything but in vain, in vain!

Then I reached for the pile of notebooks, books, brochures, and papers on the table once again—I had just looked through it all, sifting through the pages, laying them to the side one by one, but nonetheless I began again. From my touch, the pile shifted and, losing its balance, crashed onto the floor in total disarray. Textbooks, some sort of theoretical instructions, schedules of exams, tomes of Pushkin, Leo Tolstoy . . . and suddenly, one piece of paper separated itself from the rest, glided to the top of the pile, and covered all those underneath it. On it was written: Exam Sheet.

Seizing it, I jumped into the car and in half an hour had handed it off to my daughter, the suffering aspiring graduate, who immediately went to take her exam and was shortly afterwards accepted into the institute.

There were times, however, that I appealed to the Martyr Tryphon in less dramatic circumstances: the potential loss almost seemed too trivial to bother the saint about it. Nevertheless . . .

This happened in the summer while we were at our *dacha* in Peredelkino. Our daughters had come to visit me and Fr Vladimir with their children, as well as my brother Mitia with his beautiful dog. A friend of our granddaughter, Sonia, also came—the twelve-year-old Verochka, who was our neighbor's daughter. Verochka's mother diligently tried to shelter her from all the cruelties of life, and therefore handed her over to us personally, though they lived only one hundred meters from us. She even gave her a cell phone, so that she could call "if anything happened."

The children romped around to the fullest: they ran through the forest surrounding the *dacha* and played with the dog, rushing after it through the nettles, hiding from it under bushes; they only returned home when the thunder started and the rain came down.

Once inside, Verochka reached for her phone, but it was nowhere to be found. It had apparently fallen out when she was climbing through the bushes and hiding in the ravines. There was nothing to be done but to wait for the rain to die down and all go out—adults and children—in search of Verochka's cell phone; we armed ourselves with our own cell phones, and scattered in all directions. We took turns dialing her number in various places, hoping that Verochka's phone would ring and one of us would hear it and follow the sound.

The rain had stopped, the sun came out, but all we got in answer to our calls to Verochka's phone were long, plaintive beeps that weren't managing to break through the nettles and bushes. The meadow was silent, the ravine was mute, the yard was quiet, and the fir grove too.

Verochka was barely holding back her tears—it was obvious that she would be scolded for losing the cell phone: her mother was strict, temperamental, and willful, while Verochka was quiet and timid. And her family wasn't wealthy enough to view the loss of a cell phone as an insignificant problem.

To make a long story short, seeing that it was a hopeless case, we finished our search and returned to the house. The phone battery had probably died already; it had probably gotten wet in the rain, and was now lying mute under a fallen branch . . .

"Let's pray to the Martyr Tryphon," I suggested just in case. "What if he finds it?"

We stood up in front of the icon of the saint, sang his troparion, and read a prayer, adding in our own words that we hoped for his help very much. After that, we took to calling the phone again, dispersing throughout our plot of land. But this time, a steely voice told us that the subscriber was unavailable or out of range.

Suddenly, Fr Vladimir confidently and decisively walked toward the same bushes that we had repeatedly inspected; he knelt down, reached out his hand, and plucked Verochka's phone out of the thick grass.

"How? What? How did you know?" we thronged around him with questions.

He shrugged his shoulders in uncertainty:

"I just went and picked it up from the ground."

From that point on, even our little children knew who was always ready to rush to their aid, wipe away their tears, and bring them comfort surpassing even the grief that had caused their tears in the first place; and they now appreciated the value of an object that had been restored to them.

❧ *Criss-Cross* ❧

S eminarians who do not intend to take the monastic vow and who wish to become priests must enter into marriage before being ordained. But this is very difficult for them to do if they have no childhood friend or neighbor from before they went to live in the seminary who would want to be a priest's wife. Seminaries are usually located on monastery grounds and the seminarians live behind strong monastery walls. Where can they find a worthy life companion? Among whom do they have to choose?

In recent times, at least, seminaries have begun to introduce conducting courses in which young girls with a good voice and a good ear may study: this did not exist before. Seminarians, who had already graduated or who were on leave, could only walk the streets and gaze around, wondering if the Lord would send them their intended. No, really—were they supposed to find them at nightclubs? At the karaoke bar Metelitsa?

As for those young lady parishioners who attended the seminary churches, they would inspire an undignified sense of competition among the future priests. I was once a witness to that drama. A seminarian came up to a modest young girl with a headscarf and a long skirt, and asked her:

"Are you going to the holy unction service today?"

And she answered him:

"I'm going, only with Peter, not you—he asked me first."

And that same Peter hurriedly and authoritatively tugged the girl by her sleeve:

"Let's go, let's go. I saved a spot for you in the line for confession."

Thus he made his conquest of a potential *matushka*.

In addition, those emaciated, closely trimmed and shorn seminarians, in their short little suits, which always seem too small for some reason—narrow in the shoulders, short in the sleeves and trousers—looked like ugly ducklings, so that none of those young girls could even dream that they would soon become majestic swans: once ordained and clothed in a cassock and *ryassa*,[1] they would grow out their thick hair and magnificent beards and become handsome youths—one after the other.

But their chances were smaller when, while stammering and getting flustered, they tried to get acquainted with young ladies sometimes by just stopping them on the street, and because the seminarians were still in their untransformed, uncomplimentary, and even, frankly speaking, miserable-looking forms, their chances were small.

When I used to visit the Lavra, I also would be approached several times on the commuter train by young men with the characteristic haircuts and collars of seminarians, who tried to start a conversation with me. Once, when I stayed for a bit after the evening service in the Church of the Mother of God of the Sign in order to venerate the icon of the Martyr Tryphon, I had just stepped away from it when a young man stopped me and straight-out asked me:

"Forgive me, but you couldn't possibly marry me right away? I'm going to be ordained in a few days . . ."

He had obviously come to pray to the Martyr Tryphon, who they say helps people to find a good spouse, and there I was—young and with my blond braids, and by all appearances someone who kept the fasts, knew how to cross herself, prayed, and even stayed to venerate the icons after the service.

I looked at him and saw that he was almost dying from nervousness—he was all red, nearly driven to tears; but still, he was very nice, with such an exalted expression on his thin and pleasant face. I swear he might have convinced me! Had I not been married already and a mother of two, I might have agreed out of a sheer sense of adventure and the mere extravagance of such a marriage proposal!

In short, marriage was a big problem for seminarians. Even if you found a girl, who knew what she was really like? It was impossible to tell during those brief acquaintances—what's more, they always appeared pious and modest in the beginning, but what came after . . .

Seminarians would even take the young women to elders. It was said that one elder could immediately tell who would make a good couple and who wouldn't. Sometimes it even happened that two prospective married couples would come to him at the same time from opposite ends of the country. He would look them over with a critical eye and would shake his head in disapproval, as if to say no, it's all wrong.

"How can we make it right?" The couples would ask him, frozen in fear and dismay.

"Criss-cross," he would say. "I will only bless it the other way around, not this way."

This meant that the potential bride of the first young man must now marry the other young man, and the bride of the other must marry the first.

Who knows, perhaps some did find marital bliss in this manner, but I was told of one instance when the young people were obedient to this "criss-cross," and it only ended in divorce, tragedy, and pain.

There was another scandalous story of a young priest, who while still a seminarian, received a blessing from his spiritual father—who was a bishop, by the way—to marry his fiancée. However, as soon as she was a legally married woman, the modest headscarf that had formerly covered her head immediately went into the garbage, the long grey skirt in which she had gone to see the bishop went to the poor people sitting outside, and she started frequenting the gym, getting manicures and perms, putting on makeup, pulling on miniskirts and cleavage-baring tops, and going to nightclubs.

"What are you doing?" the young man would exclaim. "You're a *matushka* now!"

"Oh," she would wave her hand. "You aren't going to do anything about it—priests aren't allowed to divorce, and you don't want to be a monk. So now you must bear it and support me until the end of our days. It's supposed to be like that for you—humility aplenty, patience through trials and tribulations, but I, for one, will not waste away my youth among pious old women in those grey rags of theirs. It was almost more than I could bear while I was trying to win you over—all those fasts and prostrations, prostrations and fasting. I almost ruined my complexion! And anyway—I like the singer Madonna, that's who I want to look like!"

So the desperate priest went off to his spiritual father, the bishop who had blessed him to enter marriage. In a surge of emotion, he rushed right into his office and exclaimed from the doorway:

"Your Grace! You gave me your blessing, I brought you my bride and showed her to you, you blessed us to marry, and now she goes to nightclubs, she pierced her nose, she has tattoos . . . Why did you do this to me, *Vladyka*?[2] You sentenced me to a life of ridicule!"

And this bishop, seeing that he was in a fighting mood, went to the other side of his table just in case, in order to increase the distance and place a barrier between them. But the young priest, out of the fullness of his grieving heart, took a step in the direction of the table and began to walk around it, trying to approach the bishop. The bishop, however, kept stepping in the other direction—who knew what was going to happen? The priest took another step forward, waving his hands and gesticulating, and the bishop took another step back. So they went on circling around the table.

"Oh, *Vladyka, Vladyka*, how could you do this to me?" the priest would say reproachfully.

Finally, the bishop grew weary of backing away; he stopped, held his head up high, shook out his hair, and blurted out:

"This is not a totalitarian sect! You should have thought better for yourself! You yourself are to blame! Nobody forced you and nobody prevented you either!"

This exclamation brought the bishop's cell attendant running in; he knew the priest's story and blocked the bishop with his body, yelling at the unhappy priest:

"You knew what you were getting! You chose it, you kneaded it, you cooked it, now you must eat it!"

The poor priest, fighting back tears, turned on his heels and dashed off without asking the bishop's blessing.

"You, yourself," he repeated to himself, running down the street and beating himself on the chest, "you, you, yourself!"

✎ *The Queen's Pendants* ✑

When by the holy prayers of the Martyr Tryphon I wasn't accepted into the writer's union in 1982, my husband and I with our two little children found ourselves on the brink of poverty: we hardly had enough money for food. Nevertheless, the Lord generously and continually sent us everything we needed and more—He clothed us, shod us, fed us, and arranged holidays for us.

I had a lovely little white English fur coat given to me by a friend—the English reporter Tony Robinson—and a pair of gorgeous black knee-high leather boots, which a friend had given to me because she didn't like them for some reason.

I repeat, the boots were top-notch, warm, with only one fault: they were unbelievably slippery—so slippery that it seemed like they had been designed for clowns. A clown gets up quickly on stage, but his legs slide in opposite directions and he falls down—ha-ha-ha, how funny! So these boots required their owner to have a special talent, I would say, a balancing act with your legs, otherwise you could whimsically throw your feet up in the air and flop onto the ice or sprawl in the snow.

But that is beside the point, and my story is not about that.

My spiritual father was at that time an inhabitant of the Holy Trinity-St Sergius Lavra. His Holiness Patriarch Pimen[1] had given him an old, valuable cross for restoration and instructed him not to take the cross out of his studio.

My spiritual father restored the cross; however, being a perfectionist, he wasn't completely satisfied with the result. The problem was that at one time the cross had been decorated with precious stones, many of which were now lost. So this part of the job would have to be done by a jeweler. Only then would the cross be restored to its former beauty. Patriarch Pimen himself would be happy about that.

At his own risk, my spiritual father gave the cross for a very short time to a jeweler he knew, a considerably skilled master and a trustworthy person. But because of this, the Patriarch's instructions were disobeyed, and the cross ended up in Moscow.

Then, suddenly, my spiritual father was told that Patriarch Pimen was planning on serving Liturgy at the Lavra and might ask for his cross, if not come into the studio for it himself.

In short, my *abba* called me that evening and begged me to pick up the cross from the jeweler, then take the first train in the morning and bring it to him, or he would be faced, at the very least, with disgrace.

I picked up the cross, and around three o'clock in the morning—to catch the first train at 3:40 a.m.—I set out on foot from my house near the metro stop Prospekt Mira to Yaroslavsky railway station.

In theory, I could have cut across the park, but I was afraid to, and carefully stepping in my slippery boots, keeping my balance with my hands, I headed in the direction of Grokholsky Lane. The streets were cold, blustery, dark, slippery, and empty. There were no cars, either. The patriarchal cross of priceless value lay wrapped in a cloth in my lightweight plastic grocery bag.

I was dressed in the white English fur coat. I walked along and prayed.

Suddenly, a car slammed on its brakes to the left of me and began to drive slowly next to me. The people sitting inside were openly staring at me taking steps that were unsteady at best, wavering and wobbly at worst. I tried to increase my pace, but as a result I immediately let my guard down: my boots began to slip, my feet began to slide apart, and I tottered, almost losing my balance. I made another step—and tottered again.

"What are you, drunk?" I heard from the car. "Hey, prostitute!"

Out of the corner of my eye I noticed that it was a cop car, but this didn't bring me any comfort. I had heard that the police organized raids from time to time near the three railway stations, catching the "nocturnal butterflies," and began to imagine how they would start asking me for my documents, confirming my identity, testing for sobriety: who was I and why was I wobbling around the streets at night, barely standing? They would drag me to the station, start digging in my bag, remove the cross; I would be late for the train, and my spiritual father would be forced to face the Patriarch as a liar. I froze from fear.

"Lord, help me!" I cried out, resolving to move steadily, step firmly, look straight ahead, and not react to any catcalls.

And it seemed to me like the Lord swept me up and carried me, carried me—I simply moved my feet very quickly, taking minuscule steps, while some hidden force carried me further and further without any obstacles; meanwhile, the car continued to drive by my side with me and several pairs of eyes watched to see if I would stumble again.

So I reached the railway station, climbed onto the commuter train, and immediately forgot about my fantastical flight over the snow and ice, my foot march at breakneck speed, my speeding boots.

With my first step onto the Zagorsk platform, I slipped and with my second step, I wobbled, trying to maintain my balance. Holding onto the banisters with both hands, I somehow barely scrambled onto the bridge over the railway tracks, crossed it in the same manner, and, stepping onto the ground, understood that I could go no further: my boots had completely begun to ignore all rules of gravity.

There were almost no people around at that early hour, and the little street onto which I had turned seemed almost empty, so I started moving practically on all fours. Then I came along some roadside bushes and trees, and a gnarled stick that I could lean on like a staff, and I made it in the end in one way or another.

All this reminded me of *The Three Musketeers* and the queen's pendants that had to be delivered on time at any cost in order to preserve her honor. Many obstacles, enemies, and villains were met on the way, but the hero had to overcome all of them. The queen had to appear at the ball in her diamond pendants.

In the same way, my spiritual father, as soon as Patriarch Pimen asked for his relic back after the Liturgy, was able to hand over the antique cross, restored and adorned with precious stones, without skipping a beat.

As for my boots, I never wore them again after that—it was impossible to walk in them. But I often remembered how that miraculous power carried me in them at three o'clock in the morning from my house to Yaroslavsky railway station, while the policemen watched me from their cop car, waiting for a chance to catch me, but which the Lord did not allow.

❧ Embrace ❧

My husband, now Fr Vladimir Vigilianskii, comes from a family of many priests. His last name itself has an ecclesiastical origin—such noble names were given to seminarians who had especially excelled in their studies, and in this way, they became Blagoveshchenskiis, Vosnesenskiis, Bogoiavlenskiis, Preobrazhenskiis, Uspenskiis, or Rozhdestvenskiis.[1] Similarly, my husband's ancestor had simply been Gubin, but later became Vigilianskii.

There were three branches of the Vigilianskii priests in all. One was situated in St Petersburg: it is known that Fr Boris Vigilianskii was the spiritual father of Lermontov's beloved, Sushkova, and that he dissuaded her from the criminal idea of running off with the reckless poet, as the latter had been suggesting.

Another branch spanned the Vladimir Diocese. Fr Maksim Kozlov, the rector of the Church of the Holy Martyr Tatiana, under whom my husband served, recently showed him a photograph of either his great-grandfather or great-great-grandfather—Archpriest Kozlov, and next to him another priest with the last name Vigilianskii. It turns out that they both served at one time in the same church in Murom. What's more, just like now, Kozlov was the rector, and Vigilianskii was the second priest.

The third branch—the biggest one—was spread out throughout the Volga Region. To this branch belonged mitered archpriests and a protodeacon with great presence whose intonations of the litany of supplication had even been immortalized on a record. We were given a fleeting chance to hear this voice and see the photographs of these God-loving ancestors. All this wealth had been in the possession of a cousin of my husband, who had died suddenly and whose property had disappeared somewhere.

This illustrious tradition of priests was interrupted with my husband's father—Nikolai Dmitrievich Vigilianskii, as he became a writer and journalist who spent time in a concentration camp, was freed after the Beria amnesty, deprived of his civil rights, and moved to the countryside. He kept himself occupied with all sorts of things, even becoming a dance teacher . . .

Later, after Stalin's death, the family relocated to Moscow, and Nikolai Dmitrievich's son was accepted to the Literature Institute and became a literary critic and journalist. And so it seemed that the priestly dynasty had come to an end.

But, obviously, the devout Vigilianskii forefathers prayed for the continuation of their line, and the Lord made His choice in my husband. "You did not choose Me, but I chose you" (Jn 15:16). And in one moment, our life suddenly and drastically changed course and rushed headlong in a direction we were frightened to contemplate.

And so, in the end, my husband was ordained to the diaconate on February 14, 1995. Everything about it was miraculous—the consecration was scheduled on the day of the Martyr Tryphon, whom we greatly revered; it took place in the Church of the Mother of God of the Sign near Ryzhskaia metro—"our" church, which we had attended for many years with our children, where we knew all the relics, icons, clergy, singers, and parishioners; and His Holiness Patriarch Alexy II himself led the ordination.

Standing at that Liturgy, which was already nearing its end, I unexpectedly looked to the side, as is the case when you feel you are being watched. I turned my head and saw the left side of the church with the miracle-working icon of the Martyr Tryphon, and farther, near the window, the standing icon of the crucifixion from the skete at Gethsemane, Golgotha . . .

I had always prayed before this crucifixion when I was in that church . . . I had placed candles before it . . . I had venerated the crucified Christ, kissed the Mother of God and St John the Theologian who were suffering next to Him . . .

Now at the Liturgy, however, when I unexpectedly turned my head in that direction, I suddenly saw something new that amazed me, something unusual that I hadn't seen before—this time I didn't see the hands nailed to the Cross, the palms with wounds from the nails, but only the arms of Christ opened wide in a welcoming embrace, only a beckoning, blessed embrace . . .

A little later I wrote a poem:

> The heart is a traitor.
>> The heart is a rider and wanderer.
> The heart is the hunter in an ambush and the animal in the pen.
> The heart is an aging acolyte,
>> nasal voice droning on his commemorations,

And the wizard on the throne!

It is a pawnbroker! A swindler! A slaveholder!
A Pharisee. A man condemned to death.
    A troublemaker brawling on a third-class train.
But also—a recluse,
    A hesychast and a victim of fire.
And an academic-year-repeater manning the rearmost desk!

Through all of its knockings and beatings,
Through its leather bags and its dresses
You will understand only one thing: however you open your
    arms
You get a cross . . .
And the Crucified One opens wide His embrace!

Soon our son Nikolai was also ordained a deacon. So the line of priests, though disrupted, was again restored.

❧ About Love ❧

When my husband and I visited Archimandrite Seraphim in the Little Hermitage after our baptism, we received enough gifts there to last a lifetime. Firstly, it was the people whom we met there: priests, hieromonks, simple monks, pious lay people, holy and blessed fools—Holy Russia. One of these precious people was a hierodeacon of the Lavra who has since become an archbishop.

But at that time, with the elder's blessing, he became our spiritual mentor and enlightener, for we were notably untaught people when it came to matters of the Church.

And so, this enlightener and friend of ours, who was in those days a student of the Moscow Theological Academy and a hierodeacon of the Lavra, once brought us cassette tapes to listen to with recordings of Metropolitan Anthony lecturing to academy students and seminarians. These were lectures about God, ministry, and faith.

One day we sat at the table, on which stood a small tape recorder, and began to listen. Then, the next day, we began to invite friends, relatives, and mere acquaintances so that they could listen too. We sensed that this was in some ways a treasure that we were obligated to share with people near and far, with everyone. If no one came, we listened by ourselves. Everything which *Vladyka* said, and how he spoke—with that wonderful voice of his, his noble, old-fashioned accent, turns of phrase, and intonation—carried, without exaggeration, "indescribable pleasures" to our hungry neophyte souls, so dire was our spiritual thirst.

Here, in *Vladyka's* presence, we sensed a living and personal experience of witnessing to Christ. He spoke as one who had knowledge, who had power, who participated in the mysteries of the heavenly kingdom. We quickly grew to love him. And with this love we most attentively examined his photograph in the Orthodox church calendar, from which a handsome man with a thick black beard gazed at us with piercing eyes from underneath his white *klobuk* (clerical hat). We tried to recreate a mental image of his appearance while listening to his voice, too. This voice, daily resounding throughout our room, was soft, but also, as I said before, very forceful and inspired, and its bearer manifested himself to us as a man who was extremely dignified in appearance, of high stature, and full of strength.

We didn't dare to even dream of meeting *Vladyka* in person—it was still the time of the Iron Curtain, and *Vladyka* lived in London; we knew that his trips to Russia were problematic.

Just like our friend the hierodeacon, our father confessor lived at the Lavra at the time, and we went to him very often—sometimes once a week, sometimes even more often. He would appoint a meeting place at the monastery gatehouse, and then take us to some quiet side room or a church where there were no services at the moment, and there we would confess to him or just talk.

At that time, I was translating poems written by Georgian poets, and I left for one of my research trips to Georgia. At first light, my husband went to the Lavra to receive confession and communion from our father confessor. They were supposed to meet, as usual, at the gatehouse.

This was February 10, 1983. The winter frost was fierce, and my husband, dressed like a frivolous student in jeans and a jacket, had already managed to freeze on the commuter train ride to the Lavra.

At the appointed hour he stood at the gatehouse, waiting for our father confessor to appear at any moment. But ten, fifteen minutes passed with no sign of him. Then my husband, frozen to the bone, began to ask the monks entering the monastery to call our father confessor, explaining that he was supposed to meet him. But another five minutes passed, then ten, and still no one came. My husband, shifting from one foot to the other and shivering from the cold, felt something akin to hurt pierce his soul, and an unpleasant anxiety fluttered in his chest: maybe our father confessor set the time and then forgot? Maybe he was sitting somewhere all warm and praying, his thoughts ascending to the heights, and forgetting all things earthly? The Liturgy would begin at any moment; how was he to take communion without confession? He would, of course, have time to confess in the church near the gatehouse to another priest, but what if he would leave and our spiritual confessor would emerge from the gatehouse in his *epitrachelion* and cuffs, with cross and Gospel in hand?

So he tried to banish these varying thoughts attacking him as temptations, and began to shift from one foot to the other even more earnestly, noting with alarm that his feet were at this point completely numb, becoming wooden and disobedient.

In the meantime, the reading of the hours was announced from the bell tower, the Liturgy began, and still no father confessor came. He didn't come, but my husband, numb with cold, believed that he would appear before him at any moment. He would hate to think that he had stood there so long in vain, and he wished that his pointless wait would still somehow be rewarded at least for his exhibited loyalty with the appearance of his father confessor. A little more time passed, however, before my husband realized that he wouldn't even have time to confess in the church near the gate, and that he would not be able to receive the holy communion for which he had so assiduously prepared.

He stood a little longer, tortured by the icy, frost-ridden wind, to strengthen his sense of duty, and finally, his heart overflowing with disappointment, bitterness, and even hurt, he gave up, opting to go inside the

Church of the Holy Trinity-St Sergius and warm up a little there. He also wanted to pray that St Sergius, now and ever the abbot of his monastery, would somehow remind his prayerful monk of certain earthly arrangements of his.

And so he came to that wonderful church, venerated the relics, and, stepping down, remained close by them. There were few people, the priest read the akathist to the saint in a quiet, rhythmic voice, and several old ladies raised their breaking voices to repeat: "Rejoice . . . rejoice . . ." My husband kissed the reliquary and settled himself in the corner, leaning against a choir stall. It was warm and lovely in the church . . .

Soon seminarians desiring to venerate the saint before the beginning of their school day began to appear, then a stream of people began to pour in but soon dried up—evidently, the Liturgy had ended and those who had been blessed with partaking of holy communion had come to bow down to St Sergius, the abbot and wonderworker.

And so the church eventually became empty—it was a weekday and the weather was unfavorable for pilgrims. Having warmed up, my husband, standing immersed himself in the words of the akathist in the half-dark, illuminated only by the little flames of the multi-colored vigil lamps.

Suddenly, an old monk with a grey beard, who was not tall, or perhaps even slight, as it seemed to my tall husband, appeared in the church doorway. He held himself upright and immediately approached the shrine with the relics. The priest, pausing his reading for a moment, went up to the solea, opened the shrine with the relics with his key, and asked the blessing of the old monk, who didn't carry on his person any sign of his rank. All the old women, seeing the priest asking this old man's blessing, also began to present him with their crossed hands.

My husband, witnessing all this from his corner, decided that asking to be blessed by a man unknown to anyone reminded him of a magic ritual of sorts: neither do you know who is blessing you, nor does the other know what is on your conscience. In short, he decided not to even approach this grey-haired old man wearing a *skoufia*, the hat of a cleric.

Meanwhile, the latter was already walking toward the exit; he passed my husband and even glanced in his direction—he was the only one remaining who had not received a blessing—but my husband lowered his eyes. And then he caught one of the old ladies answering another's question and whispering something like "from England . . ."

My husband started: from England? Could it be that Metropolitan Anthony was here, now? But he hadn't heard anything about this, and what's more, this small grey-haired old man with a straight back didn't look anything like that stately youthful bishop from the calendar. Nevertheless, he understood that if this was truly *Vladyka* Anthony, his favorite bishop, he would never forgive himself if he had been near him and hadn't asked for his blessing. So he rushed after him.

The bishop was already at the doors, and in his agitation, my husband yelled at him with an impertinence that even he didn't expect from himself:

"Wait!"

The old man in the *skoufia* stopped and turned around, looking at this strange young man with amazement.

Here my husband again hesitated—he was so small, so grey, where was his force of presence? Where was his strength? His energy? And finally—where was his *Panagia*?[1] Only a certain unique sparkle in the eyes of this still-unidentified monk could attest to the fact that it was indeed Metropolitan Anthony.

Stammering and discouraged, my husband suddenly asked even more impertinently:

"What is your name?"

"Anthony," the old man calmly replied. "And what is yours?"

"Vladimir," answered my husband, and immediately bent down, asking for a blessing.

But *Vladyka* Anthony didn't even glance at his extended hands. Instead he raised his own, took this insolent, bewildered, and dismayed young man burning with shame by his cheeks, or rather his ears, pulled his face down in order to reach it, and kissed him three times.

At this my husband—who, I must say, is a completely unsentimental man and nowhere near inclined to expressing even the most strong emotion, especially by way of tears—felt such a joyful rush of excitement that his eyes welled up with tears, and he began to prattle on excitedly:

"*Vladyka*, we love you so much, you have done so much for my family and for me personally, we listen to your lectures on our tape recorder, they are so important to us, such a joy, *Vladyka!*"

"Vladimir, we will pray for each other!" said the metropolitan, his face radiant. "Now we will pray for each other forever!"

"Will we ever see each other again?"

"We will definitely see each other again!" the metropolitan promised.

"And we can talk then?"

"We definitely can!"

My husband went outside and, not feeling the cold, went to the monastery entrance. His soul rejoiced. There! he thought, a person can undergo a trial, but then the Lord will comfort them so much that the trial will seem like nothing at all.

Now desiring to share his joy with our father confessor, who also respected Metropolitan Anthony very much, he asked a monk who was just about to disappear into the gatehouse to call our priest.

"But he's sick. He's lying in bed with a temperature near one hundred degrees. It's probably the flu. How am I supposed to call him?"

That evening in Tbilisi (the time difference with Moscow was two hours), my phone rang.

"Do you know who I saw at the Lavra today and whose blessing I received?" my husband asked animatedly.

"Yes, you saw our father confessor."

"No, he's very sick—pray for him. But who did I really, really want to see but didn't even dare to imagine . . . ?"

"*Vladyka* Anthony?" I asked, feeling my throat seize up with joy.

"Yes! Tomorrow he's serving vigil at the Church of the Three Hierarchs, Liturgy the day after tomorrow, and I will see him again!"

I started to cry. This was a true miracle, a gift from God! For some reason, it seemed then that the Lord was strengthening us in this way for impending persecution. I will remind you that it was 1983, the very beginning, and all the spiritual blessings were received and multiplied in view of the forthcoming adversities.

Even in 1986, as strange as it would seem at present, all monks, including those at the Lavra, prepared themselves for great trials. At that time, either in the *Komsomolka* or in *News Bulletin,* a blatantly atheist article came out on the front page, and all monks—young, middle-aged, and old—prepared, just in case, to retreat to the forest, learning by heart the Gospel and church service texts, while others—former concentration camp prisoners—even began to dry bread to make crackers.

If you came to the Lavra, you could see the old, bent-over Hierodeacon Filadelph leaning on the hand of the young Hieromonk Porfirii as they came out of the monastery to go to church:

"How are you, Fr Filadelph?"

"We're making crackers. Have you read the papers? It's beginning again . . ."

Or you would see the former camp prisoner Archimandrite Zosima, whose eye had been poked out by an NKVD[2] agent and who had been sentenced to many years at Solovki. He would sadly shake his head when I approached for a blessing:

"Yes, yes, evil times are ahead . . . Did you see the article?"

There was a story about him, that when he became ill with the flu and ended up in the monastery clinic, his young nurse tried to take his blood sample, sighing heavily:

"Why isn't your blood flowing at all, grandfather?"

"It's because the Bolsheviks drank it all, child, the Bolsheviks!" he replied.

But I must return to my story. My husband did go to that vigil, and to the Liturgy; he came up to the bishop to be anointed, and he partook of communion from him, and kissed the cross in his hands. Every time, *Vladyka* would call him by name, "Vladimir," and say two or three words to him. But to actually speak to him, to ask him a question and hear the answer, was not yet to be.

And so the new age approached, 1988. Metropolitan Anthony came to Moscow and invited us to join him at his hotel, the Ukraine.

Excited and timid, we came to his hotel room. And even though I saw him then for the first time, I had a feeling that I had known this person for such a long time and had loved him for all that time, that he was so near and dear to me that I was struck by the accuracy of the expression "He is a man after my own heart."

Our conversation, too, flowed right away: it was so lively, sporadic, joyful—as if we talked about nothing at all—it was like when people haven't seen each other for a long time, and they are happy just to be together, happy for the sense of being in each other's company again.

Finally, I approached *Vladyka* with a few of my problems —specifically, Orthodoxy and creative work. Well, Berdyaev wrote that humility and creativity, like genius and villainy, are two incompatible things. Looking at creative work from a spiritual point of view, I was always wary of the fact that the process itself (all right, let us call everything by its proper name: the inspiration) completely devoured a person. When I wrote poetry, I practically ceased to notice the world. I literally stopped watching the clock. What should I do then about the virtue of sober-mindedness? How could I keep watch over my passions?

Moreover, I felt energy and strength inside myself that were impossible to attribute to my own physical being—in this state I could work the whole night through. But how could I learn to distinguish between the spirits, how could I be sure that it was not the evil one giving me strength?

In addition—sometimes I wrote something that surprised even me: it was as if I didn't know a thing before I named it, and having named it, then I knew it. It was as if the creative soul saw more than my daily quotidian "I" ... and yet—perhaps it was not the creative soul but a suggestion from the enemy? Could it be that I was falling into some sort of delusion, God forbid? Could it be that while the poet in me was in a state of bliss, the Christian in me was dying?

All this I imparted to *Vladyka* Anthony. I also added how I sometimes tried to fight this so-called creative energy: one, two!—and I resolved to cut it off with a willful gesture. How I tried to insert my Orthodox consciousness, or call upon it as a censor; how I tried to place the sign of the cross over all the dark corners and recesses of my soul, how at times I twisted the end of a poem in order to crown it with something tried and true, something spiritually beneficial: an allusion from the Gospel, or a veiled quotation from the holy fathers, or a simple moral. But the poem would only be distorted from these intrusions; it would collapse like a man whose legs had been tied; it would lose its vitality.

Here *Vladyka* stopped me and said strictly, almost severely:

"Don't you dare do that! You will ruin everything that way! I don't say this in general, but only to you. Remember that there is a parable in the Gospel about the grains and the weeds. A man planted a good harvest in the field, but his enemy came and planted weeds among the wheat. When his slaves offered to pull out the weeds to their master, how did he answer? He answered: 'No, lest while you gather up the tares you also uproot the wheat with them' (Mt 13:29).

"It is the same with you in that moment: when you begin to artificially destroy what you wrote, feigning virtue and wonder, and inserting something universally known and acknowledged, you ruin your wheat, what may be your good harvest. Leave everything as it is, even if it has some weeds, and it will fall to you to be the judge of it."

Thus Metropolitan Anthony spoke to me, so that I would understand that wherever there is the spirit of Orthodoxy, there must be freedom. But where there is freedom, there is always risk.

Fr Vladimir, on the other hand, who at the time was not yet Fr Vladimir, asked *Vladyka* among other things what to do: the publishing council of the Patriarchate had asked him to compile Dmitry Donskoy's life for his canonization. But he was dismayed by several facts of his biography that seemed to him inconsistent with sanctity, and so he declined. And now that the right-believing prince had been canonized, what was he to do with these doubts?

Vladyka answered with authority:

"You must sort it out with him in your prayers. He is a saint, after all!"

Thus we sat, so wonderfully—asking, listening, and wondering—when suddenly the telephone rang. *Vladyka* took the phone, broke out into a smile, and cried out joyfully, affectionately, even:

"Dear *Vladychenka!*[3] Come in, come in!"

Then he turned to us:

"You will not object if a bishop who is a very good friend of mine joins us right now? I know that he is looked upon in different ways here, but I love him very much. He is a very spiritual person—Archbishop Ioann Snychev." (At that time Ioann Snychev was the Archbishop of Kuibyshevsk.)

"How can we object?" we answered, taken aback, especially since the name meant little to us.

In three minutes flat there was a knock at the door, and the archbishop entered. They kissed each other in greeting, gave each other the mutual blessing, and it was obvious to us that their relationship was one of warm and touching brotherly love, as between two people who are very close to each other. They slapped each on the shoulder, called each other "*vladychenka*" and "*vladychka*," addressed each other in more familiar language, smiled at each other, joked with each other. It became joyful, hot, and crammed in the room. We received the archbishop's blessing, while the manager of that hotel, now transformed into a monastic cell, introduced us, pointing at me and saying, "She's a poet."

At that moment, *Vladyka* Ioann noticed on the table a pile of journals with my poems that I had brought to show Metropolitan Anthony, and he said:

"What do you have here? Let's take a look," and taking one of the open journals, he began to read them aloud, chuckling and tripping a little over the words.

In that moment, I caught the disconcerted glance of *Vladyka* Anthony and understood that he worried that his amiable friend would begin to treat my work with irony and offend me with his sarcastic tone.

In theory, I can say that I would not be against such a recitation of my work, especially considering it was the poem "The Correspondence of Ivan the Terrible and Kurbskii"—aggressive, indicative, shall we say "in the manner of a holy fool." Every line begins with either "Kurbskii to Ivan:" or "Ivan to Kurbskii:", and after each respective colon—endless quarrels, the eternal debate of Westerners and those bound to their home, liberals and nationalists.

But *Vladyka* Anthony didn't know this and hurried to my defense.

Recovering from his momentary discomposure, he tried to take away the journal:

"That's not for you, it was a gift to me, you don't understand things like this!"

Archbishop Ioann, in the meantime, began to turn and hide the journal behind his back:

"No, no, let's take another look, let's see what they've come up with, those pen pushers!"

So they stood, waving their arms and trying to take the journal from each other. Finally, *Vladyka* Ioann emerged the victor: he grabbed the unfortunate edition from Metropolitan Anthony's hands and ran away from his friend to the other side of the small desk standing next to the couch, trying to read on the run despite being hotly pursued. After having run several times around the desk, laughing and out of breath, *Vladyka* Anthony suddenly jumped onto the couch, positioning himself over the very head of his guest, who in turn momentarily lost sight of him, and, victoriously taking away the journal, even lightly tapped him over the head with it.

The hierarchs laughed, panting for breath, while my husband and I were in tears from laughter—it was all so joyous, so wonderful, performed with such happiness and the type of love that only exists between close friends and brothers. They were both: friends and brothers.

Only several years later did I learn that it was a habit of malicious members of certain parties to pit these wonderful archpastors of the Church against each other, saying that *Vladyka* Ioann was a spiritual leader of the "patriots," while *Vladyka* Anthony was the spiritual leader of the "liberals"—although what kind of a liberal was he, a monarchist, a traditionalist, anti-Catholic, anti-ecumenist?

I even came across informal secular and "Orthodox" questionnaires that attempted to sort the test takers into categories using questions such as: "How do you feel about *Vladyka* Ioann? And what about *Vladyka* Anthony?" And if you answered: "I have much respect for *Vladyka* Ioann," then you would immediately be categorized as an extreme reactionary, but if you admitted that you will eternally love *Vladyka* Anthony, you would be practically labeled a Mason.

Alas! This habit of thinking in Party categories turned these two lovely and bright archpastors into flat token figures, scarecrows to frighten off adversaries, a trump card to defeat opponents.

In reality, of course, they stand immeasurably above these human—too human—accounts, divisions, and groupings. They stand higher than both Kurbskii and Ivan the Terrible, who ever continue to quarrel.

That poem of mine that *Vladyka* Ioann had so futilely tried to read ended thus:

... And such discord rushes through the centuries,

Echoes within the Russian soul, multiplies,
Its apparitions are troubled:
A halfwit tyrant has lodged in it visibly,
A turncoat, *oprichnik*,[4] a spy from Rome,
And the innocents cry out that they are killed.

Rivers spill, uncontained by their banks,
The earth bellows, and the earth burns underfoot.
There is a full moon. A solar eclipse . . .
But out of the groans and wailing arises
The miraculous image of the Martyr Philip,
And Cornelius hails from the smoldering embers!

Somewhere there, next to the most blessed Metropolitan Philip and the humble Abbot Cornelius, or at any rate in the same row, so to speak, from the point of view of heaven but not of earth, we should contemplate the wondrous images of these archpastors, alongside whom the Lord has allowed us to live, create, repent, rejoice, sorrow, celebrate, and sing with a single mouth and heart the creed and "Hallelujah!"

After *Vladyka* Anthony died, my husband and I received some comfort when we were given a remarkable photograph. On it were two young, fresh-faced, wonderful bishops. Looking at them, my heart comes alive, my outlook is brightened, my soul rejoices. It is Bishop Alexy, the future patriarch, and Bishop Anthony, the future metropolitan. Two Russian bishops—von Ridiger and Bloom—each "an angel in the flesh, a man of heaven."[5] We look at them, and they in turn look at us with their fixed gaze.

In the end, you begin to understand that the main treasures of this earthly life are people whom you've met, come to know, gained as friends, and grown to love . . . And this is something nobody can take away!

❧ *"You Do Not Know What You Ask"* (*Mk 10:38*) ❧

M y friend Nadiusha ardently dreamed of getting married. She was, as they say, a divorcée, a single mother past thirty years old, and this caused problems.

Discovering that there was a wonderful saint called the Martyr Tryphon, to whom people prayed specifically to help them get married, she began attending the Church of the Mother of God of the Sign that had his miracle-working icon and ordering prayer services to him.

And so, one day after the prayer service, some guy came up to her and asked:

"You were also praying to get married?"

She fixed her gaze at him in amazement and mumbled something unintelligible.

"Well, there you go," he continued happily, "I was too. Let's get married, apparently God sent us to each other!"

Nadiusha looked him up and down and arrogantly shrugged her shoulders: the man seemed extremely simple, a manual laborer, completely not her type. Nadiusha had an entire checklist: her husband should be intelligent, able to support himself, on the right social level . . . She, herself, was attractive, elegant, highly educated . . .

"Oh, goodness me, no!" she shrank back from her unexpected suitor.

"Why not?" he said in genuine disbelief. "This is not the first time I've seen you here. You asked for a husband yourself! Well, here I am."

And he squared his shoulders.

"No," wailed Nadiusha, "I didn't ask for you at all!"

For two days she was in a state of spiritual stupor—she felt terribly hurt. How she had pleaded, only to get such an unsuitable commodity!

Then someone taught her: when you ask for something, ask for something more concrete—this and that.

And she began to ask not simply to get married, but for her husband to be smart, rich, preferably a foreigner, even more preferably a Western European or an American (but only of a certain kind).

And soon such a man (smart, rich, foreign) did indeed appear in her vicinity. Everything happened just as she had asked: he proposed to her, she married him, and left with him to America.

But—alas! This did not bring her happiness. First of all, her former husband, the father of her child, categorically refused to allow the boy to leave Russia or to sign his release. So she was forced to leave her child with his grandmother. This was payment for the fact that her husband was a foreigner.

Second, it turned out that Nadiusha herself didn't have anything to do in America—she didn't need to earn any money with a rich husband, after all! She began to attend a university and graduated with a degree in conversational Russian.

Third, the American decided to divorce her, but he did this stealthily and secretly so that she wouldn't get any of his money. He found some place where it is legal to get a divorce without paying the spouse alimony. His lawyer simply presented the divorce documents to Nadiusha. And that was all. This was payment for the fact that her husband was smart.

So Nadiusha came home. Now she was reunited with her child, and on her wall hung a diploma awarded for excellent knowledge of conversational Russian. But now she spoke this language in a broken voice, with an intonation that suggested the suffering she had experienced.

How are we supposed to understand this? It can be said that you can get a masochistic sort of high from taking every little bit that you can from life, seemingly enjoying your misfortune ... As for me, I was reminded of this story when I read something by St Nil Sorsky:

"Pray with the words: 'Let Thy will be done in me.' In prayer, I often stubbornly asked for myself alone, for what seemed good to me, foolishly coercing the will of God and not allowing Him to arrange everything as He best saw fit. But, when I did receive what I had asked for, I would grow extremely despondent—why did I ask for my will to be done, for something that turned out completely differently for me than I had imagined?"

And so? If we were to look dispassionately on our disappointments and failures, it would be impossible not to see that many of them were elicited by us, blindly snatched from life.

❧ Wishes Come True ❧

One glorious September day, we—the poet Oleg Chukhontsev, critic
Sergei Chuprinin, and I—walked along Nevsky, chatting happily. We
had come to St Petersburg on a business trip and were staying in a fine hotel;
there was plenty of time left before the evening, when we had a literary event
scheduled, and so we were simply walking around and enjoying ourselves.

"If you think about it, our dreams have essentially come true," said Chukhontsev suddenly. "I, for one, always dreamed not to have to labor hard for
my work, not to go around to all the editors, but just sit at home and they
would call me from their offices and ask for my poems. That's what happened. Now they call me and ask me—I don't even have enough poems for
them."

In his youth, before the collapse of the Soviet powers, he was barely
published; he was censored, and every published work, for which he had to
wait years only to see it in a butchered state, was acquired through heartache
and agony.

"What about you, Sergei Ivanovich, what did you dream about?" Chukhontsev asked Chuprinin.

"I?" he hesitated, a little disconcerted, and said: "Well, I began in Rostov.
So I really wanted to be the chief editor of a thick literary magazine."

"Oh, how perfectly you achieved your goal!" laughed Chukhontsev.
"How many years already have you been the chief editor of *Znamia* now?
Twenty?"

"What about you? What was your dream?" they asked me.

"Me?"

A cool wind blew from the Neva, blowing through the skirts of my thin
raincoat. Golden rays flowed down from the dome of the Kazan Cathedral
and flooded our faces. There stood a red-cheeked and slightly tipsy Peter the
Great with some important lady in a curled wig and crinoline—you could
take pictures with them as a souvenir. Next to them appeared a carriage with
a coachman—did we want a ride? All over Nevsky Prospekt there were a
thousand possibilities for entertainment.

"Yes, yes, of course, you! What did you dream about?" they asked again.
"What were your desires?"

I remembered how many years ago—twenty? twenty-five?—my spiritual father had asked me the same question.

I had answered him then, grimacing from the impudence and improbability of my desires:

"I would like to live among the pines, somewhere in Peredelkino,[1] write poems, and listen to classical music!"

"So you want to find yourself in heaven on earth!" he laughed. And his eyes became clouded over with doubt: he knew—here, on earth, man is doomed to experience many trials . . . Where is there room for classical music among the pines?

"Well, at least tell us—did your dreams come true?" my companions now demanded.

"Well, yes, yes!"

For some reason, I was too ashamed to admit to them about the pines, the classical music, and Peredelkino.

My husband had recently bought a magical computer unit on which we could listen to music from all over the world. And now Mozart, Bach, Schubert, Handel, Vivaldi fill the surrounding air, sometimes competing with the birds singing, sometimes joining voices with the wind rocking the old, creaking pines, and my liberated heart sings along with them.

At the same time, I always approach any "dreams come true" situation with a certain suspicion. After all, you should ask with reflection and care, for you never know what cross you are taking on yourself. As the holy fathers say, the cross for which you asked is the heaviest to bear.

For example, my mother always dreamed that she wouldn't have to wash dishes and clean the house.

My friend Liulia, an actress and singer, dreamed of emigrating ("If only I could escape this cursed country!").

My acquaintance Lenia Zolotarevskii wished to become immensely rich.

The beautiful Iren dreamed of learning to drive a car and buying herself something like an Alfa Romeo.

And so, my mother had a stroke, and in the last ten years of her life, she didn't wash dishes or clean her house, but simply lay in bed.

Liulia left for Israel and settled in a kibbutz; every day she—an actress, singer, ballerina—would earn her bread by going to remove trash from the forest and pick up branches. The artistic career abroad that she dreamed of boiled down to simple amateur performances: at parties she would sing at the table and artistically and expressively tell stories.

Lenia Zolotarevskii became impossibly rich, but someone kidnapped his child and demanded a ransom. After he paid the ransom in exchange for his son, the latter developed a heavy stammer, and Lenia himself soon died of leukemia. The doctors said it was a result of stress.

The beautiful Iren learned to drive a car, but since she didn't have any money, she sold her three-bedroom apartment in a new building and bought an Alfa Romeo with that money, renting a two-bedroom apartment in the city center. Then the landlord suddenly and unexpectedly raised the rent. Iren became nervous and got into an accident, and as a result was forced to move in with her former husband. He lived with his young wife and two small sons, who were born a year apart. Iren lived in their storage closet for half a year, and then disappeared somewhere.

I honestly sometimes think: "Glory to You, O Lord, that You didn't grant some of my crazy desires!"

Vladyka Anthony of Sourozh remembered with a touch of irony how in his childhood, when he saw his uncle's dentures that he took out at night and put into a glass of water, he would passionately dream of having the same.

As for me, in my childhood, when I was visiting my grandmother, I saw an old woman who had spent time in one of Stalin's concentration camps as a political prisoner. When I watched her cavalierly smoking a Belomorkanal cigarette and rather expressively describing her ill-adventures in a pleasant bass, I passionately desired to be like her—to suffer, to live out my years in innocence, to be measured on God's scales and be deemed significant in this life.

As a young adult, I listened to my fill of the stories of my mother's friend, the director Inna Tumanian, relating how she was forced to fight for her movie that had been shelved by the State Cinema Committee, and I also dreamed of being a director and fighting for my work in the same manner. Inna Surenovna had a boyish haircut, so in the ninth grade I also cut my hair like a boy. Inna Surenovna had a gloriously low voice for a woman, so I also began to speak in a low voice. And when I wrote a directorial analysis of *Neznakomka* as my term paper for an introductory course on the basics of cinematography at the Literature Institute, a course taught by the famous L. Trauberg (*The Youth of Maxim*), and he asked me to stay behind after class since he had thought my paper to be excellent, I was not at all surprised, and simply considered it a logical turn of events.

Everyone left the class, and we two remained in the empty auditorium.

"You have talent," said the maestro.

Flattered, I nodded with modest dignity.

"You have true directorial vision. Do you at least understand that?"

I sniffed in embarrassment and anxiously scratched my nose.

"Talent should not be buried!" He even stomped his foot a little, as if suspecting that I already had a shovel hidden and a hole dug out, into which I would jump at any moment . . .

"It's my dream," I earnestly admitted. "I dream of being a film director! To attend the All-Russian State Institute of Cinematography . . ."

"Well, that is where I teach! Let me seek to assist you. But for now, you will study with me," he firmly took my hand, "individually."

And he looked meaningfully into my eyes.

Here I was taken aback at the suggestion in his eyes. The maestro was old, very old, even decrepit. He was so old that, honestly speaking, when he went up to the second floor of the auditorium, dust would fall from him little by little. He was falling apart! But it was exactly for this reason that he remained above any suspicion of immoral behavior.

"But," he continued, releasing my hand, "nobody can know about this! Not one living soul! As they say, save your breath to cool your porridge."

And again he looked up at me with meaning, for on top of everything he was short in stature—he barely reached my chin.

"Right now we are going to leave," he said, handing me a piece of paper with his telephone number, "but you must pretend that you don't know me at all. I'll go first. And then—in three minutes—you go. Do you understand? Shh!!"

I counted exactly three minutes after he left the auditorium and rushed home. But I hadn't even reached the front entrance when I overtook him: he was barely shuffling along. What's more, it was slippery, and his legs were constantly sliding in opposite directions. Suddenly, he faltered and waved his arms, trying to keep his balance.

"Can I help you?" I asked him compassionately, skipping up to him, just like a young Girl Scout would ask an old woman who was planning to cross the street.

He understood my tone correctly. Looking up at me with hurt and anger, he firmly started forward, slipped, and fell.

After that he never invited me anywhere—not into the All-Russian State Institute of Cinematography, not to study with him individually, not into the world of film in any way.

So my film career was over before it had even begun . . .

Another instance . . . My mother had a friend called Lucy—a wonderful loon, a lady of the secular world, the wife of an old writer. She wore fabulous costumes—wide-brim hats and long scarves—she drank champagne, and was wont to appear at my mother's at any moment—even at three o'clock in the morning, with heaps of fanciful stories, announcing from the threshold: "What? You're already sleeping? How can you sleep?" In a word, she was a very inspired and extravagant lady, and very attractive. She would continually "issue a challenge to this world" and would find herself in considerably complex, passionate, and tense relations with it. For this reason she loved to say: "Children? Mercy, I cannot reproduce in captivity!" And I must admit that I liked this very much at the time. I also planned to "not reproduce in captivity" and to "issue challenges to this world." There was a time when I simply dreamed of being like Lucy!

However, my fate unfolded otherwise and led me down a different path. Soon I got married, and had two children in two years. Lucy looked down at me with condescending haughtiness and lost any interest in me. So does a magnificent bird fly by itself in the sky, not desiring to know anything about the provident little hamsters or badgers toiling near their burrows . . .

The years passed, during which Lucy continued to issue challenges to the world, and in the end, she remained completely alone. I recently heard from my acquaintances that they often saw her—old, tipsy, and shabby-looking—in a deli near their house. And later, the news came that Lucy had died. She had fallen asleep, the poor thing, on a bench at the end of October and had frozen to death.

All in all, I had many such occasions for daydreaming, desiring to imitate many people such as these, but thanks be to God that He chose not to hear me at times, nor to respond to all my wishes.

It is truthfully written in the *Great Canon the Work of St Andrew of Crete*: "Skillfully hast thou planned to build a tower, O my soul, and to establish a stronghold for thy lusts; but the Creator confounded thy designs and dashed thy devices to the ground."[2]

Glory to Him Who holds us back from the abyss, glory to Him Who overthrows our wicked plans!

And the music rising above the roof of my house, above the crowns of the pines, proclaimed this truth aloud.

> You, O soul, would contrive to erect
> an entire column of your passions
> and lusts, if the Creator did not
> stop your plans and did not
> overturn your undertakings.

∾ *More Than Enough or Nothing Extra* ∾

My godmother Tatiana, who was the wife of my friend the children's author Gennadii Snegirev, was remarkably generous. And yet you couldn't say that they were people of means. It's always like that with writers—feast today and fast tomorrow. But Tatiana, whether it was a time of feast or famine, always tried to give something to her guests, so that they wouldn't leave empty-handed. One person would depart with a packet of dried apricots, another with books by Snegirev, another with a piece of chocolate, and yet another, like the Georgian archimandrite, Fr Georgii, with a lynx fur! "It is better to give than to receive," Gennadii Iakovlevich liked to say.

It was no wonder that sometimes, even often, the reserves of that house were completely depleted, and Tatiana would ask us for a loan on more than one occasion, in order to survive until her husband's next paycheck.

Thankfully we lived in the same house—either the Snegirevs would borrow money from us or we from them. And very often Tatiana would sigh dreamily:

"If only the Lord would send us some money, Genka and I would go on a pilgrimage to the Holy Land, or buy a house next to the monastery!"

To this Snegirev would reply severely:

"God is no bursar! 'Give her this, give her that!' And no accountant!" he would add in an edifying tone. "And in general—even if you had a million dollars in the desert, you would somehow manage to spend it all immediately, even there!"

Then Tatiana began to formulate her request in a more spiritual setting:

"Lord, tempt me with money!"

This reached the ears of our friend Fr D., a Lavra hieromonk who later became a bishop.

"The Lord Himself disposes of money," he said. "He sends to each person exactly what their spiritual nature demands."

But Tatiana decided that her spiritual nature was such that she would have enough strength to overcome just such a temptation: she would give so much money to the sick and poor, so much she would use to feed others, so much she would donate to God's churches! And she would only leave a little for herself and Genka—for good deeds.

Since their house was in the backwoods, it was constantly being robbed: the oven was broken, the stovetop stolen, the pots and dishes carried off, all in spite of the fact that Tatiana locked the door. Finally, even the front door was stolen, together with the lock. In short, they lost the house. And now she wanted to buy a dwelling place in a more inhabited area, ideally in a small town next to a monastery.

But as soon as they broached this topic, Snegirev would again cut her off:

"God is no bursar for you!"

One time a famous Moscow conductor named Sergei was visiting them—I dare to add that he was one of the best choir conductors—and he said to them:

"How are we to look at this, Gennadii Iakovlevich? If we look at it from the point of view that the Lord gives us all that we need, then in the metaphysical sense that's how it is! In any case, I present as proof that the Lord sent me fifty rubles in a dire moment, and this money saved me and turned my whole life around. Would you like to hear the story?"

"Yes, we would, tell us!" everyone expressed interest.

"With pleasure. I used to be the very worst kind of punk, so low did I sink—I would get drunk with my girlfriends, paint the town. One time we were so drunk that we robbed Durov's Animal Theater. Broke inside and stole—"

"—a guinea pig?" one of us attempted a joke.

"Well, no, we lifted a radio, traded it in for drink . . . By the way, I already had a wife and two small children at this point. And so my wife told me:

"'I don't have any more strength to put up with you; if only I had never set eyes on you! Your children are starving here, we need to feed them, and all you do is drink from morning to night. Go away and don't come back without money!'

"Then she kicked me out.

"I wandered the streets for a long time, because I had nowhere to go, no way to get any money; I just floated around like a dry leaf in the wind. Suddenly, I saw a little old woman with a cane, barely moving her legs trying to cross the street, while the cars continued on in an endless stream, making it impossible for her to cross. I came up to her: 'Here, granny, let me help you.' 'Do, dear boy,' she said, 'or I'll never make it to church.' I led her across the street, placed her right next to the church, and she thanked me: 'May the Lord save you, may He give you health! But why are you so sad? It seems like something is troubling you?' 'Well,' I answered, 'my wife kicked me out and told me not to come back without money, but I don't have a job or anyone to ask for help.' 'Yes,' the old woman sighed, 'this is trouble indeed. What is your name?' I told her. She nodded happily in return: 'Then you must go to St Sergius right away in the Lavra. Turn to him—he will help you!'

"I parted ways with the old lady and thought, maybe it was worth going to St Sergius after all, especially since I didn't have anyone else. I reached the train station—ugh! I didn't even have enough money for the ticket! So I decided to sneak on without paying. I arrived, and it turned out I would still have to walk a long way. Here I became filled with doubt—why did I listen to that old biddy? What had I done! I was not happy.

"But still to the Lavra I went—since I had come this far, what was the point of turning around? I learned where the relics lay, parked myself next to them, and stood there, mentally crying out to the saint.

"Soon, however, it was time to go home: the church was being locked up, the people were going their ways, and I turned homeward. I somehow reached my house, thinking—what if my wife kicks me out again? I still wasn't bringing her back any money! Well, what was I expecting, really, when I went to the Lavra? I came up to the entrance and suddenly saw there an old friend whom I hadn't seen in a long time pacing back and forth.

"'What are you doing here?'

"'Well, I came to see you, but your wife kicked me out. So I've been waiting for you here at the entrance. I brought you some money. Here. Fifty rubles. I borrowed it from you at one point and wasn't able to pay you back, but now I came into some money. Here you are.'

"And he handed me the fifty rubles. I couldn't even remember that he had ever borrowed them from me!

"I took the money, brought it to my wife, and we made up. The next day I was asked to sing in a small church choir. And so my life began to straighten out more and more ... All this thanks to the venerable Sergius! Fifty rubles!"

"Well," I said, "I also have a story about exactly fifty rubles. But it involves St Nicholas the Wonderworker, not St Sergius."

"I don't doubt it," said the conductor. "I am Sergei, after all, and your last name is Nikolaeva. So go ahead."

"The children and I really wanted to visit our spiritual father in the Pskov Caves Monastery. It was summertime by then, and the children were just sitting around in humid Moscow—I needed to take them away somewhere, but the problem was that we didn't have enough money. More to the point, we weren't expecting to get any in the near future. So it was impossible to even borrow it from anyone.

"At the time, we were attending the Church of the Mother of God of the Sign, which had many miracle-working icons. One of them—St Nicholas the Wonderworker—hung in the portico. Two priests who served in that church, Fr Vladimir Rozkhov and Fr Vladimir Rigin, had told me of its power to work miracles—'Go to our icon of St Nicholas the Wonderworker there, he will help you.' And so it was. He had helped me before in a difficult moment.

"So I turned to him once again. I stood before him, lit a candle, and told him everything: this and that, my little ones were suffering in the city, our spiritual father was inviting us, my soul was longing to go there, but there was no money. Help, us please!

"And my heart felt so light, as if I had just spoken to a close and beloved friend—he would definitely help us!

"I came home, and at that moment, Igor Isakov, a good friend whom I had hardly seen in the past two years, arrived, and stood there smiling.

"'Here you go,' he said. 'I'm paying back an old debt.' And he placed fifty rubles on the table.

"'What do you mean, Igor, when did you borrow money from us?'

"'Two years ago, maybe three—I don't remember.'

"'I don't remember either. Maybe you borrowed it from someone else?'

"'It was from you for sure!'

"'Fifty rubles?'

"'Fifty! When you loaned me the money, I even told you, I don't know why, that I was taking a math class that had two smart Jewish boys and only two smart Russian ones, and even those were called Abramov and Isakov. I remember that you laughed . . .'

"I took the money with great disbelief and immediately took off to the station with it. There I bought four tickets in a sleeping car (for one adult and three children) for the Tallin train to Pechory[1] for the way there, and for the way back—no sleeping cars were available—four economy-class tickets for the Pskov train to Moscow. I paid in advance (that was possible then) for the beds. The cashier counted it all up and pronounced:

"'Fifty rubles for everything.'

"Down to the last penny! No more, no less!"

"You see, Genka?" sighed Tatiana, "and you said that God was no accountant! And here we have both credit and debit! He has everything counted, measured, and weighed, even the hairs on our head are all accounted for! (Mt 10:30). Nothing extra!"

And more than enough, I thought, remembering the Pskov Caves Monastery and how wonderful was the time we spent there.

❧ *Come and See*[1] ❧

I n the middle of January, around the year 1991, the poet Iurii Kobula-
novskii called me and downright ripped into me:

"There you are sitting in your home in Moscow, when Fr Sergii Vish-
nevskii is perishing from cold and hunger in his remote village . . ."

"Wait a minute—Fr Sergeii—isn't he the rector of the Church of the
Mother of God of the Sign on Ryzhskaia Street? Why is he in a village and
why is he perishing?"

"Little do you know! He asked to be sent to restore the church where he
used to be an acolyte in his childhood. But this church is in the wilderness,
deep in the forest, and there are no residents in the entire region during the
winter! No stores, nothing! We need to save him!"

"But where is he? Where is this wilderness?"

"Well, listen. You need to get to Rybinsk, my native town—there you
will be met by Boria, my childhood friend. He is not a believer, and is soon
planning to emigrate to Israel, but he will help you to find Fr Sergii. So take
some food and go."

As it was, I had already planned to go to the Pskov Caves Monastery
to see my spiritual father! However, since Fr Sergii was perishing there in
the snow, we must help him. I gathered all kinds of grains, pastas, flour,
sugar, sunflower oil, salt, matches—all the necessities—and set off directly
for Rybinsk.

It must be said that the weather in Moscow was, despite the fact that
it was Christmastime, very sluggish: everything was melting, leaking, drip-
ping, and so I, in response to this weather, went dressed in a flimsy jacket,
thin tights, and a light scarf.

But by morning, in Rybinsk with Boris (Boria)—who was already mentally in blooming Israel—I was greeted by our renowned chieftain, Father
Frost.[2] While I slept on the train seat, thundering ice fettered the waters
and stiffening snows engulfed the earth; my breath produced huge amounts
of steam when I stood on the platform and introduced myself to Boris, and
he hastily described to me the various turns in the road, legs of our journey,
and layovers still to come.

At first, we were supposed to ride on a trolley bus to Myshkin. There we would transfer to another bus until some turn, and then we would walk along the highway, trying to hitch a ride from a passerby. This way we would reach the village. But from the village, we would have to walk on foot through the forest with no road for several kilometers. Then—a wonderful view would be revealed: Fr Sergii's church on a curving river bend, glistening in the ice!

First and foremost, I gave Boria some of the bags with provisions, and he, staggering a little, courageously took them out of my hands. His frail figure was slightly distorted, but he managed to preserve his balance, and we trudged along to the bus stop.

It was an old, rattling bus, toiling away at a speed of fifty kilometers or so per hour and shaking so much that it could have fallen apart at any point during the journey, and we with our pastas and buckwheat could have ended up in a ditch buried under the snow. But all this was nothing compared to the cold that devoured the warm air escaping from the bus heater, and took the immobile passengers prisoner, fettering their hands and feet with its chains.

Here I finally realized that instead of a happy journey in the flurries, instead of a Russian fairy tale with festive frost lining the trees, instead of a warm meeting with our kind and beloved Fr Sergii, I instead faced icy torment, the sensation of my cold and smarting spinal cord freezing to my very skull, and frostbite in my extremities, which were barely covered with cloth gloves and light booties. My companion, however, was not much better off—he was all crumpled and shriveled up, as if he wanted to squeeze into a little crevice and preserve all the remaining heat in it. I immediately repented of the fact that I didn't take a few bottles of good old cognac along—how we would cheer up then and warm ourselves up a little!

In the meantime, we reached Myshkin, where we were supposed to transfer to another bus, but first we decided to warm up a little and went into a hole-in-the-wall shop near the bus station. There stood something like a cast-iron stove, and, laying our bags all around us, we settled down at a table. Boria looked wretched—his lips had turned blue, his eyes were rolling back in his head, and he needed to be fed immediately, but there was nothing in the run-down little shop except some dirty, brown *pirozhki* with fruit filling, so we ordered two cups of hot tea each, served there exclusively in mayonnaise jars.

Finally, having warmed up to a certain extent and wrapping our scarves several times around us—I around my head and Boria around his neck— and loaded with bags, we hobbled off to the local bus. As soon as we climbed aboard, we realized that it was a far cry from that Rybinsk bus that we had so abused in our hearts, which had at least tried to fan us with a warm stream of air. But no sooner did we express our disappointment than the driver, having just left the borders of Myshkin, where we had everything—even a café with a warm stove and tea—and finding himself amid vast and many-layered forests, came to a sudden stop.

"Halt!" He said. "Everyone out!"

"What do you mean, get out? How, get out?" The people grew anxious.

"Get, out, I said," he repeated, waving the disconnected gear unit with his hand, "the bus will go no further."

So we all piled out onto the highway. Boria tightened his scarf and tied it around his skullcap, which made him resemble one of the Frenchmen fleeing Moscow in disgrace in the past.[3] His eyes, in which all the trials of the Jewish people seemed to be reflected, were fixed somewhere in the distance—probably where the blessed Promised Land appeared to him, where the warm Red Sea that had sunk Pharaoh the persecutor along with his horses and charioteers gently lapped . . . [4]

"Well, Boria, we must go on!" I said.

We walked several scores of meters along the deserted highway, avoided a ridge, and began to slowly descend down a hill. Suddenly, I noticed that there was nobody around. The broken-down bus had somehow disappeared from view, and the passengers who had also set out on their journey vanished. Boria and I were all alone in the snowed-over expanse.

"Let's pray to St Nicholas the Wonderworker," I said, "and some car will come by to pick us up. That's what I always do."

"I'm not a believer," responded Boria in a weak voice. "I'm an agnostic. I'm afraid it won't work."

"What do you mean, it won't work!" I mumbled with frost-covered lips. "Let's try and see!"

And I began to recite "The truth of things revealed thee to thy flock as a rule of faith . . ."[5] in a cracked voice. Surprisingly, my voice began to get stronger, and I seemed to get warmer. "An icon of meekness," I barked out.

"Iurii Mikhailovich Kublanovskii also tried to lead me to the faith, but nothing can be done with me!" admitted Boria. "I don't believe, that's all!"

"A teacher of temperance," I continued.

"He made me feel so ashamed! He told me: come and see! Here, with you; he sent me to Fr Sergii."

". . . Therefore thou hast achieved the heights by humility, riches by poverty," I articulated.

"So I'm coming and seeing. Coming and seeing," Boria uttered somewhat helplessly.

"O Father and Hierarch Nicholas, intercede with Christ God that our souls be saved," I finally finished.

"So said Iurii Mikhailovich: come and see . . ."

At that moment, a car appeared from behind the hill. I went onto the road and blocked its path. It was an old jeep with a canvas roof. The driver unhappily opened the door:

"Where to?"

"We would be grateful for anything," I answered.

So we reached the village from where the long journey through the forest awaited us. However, we were already so frozen stiff that it would have been total madness to set out on that road right away—we wouldn't have gone a hundred meters before freezing like the coachman in the desolate steppe.[6] So we knocked on the first door we saw:

"Will you let in some travelers to warm up?" I mumbled with great difficulty.

At that time they still let strangers in. And we settled down near the lit stove. An hour we sat, two . . . but we had to go on to reach Fr Sergii before dark . . .

Again, we loaded ourselves with our bags, now lightened a little by the several kilograms of buckwheat and millet we had given as a gift to our hosts for their hospitality, and trudged on farther—two pilgrims.

Happily, there was some sort of road through the forest after all. Of course, a light car would not have been able to go through, but a tractor could. It was a tractor's tread—and along that we went.

Meanwhile, the chieftain Father Frost was no longer trifling with us—everything had been prepared for him before the feast of Theophany: glistening snowy garlands had been hung up everywhere, the fir tree skirts shone . . . His presence there was so palpable! He himself, it seemed, would emerge at any moment from the forest brush: "Are you warm, maiden? Are you warm, dear?" And I would answer him: "I'm warm, grandfather! I'm warm, dear one!" And I would sit down on my bag under a bush, curl up, and go to sleep.

"Boria, why are you going to Israel if Iurii Mikhailovich is guiding you to the Orthodox faith?"

He was barely stumbling along after me.

"My wife is Russian. She's the one who wants to live in Israel. I myself don't."

"Boria, you should turn to God, ask Him to reveal Himself to you. And ask Him to show you your path."

"No," he whispered faintly. "It won't work. I am an unbeliever. An agnostic. Iurii Mikhailovich said to me: come and see. But to turn to God, to ask Him—he didn't tell me to do that. I'm coming and seeing."

But even if he was still somehow coming, it was clear that he wasn't seeing. He was automatically opening his unseeing eyes and helplessly blinking. It seemed like the Snow Queen had already put blinding icy lenses over his eyes.

"I heard that there are still wolves in this forest," he finally said. "Hungry ones . . ."

"Come on, let me recite the Christmas troparion to you. Did Kublanovskii at least tell you about Christmas?" I said, surprised at my own self.

"I read about it on my own," I barely heard him reply.

In the meantime, it had gotten darker, the wind grew stronger, the snow on the ground came flying up, and it seemed that everything around us began to howl—either it was a snowstorm or really a wolf. I couldn't feel my body, it was so frozen solid and covered with frost that it was like glass.

My feet seemed brittle and fragile: if I fell down, I would break into little pieces.

I remembered a story that told how one Muscovite drove his wife to the airport. This was on a winter evening, and he went in light shoes, because the heater worked well in his car. And so he escorted his wife and turned back home. Suddenly, his engine overheated. He got out of the car, took a water bottle from the trunk, and began to walk "toward the lights"—he thought there was a settlement there. Meanwhile, the frost got harder, as they say, and the lights teased him with their seeming proximity. In the end, while he walked, knocked on doors, explained his situation, walked back, and poured the water in, he got frostbite in his foot—so badly that it needed to be amputated. This story was told to me by Dr Krotovskii, who had treated the poor man. It served as an example of how sometimes, a fatal storm can arise from a small little cloud, how an innocent episode can grow into a tragedy. As for me, by the way, I could develop bronchitis or pneumonia from the slightest draft. I became afraid. I began to pray . . .

But while reciting the Christmas troparion to myself, I stumbled over the words "the light of knowledge," repeating them several times. And this light, it began to radiate within my body.

"That's it!" said Boria. And he sat down on his bag. "I can't go any farther."

"Let's build a fire?" I suggested. "Maybe someone will notice us here and pick us up. You know, the people with the tractor."

And I sat down on my own bag next to him.

"Do we have much farther to go?" I asked.

He turned his head:

"How should I know?"

"Do you mean—you've never been here?"

"No."

"So all this time we've been guessing our way?"

"I was told—from the village via the highway to the forest."

The wolves began to howl louder. It became completely dark. We were going to freeze any minute now, and Boria would find himself at the warm sea in the Holy Land. And I would come home . . .

Then, through the trees, a light seemed to flicker. I closed my eyes and opened them: it didn't disappear, but kept burning and burning . . .

"Light!" I exclaimed. "There are people there!"

"It's a mirage," my companion uttered hopelessly. He had no desire left to go anywhere . . .

Nevertheless, we dragged ourselves in that direction.

The trees parted, and an enormous church rose before us. Small houses pressed around it, and inside one a light was burning. Fr Sergii opened the door to our knock.

Well, first of all, he was not alone, but with his kind *matushka*, Alexandra. Second of all, he was not starving or perishing from the cold because the Lord had fed him already without our help: he had millet-buckwheat-pasta and vegetable oil in reserves to spare, as well as rice, salt, and matches. Third of all, it was warm and festive in his and *matushka's* home: the lit stove sputtered, the decorated Christmas tree glowed, it smelled of fresh pirogi. Fourth of all, Boria and I caused them not a little worry. We were immediately sent to the heated stove to warm up, fed tea with raspberry jam and pirogi, pampered and nursed. Fifth of all, Fr Sergii could not understand for a long time who Boria was, who he was to me, and why he had so suddenly come to his door. He kept telling him of the night service he would arrange tomorrow in his church in honor of the feast of Theophany, and expressing his readiness to entrust Boria with the role of acolyte.

The next morning Fr Sergii, wrapping me up in some sort of coat, took us to show off the surrounding area—the river from which he drew water in buckets with his own hand, the tree on which the miracle-working icon of the Mother of God had been found many years ago, and the church itself—two stories, for winter and summer, with two altars. The summer portion had been completely destroyed and defiled by atheists, but the lower portion Fr Sergii was slowly restoring. Despite all its neglect you could sense the presence of the Holy Spirit there, because the Divine Liturgy was served in it.

Then *matushka* and I read the prayers before holy communion and the canons, and towards nighttime, Fr Sergii set off to prepare for the service, disappointed that he would remain without an acolyte on such a great feast, as Boria had already admitted to him that he was merely "coming and seeing" for now, according to the advice of Iurii Mikhailovich Kublanovskii.

Fr Sergii blessed me to take a few blankets to church in addition to the coat, since the frost had become considerably acute, a real Theophany frost, and the church was quite expansive, while the metal stove that only weakly warmed its surroundings proved to be very small. So *matushka* and I stood by this little stove in the middle of the church in our blankets. The service began. Here I realized that *matushka* and I would be the readers, and the singers, and she would also play the role of altar server. She and I were quite hoarse by the end of the vigil, and I shivered from head to toe like an autumn leaf, despite the coat, little stove, and blankets. Fr Sergii, who came out to hear my confession, noticed this and threw his winter *ryassa* over me as well.

"As for the Liturgy," he said, "let the angels sing it for us."

And he simply turned on a recording in the altar with a church choir singing.

But the angels also sang there ...

When Fr Sergii gave me holy communion, my tongue stuck to the spoon from the frost ...

Then came the blessing of the water ... the appeal to the Holy Spirit: "And the Spirit in the form of a dove."

"Come ye all, and receive the spirit of wisdom, the spirit of understanding, the spirit of the fear of God, from Christ Who is made manifest." [7]

Having blessed the water, Fr Sergii brought the cross out to me and *matushka*, and ordered us to go home and lie down on top of the stove while he cleaned up in the altar.

At the house, we were greeted by Boria, sleepy and radiating warmth.

"You slept through the whole thing!" I said to him.

The next morning he and I set off on our journey home. I told Fr Sergii what terrors we had endured in the icy desert and how close we had come to despair. But he simply waved his hand:

"Right now you will reach Rybinsk very quickly. You won't have time to freeze, or get tired, or be afraid."

And he blessed me with a wide sign of the cross.

"As for you," he said to Boria, "come and see again!"

It was light, sunny, quiet, and frosty. The snow shone in the sun so much that it hurt to lift up our eyes to it. Lightly packed with pirogi from Fr Sergii, we reached the tractor trail, now generously swept over with snow, and went along it.

However, how we went! Oh, how we went! As if someone picked us up by the armpits, we began to lightly and intently approach the highway, flying over the ground in enormous leaps and bounds. Even the agnostic Boria admitted that something miraculous was taking place.

"Boria, don't you feel like something is carrying us? Like we are flying?"

He gazed around in wonder.

"Boots of swiftness!" he recalled the fairy tale.

And he looked around with the wide-open eyes of a child. In them the large pieces of ice had melted and were now replaced with swimming, joyful golden fish.

As soon as we reached the highway and climbed out of the ditch, a Zaporozhets pulled over.

"Where are we going, young folks?"

"Where are you going?"

"To Rybinsk."

And so we drove along in that cozy warm Zaporozhets, not rushing anywhere, simply taking in the surrounding view—the enormous forests of fir trees, the mighty pine forests. And the sun! And everything covered by the newborn snow! The purity! The clean air! The blessed waters! "The earth is the Lord's, and all its fullness!" (1 Cor 10:26).

The next day, I was back in Moscow.

"Well, did you feed our dear Fr Sergii? Did you give him some support?" asked my husband.

"No," I replied. "He has everything he needs there! He's the one who fed and supported me. I simply came and saw."

❧ *Bring Back My Husband* ❧

My friend Asya's husband left her, and it happened quite dramatically. Not long before that, they had moved with their two teenagers to Moscow, since with the beginning of *perestroika*[1] there was growing unemployment in their native town, and in any case it would be better for their gifted children to study at a big city university.

They were renting a small apartment in a Khruschev-era prefab on the edge of Moscow; the husband was trying to start some sort of business, but it wasn't working out well, and their main concern was now to earn enough to survive. In addition, it came to light that he had taken a lover. You couldn't say that she was rich, but she was a Muscovite, with an apartment, work, and a good career. She supported herself. And most importantly—she was young.

There was no end to my friend's despair. It completely filled her and seemed to spill over the brim, threatening to flood everything and everyone around her—first and foremost, naturally, those who were in her immediate vicinity. When I was around her, I physically sensed that I was being drawn into some sort of depressing, heavy force field. We had to do something about it.

"I think you should fight it!" I would tell her. "Imagine that you are a maiden warrior, and you are going to battle with a dragon who has bewitched and taken prisoner your Ivan the Fool."

"But how do I fight it? How?" she would ask, wiping away a tear. "I only want one thing—to take a stick and hit this young thing several times over the head! We lived so well, we loved each other so much, we have wonderful children, and then she came along . . . that tramp!"

So Asya's dream went no farther than beating up her rival—only the weapon changed—whether it was sticks, stones, or simply fists.

"That's a bad plan. It won't get you anywhere," I would categorically protest. "First of all, you would be found the guilty party. You would look like a crazy troublemaker, and she would end up the victim. And then, if you attack her, it's not clear who would come out on top: look how fit she is, she probably knocks down bowling pins every evening at the bowling alley; look at her biceps, calves, strength, height, and finally, age. What if she takes away that stick from you and cudgels you over the head with it?"

"Well then, how am I supposed to fight her?" sobbed the frightened Asya. "As it is, I'm fighting her with dignity."

"That's good. But it would be even better to fight her on a spiritual level. Pray to the Lord, to the Mother of God, to the saints, go and complain to them: help me with so and so! But you must pray for her too—what a sin she is committing!"

"No," Asya firmly shook her head. "I will of course pray and ask God for help, but I will never pray for that adulteress! Let God punish her! Do you happen to know any stories where a husband left his wife and children for a home-wrecker, and then by the prayers of the wife the Lord brought back the husband?"

"Yes, of course I do. I know a story just like that."

"Well, tell me!"

"I had two classmates, Petya and Masha. Even before kindergarten, they were in the same preschool group, and Masha, as she tells it, sitting on the potty next to Petya, fell in love with him then and decided to become his wife. But she never really managed to get his attention in school, and no romance developed then. After their graduation ball, they went with their former classmates to someone's *dacha*, spent the night there, and Masha, as they say, begat in her womb, which she soon announced to the future father.

"Petya was devastated, but, as an honest man, he promised to marry her. He said as much to his parents:

"'I am going to have a child. As an honest man, I am bound to marry.'

"His parents were, honestly speaking, horrified. The seventeen-year-old Petya—a musician who had just been accepted into the conservatory—what good could come of his getting married? Of course, they immediately began to hate Masha. But what was there to do? They hosted the wedding, Masha gave birth, and their baby died right there in the birthing clinic.

"And so everything returned to the situation as before: Petya lived with his parents, Masha with her grandmother, living their separate lives. Now and then Masha would visit her young husband and bake pirogi for him.

"So a year passed, then another. Petya had various friends, girlfriends, his own circle: artists, musicians, no match for that poor Masha. But Masha still came over sometimes, and baked pirogi. And so, at one point, his parents were leaving on vacation, and Petya was also supposed to go on tour, leaving their cat and many plants unattended at home. So they asked Masha as part of the family to stop by from time to time in their absence to feed the cat and water the plants. And Masha did. One evening, she came across Petya, who had just returned from his trip; they drank some tea together, talking about this and that. Well, in short, she conceived again after that. Well, what about it? She was his lawful wife, after all!

"She gave birth to a daughter nine months later, although she and Petya continued to live in separate places as before. Now she came to his house with their daughter, baked pirogi, and went home.

"But then Petya fell in love with his classmate, fell so hard! She was such a beauty! Also a musician, a violin player. And he simply radiated with joy. Now this musician hardly ever left his side. Then, Masha and her daughter appeared on the doorstep. What's more, some fool had advised Masha to shave her daughter's head, saying that her hair would grow better that way. Her daughter was such a thin, pale, sorry, scared little thing, and now bald on top of it all! And Petya threw them out. He told them not to come again without calling first.

"I saw them then, since we shared an entryway with Petya. There they stood, God's little birds, in old clothing, both of them skin and bones, tears in their eyes, lips trembling. I brought them inside. We sat with Masha, talked, she told us everything about herself and I about myself: how I had recently been baptized and baptized my children. Then Masha said:

"'Help us to get baptized too! We are also Christians.'

"I took them to church, where Fr Valeriian Krechetov served, and he baptized them. Before baptism, Masha looked like a plucked chicken, all slouched over and clumsy, but she emerged from the font a beauty: her eyes shone with heavenly light and purity! Never again did I see such a clear transformation in a person, though I witnessed many people's baptisms.

"Masha began to visit me often with her daughter. One time, she ran in, completely in shock, crying. What happened? It turned out that she had run into that musician-girlfriend of Petya's in the entryway—violin in hand, looking the victor, all in white, radiating happiness, success, freedom, love. While Masha, the wife of sorts, if at all, with a small anxious child, stood before her in mended tights and an old faded skirt. The former said to her:

"'If you are coming to see us, then we are leaving!'

"Masha only said:

"'We're not here to see you!'

"And she broke into tears on my doorstep.

"We began to pray together. We went to the Martyr Tryphon, both in tears, and to St Nicholas. We shed tears before several miracle-working icons of the Mother of God.

"Some time passed. By all accounts, the violinist left Petya —I suddenly stopped seeing her in our entryway. Petya's father was taken to the emergency unit. His mother suffered a stroke. Petya would rush back and forth between the hospital and his patient lying at home. And then he saw Masha with their daughter in the courtyard ...

"Masha moved in with Petya to look after his mother. They released his father from the hospital—she stayed to cook for them. Suddenly, Petya received a notice to appear for military service—they threatened to take Petya, a musician, with his golden fingers, into the army!

"What was there to do? Masha successfully gave birth to his second child in nine months. Now with two children, Petya feared no military enlistment office. And while Petya hid from the army in the small hospital, Masha got so settled in his house that she gave birth to a third child.

"Now they have been married for thirty-five years. Their children have grown up, and they have children of their own. Now it's difficult to even imagine that this family had been in such chaos and disorder at any time."

"Well ..." said Asya. "Now I understand how I need to fight!"

She took down my list of those wonderworking icons through which Masha had received God's help, and committed herself to feats of prayer, begging God to bring back her husband. I believed that the Lord would help her.

But then she met an "interesting man" whom she liked and who began to court her; they even spent the night together at his place. Afterwards, they parted ways in bad blood, and her husband never returned to her.

"You see," Asya told me recently, "the Lord helped your Masha, sending her trials through which she could prove herself a true wife. That is why she emerged victorious. But I tripped over the first temptation and have remained alone. After that I couldn't even bring myself to ask God to bring my husband back to me, since I myself had shown him that I didn't really need him, that there were other options, that maybe there was someone else for me!"

That was how she understood it.

❧ *The Apple of My Eye* ❧

S ince Soviet times, a strange prejudice against priests became rooted in the consciousness of our citizens. I have heard several times from considerably enlightened people that those "pops"[1] have "epaulets under their cassocks"[2] and that all they do is look for opportunities to give away secrets collected during confession to the appropriate authorities: this man confessed to weakness of faith, this one breaks the fast, prays indifferently, gets annoyed easily, fights with his neighbors, is vainglorious, is guilty of idle talk . . . then those authorities use this good information, etc., . . .

I even found myself in situations where I couldn't convince believers in dire need of a priest's help to turn to one of the kind pastors that I knew well.

I remember when in the 1980s my former classmate at the Literature Institute, Pavel Protsenko, was arrested, and his wife came to Moscow to appeal for his release. I could not convince her to go to see a priest. It was surprising, because Pavel himself was a believer even before I had been baptized. Also, he had been arrested for gathering materials for the canonization of the New Martyrs, who had suffered bloody persecution at the hands of the Soviet atheists, and this wife of his was more or less a church-going person. But to each of my offers to go to this priest, who was completely trustworthy, or that elder, who had been imprisoned in Stalin's concentration camps for the faith, she firmly shook her head:

"That one? He sold himself to the authorities a long time ago! As for the other one, you can't pin him down as one thing or another!"

Strangely, she placed more hope in Soviet writers and asked them to collectively gather signatures on a petition in defense of Pavel. This letter was signed by Yevtushenko, Bitov, Averintsev, and several others, and soon his release was indeed secured.

A similar attitude toward the godly priests was also adopted by the recently returned from exile Zoya Krakhmalnikova. She had asked me which priest she could go to for advice, and I named quite a few who had prayed for the "imprisoned Zoya" at Divine Liturgy every day during her confinement, as was the case at the Holy Trinity Lavra of St Sergius, where the deacon read out her name from the solea.

Yet whomever I named, in her eyes they were all "agents," "secret informants," or "former KGB." Rejecting the candidacy of the holy person and elder Archimandrite Kirill Pavlov ("Olesia, he is a father confessor at the Lavra, how do you think he got that position?"), she rested her choice on Fr Ioann (Krestiankin) ("He did time? Good. He serves in the countryside? Good.") and wrote him a letter with the request to come and speak with him.

I delivered this letter to Fr Ioann, and he needed no explanation of who Zoya Krakhmalnikova was.

"Zoinka! Zoinka wrote me a letter, well, I will write her one back! Here are some holy items for her, and some gifts!"

And he began to circle around his cell, assembling a package "for our favorite Zoinka." He gathered a whole packet of little icons, booklets, spiritual sayings of the holy fathers, little bottles with holy oil and holy water, and candles, and wrote her a note "with blessings." With all this, I departed.

But "Zoinka," when I handed her these gifts, was disillusioned. As it turned out, Fr Ioann did not advise her to come to him in the Pskov Caves Monastery. Why not? God knows. He obviously had some spiritual reasons of his own.

But Zoya Aleksandrovna understood it to mean one thing: the elder was simply afraid to see her. Yes, this was her typical, if not conclusive, disappointment in "churchgoers!" Before that, she had already become disillusioned by *Vladyka* Anthony, Metropolitan of Sourozh, himself.

My husband and I were shocked by this confession, as we loved and respected *Vladyka* very much.

"What did he do to disappoint you so much?"

It turned out that those near and dear to Zoya Aleksandrova had asked *Vladyka* to write a letter of protest after her arrest, and he said that he would write no such letter, but that he would pray for her at the altar table. This was the reason for her disillusionment in him as a pastor and bishop! Zoya Aleksandrovna assumed that he "got scared."

Knowing the power of *Vladyka's* prayer, my husband and I couldn't help but simultaneously cry out in protest:

"Render therefore to Caesar the things that are Caesar's, and to God the things that are God's! (Mt 22:21). Maybe that's how *perestroika* came about, so that you would be released, Zoya Aleksandrovna, by *Vladyka's* prayers!"

But, alas! She did not reach the same conclusions. The whole paradox—and this was to her detriment—was that, having indeed suffered for the sake of God's word, which she had spread in a godless country by releasing the underground journal *Nadezhda*[3], she still didn't manage to become a church-going person. Having gone through the journey of a martyr and confessor, she was at best a neophyte. Before her arrest, she had by all accounts not had time to partake of the spiritual life of the church, to perceive it specifically as the mystical Body of Christ. And after her arrest, her Soviet dissident prejudices stood in the way of her spiritual journey: "All those pops have epaulets under their cassocks."

This is the only way I can explain her ultimate fate, when first she angrily denounced the Church on the pages of liberal newspapers, and then later completely turned away from it and joined a sect.

Bulat Shalvovich Okudzhava[4] was even afraid of her after she took to aggressively accusing and instructing him. He showed me how he would weakly shrink back into an armchair while she stood in front of him, waving her arms and accusing him like an enraged Fury. By the way, when he and I spoke about Orthodoxy and the Church, he, cringing nervously and remembering Krakhmalnikova, spoke of church aggression, forcefulness, "stylistic Sovietism," as all being in contrast to, for example, the elegance and intellectual refinement of émigré nuns and aristocrats—by this he was recalling his visit to the Monastery of St Mary Magdalene, Equal-to-the-Apostles, belonging to the (non-Soviet) Church Abroad. I even suggested to him, since he felt that way, that he be baptized by the Church Abroad.

In short, the opinion of the "outside world" about priests was often very unflattering and derogatory. But I, being personally acquainted with numerous priests—in Moscow, in the countryside, in monasteries, in cities, in villages—want to say that this was very unfair.

Yes, I, too, had instances when a priest's behavior proved unworthy of his rank. But either these were isolated instances—"slip-ups" uncharacteristic of that person, even—or as if the Church itself was purging him from its body.

In addition, a priest as a sinful man is one matter—"He who is without sin among you, let him throw a stone at [him] her first" (Jn 8:7)—but a priest as a celebrant of Mysteries is another matter altogether. There have been times when a person was in his own way rather primitive and flat, but as soon as he put on his *epitrachelion* and cuffs, and came out, let's say, for confession or to celebrate a Mystery, he would be transformed and become a beholder of the mysterious and spiritual. The power of God would dawn upon him and prophecies would issue from his lips.

Unfortunately, I can't relate all of these personal revelations. But I can tell you of two such instances . . .

Once, I went to see my father confessor in Pechory. I knew that he was planning to hear confessions during the early Liturgy next to the relics of the holy Martyr Cornelius. I arrived early and was first in line before the analogion. Confession had not yet begun. Suddenly, much to my dismay, an entirely different priest came out to that very analogion holding a cross and Gospel in his hand, and began reading the prayers before confession, and there was no sign of my father confessor. I was hoping to go to communion. So there I stood—again, first in line—before a priest whom I knew well and to whom I had no desire to confess. But it seemed wrong to turn around and walk away; that would be too pointed on my part. So I continued to stand in great doubt and uncertainty.

On the one hand, this priest sometimes started literary conversations with me and even wrote a few poems himself. By doing this he annoyed me and even tempted me with his hopeless literary dullness, and, God forgive me, his dismal lack of talent. What could he tell me during my confession? What spiritual advice could he give me? On the other hand, I thought, he is still a priest and will absolve me from my sins with the words "through the power given to me by Him . . ."

In the end, I decided to humble myself and go to him for confession.

He approached me after the service and unexpectedly began to speak to me about lying. Yes! This was one sin I knew I was guilty of, but at the same time did not consider to be of great importance, and his speech about this seemed to me to be at an entirely theoretical level.

If I do tell lies, they are, as it were, white lies, without interest or principle, simply in order to avoid giving long explanations or being a pest. Moreover, I didn't consider that to be my greatest sin, but he gave me an entire sermon on the subject. Inspired and giving way to an internal revelation, he gave me such an explanation of this sin that he literally overturned my perception of myself and of the world.

"The horror of this sin lies in the fact that it devalues words. Words cease to have meaning, they lose their essence and become empty. In addition, according to the law of psychological projection, a person who lies stops believing other people's words. They stop believing anything. Not believing words, they stop believing the Word. They read the Gospel and don't believe in Christ. And this is the most terrible thing, because 'even the demons believe—and tremble!' (Jas 2:19), while the liar is punished with emptiness. They are surrounded completely by deceit, behind which there is nothing. Even in life they find themselves in hell."

This explained much to me about the modern world, that lives completely by externals, appearances, pretenses, hypocrisy, and falseness; that wears different masks, lays decoys, tries to mimic, tries to give favors in return for benefits, and carries the punishment for its own deceit: it doesn't believe in itself, or others, or the Word of God.

As for the poems of this priest, who impressed me for the rest of my life with his instruction, they remained the same—terrible. Literally the following day, meeting me in the monastery, he handed me a large notebook:

"Here you go, read it in your spare time!"

Inside, every poem was creatively formulated in the same way: on the opposite page was glued a postcard from the Soviet times depicting the appropriate season. So, if the poem was about autumn, the postcard showed "golden autumn"; if it was about spring, the postcard showed melting snow and nesting rooks . . .

Here is another instance that clearly witnesses to the fact that during a Mystery, a priest is guided by the Lord Himself.

I had a classmate at the institute who, having just given birth to a baby at a very young age, grew very ill: she contracted cancer of the brain. She was admitted to the Burdenko Clinic, her head was shaved, and she had a craniotomy in order to extract the tumor. After the surgery, her face was distorted, and her mouth ended up somewhere close to her ear. Her husband left her for another, and she found herself completely alone with a tiny daughter in her arms.

She was a unique woman, though, because not only did she not despair, but on the contrary, she began to assure everyone who tried to empathize and help her that she had it "better than anyone": she could sit with her daughter at home, she sewed dresses, skirts, and blouses for small change, she had a perfectly clean home with homemade *pirozhki*, her mouth was returning to its proper place, she was slowly beginning to get out of the house, and so on and so forth . . .

To be honest, I thought that she was a saint: I had never seen such gentle patience, kindness, generosity, charity, and most importantly, such gratitude to God for everything that destiny sent her way, except in the lives of the saints. The only thing she lacked was to be baptized, but that was taken care of, too. One beautiful day, my husband drove her and her daughter to Fr Valeriian Krechetov in Otradnoe village, and there he celebrated for them the mystery of baptism.

After this, however, her troubles didn't end—a tumor was again found in her brain and she had another operation, but she still had it "better than anyone": her daughter was so smart and beautiful, she was growing as fast as a flower in the field, her friends were so wonderful, her orders for dresses and skirts were increasing. The only bad thing was that she hadn't received holy communion since her baptism. I spoke to her about this several times, offering to bring a priest to her, but she declined.

"No, Lesechka, I'm not ready. And then—what could he tell me? I would have to explain so much to him . . . No, no, I don't want to."

Ten years must have passed. In that time she had another craniotomy, but again she rose up with a bright outlook and a firm resolution in her soul—she did not bend or break, which might have happened with so many others.

Finally, I managed to convince her to go to confession and communion, or perhaps she herself came to that point. Either way, it was clear that the Lord enlightened her. She even desired to come to church and attend a service—I only had to bring her and take her home. She also asked me to choose for her a good priest who would help her discover some new sources of life. I was to go to him first and tell him about her life and situation, so that he would understand the context when she came to him for confession.

I did just that. I went to our Church of the Mother of God of the Sign, and asked the wonderful and discerning priest Fr Vladimir to give a life confession to such and such a servant of God, living in such and such circumstances, keeping in mind that she was confessing for the first time.

Fr Vladimir looked over his schedule and chose a day.

I told her that I had arranged everything with a wonderful, wise priest who would carefully consider her life and help her.

"And you told him everything about me? You warned him?" she grew anxious.

She began to prepare several days ahead of time, fasting and reading the communion rule. I picked her up early in the morning, and we went to the church. We stood at the analogion, waiting, and suddenly . . .

Someone completely different came out. Now, he was also a good priest. Just simple, what they called "a country priest": beady eyes, a funny potato nose, a fat belly. Terrible diction—half the prayers he read were not understandable. He was disjointed—when he began his sermon, he would inevitably wander into such a syntactic labyrinth that it was impossible to follow him! But, he was kind and pure at heart. Such spiritual warmth emitted from him that even our literary ladies from the nearby writers' house—and such ladies!—Bulat Okudzhava's wife, Oleg Vasilevich Volkov's wife (he was the author of the famous novel *Descent into Darkness*) only went to him, a simple man, for confession, despite the fact that there were more intellectual, better-looking, more educated, and much more polished in speech and manners priests at the time in that church.

And so, this father came out and began to drone, swallowing the words of the prayer before confession.

"You're sure you told him everything about me?" my friend asked one more time.

"Sure, sure," I said dismissively, frantically trying to think what to do: should I go and look for Fr Vladimir, or should I admit to her that this was SOMEONE ELSE, and still try to convince her to go to him, for chances were that we would not be able to come back for a long time: she lived on the opposite side of Moscow, after all. Or should I say nothing and see what would happen?

Suddenly, this father, having finished reading the prayers, uncharacteristically began to recite a sermon. I listened to him with one ear, as I was being torn apart by a terrible worry for the novice confessee, while some unintelligibly nasal sound reached me from that kind and dear simple priest. But he finished, and my friend stepped toward the anagolion. I walked away so as not to embarrass her, worried that she would discover my lie at any moment: for that priest didn't know anything about her.

Finally, she came back to me in amazement.

"Did you hear what he said during his sermon? It was like he was speaking directly to me, as if he knew in advance all the questions that I had come with today! That was because you told him everything, right? But he also talked to me about things that you don't know, he must have been divinely inspired, right? He understood it through the Spirit?"

"Of course," I sighed with relief. "Of course, through the Spirit!"

While we drove home, my rejoicing communicant couldn't stop talking from her fullness of heart.

"He is simply spiritually clear-sighted, that priest of yours! Who is he? An elder? A wonderworker? How he saw everything, everything inside me to the very bottom!"

These are the miracles that occur with the priests of our Church. Not in vain did the Lord say: "He who touches you touches the apple of [My] eye" (Zech 2:8).

❧ *The Thrill-Seeker* ❧

I love monastics in general. Even aesthetically, their manner is appealing to me. Their way of life, allegorical thinking, and style of speaking, which constantly hearkens back to the primary sources—Sacred Scripture and the holy fathers—but which is also alive and full of metaphors and oxymorons, sometimes with features of the holy fool, sometimes with a metaphysical subtext.

In the society of monastics, to which I was occasionally given access, my soul completely blossomed. Sometimes the monastics themselves would grant me their trust and tell me incredible stories from their lives, in which, of course, the leading figure was divine providence.

Here, for example, is how the Lord brought Lesha to monasticism, also known as "Mayonnaise," and who later became the humble Hieromonk Flavii.

Lesha had the nickname Mayonnaise for a very simple reason: he had a small mayonnaise production business. His two-room apartment served as both his office and his production facility, and there he made his mayonnaise with a single hired worker, who was also his nephew. Lesha himself—the owner of the company—bought all the materials, including packaging, and then distributed his ready-made product to his points of sale. This was all in the early nineties.

One day, he was driving on the highway in his overstuffed pickup truck when it broke down. It was terribly cold—minus twenty-two degrees Fahrenheit, and the fact that the truck had started that day in the first place was both a surprise and a mystery. There stood Lesha in the cold with the car hood open, his teeth chattering, shivering and trying to hitch a ride, but nobody stopped—who would want to—and he felt that just a little longer, and he would freeze to death on that bustling highway like the coachman in the steppe.

It must be said that, in general, Lesha was a thrill-seeker by nature; he would always set out on expeditions not suitable for beginners—either he would climb up Mt Elbrus[1] or Communism Peak,[2] or he would go out on a catamaran with other like-minded thrill-seekers on all the mountain rivers, or he would go skydiving. And now, stiffening in that frost, his thoughts began to head in the direction of realizing that against all expectations, he had finally achieved his ultimate thrill. In a minute, like General Karbyshev,[3] he would turn to ice and would remain a monument on the highway. He chuckled to himself to raise his spirits, but he felt sick at heart. He couldn't feel his arms or legs, his ears ached, there was sand in his eyes. Oh, he thought, what was the use of standing in the wind like that, let me climb into the car, curl up into a ball, and sleep, and God will take care of the rest. And if I die—then it's my time.

And that very same instant, as soon as he remembered God, a red Lada pulled over and out came a priest with the face of an angel who went directly over to him. He took him to his car, turned the heater on full blast, drove him to the Holy Trinity Lavra of St Sergius, placed him in the infirmary, and fed him tea with raspberry jam. There Lesha was rubbed from head to toe with alcohol, while one of the Lavra mechanics towed his truck to the garage.

And so, Lesha drank his tea with raspberry jam, was treated with medicinal cognac, and during the interim, his saviour-monk brought him back to life. In the end, Lesha asked to be baptized.

After that, he continued to visit his spiritual father in the monastery—for confession as well as spiritual counsel. Then his life took him for a ride—inspections of his mayonnaise business apartment by the Sanitary-Epidemiological Service, attempted bribes, extortion, etc. He tried to restore his business, the bank gave him credit and then took it away, his business expanded, and all this time he completely stepped away from the Church, only attending on Pascha and Christmas. As soon as he had any free time, off he went to the mountains, or on a kayak to the White Sea, or on a catamaran to the Altai mountain rivers. He even managed to climb Mt Kilimanjaro.

Then he began to feel that God was pushing back. He went skydiving and broke his leg in two places, a compound fracture. As soon as his leg healed, he decided to scale Communism Peak one more time. But at his last mountain encampment before the ascent, a horse stepped on his hand and shattered several fingers. As there were medics present, they immediately attached splints to his fingers and bandaged up his hand. One might think, "Lesha Mayonnaise, it is time for you to go home!" But he was stubborn: I will conquer this peak even with my crushed fingers!

He had the supplies he needed, climbing shoes on his feet, a backpack with provisions on his back; he set out in the morning with his companions, and they began to ascend the mountain recesses. They went on and on, climbed and climbed, the day flew by and still they clambered up; the second day was almost over, night approached, when suddenly—what was this vision?—a girl in red shorts skipped on the rocks past them. Well, Lesha increased his speed to go after her, but she went hop, hop, hopping farther and disappeared. He looked and saw a bouquet of forget-me-nots on a boulder. What was this parable? He was amazed.

Finally, they stopped for the night, when suddenly, a man crawled into their tent, wearing jeans, a light fabric jacket, and plastic sneakers:

"Hey guys, we found some supplies and provisions in the crevice there—are they yours? Ours are all out."

Who were they? And there was that girl—also not dressed for the weather or the circumstances, as if she was getting ready for a picnic outside the city. Lesha and his friends—tough people, rugged, experienced thrill-seekers—even got worked up a bit. They told them:

"What are you doing, without supplies, dressed like that in plastic shoes?"

They responded:

"What's it to us, we just wanted to conceive a child on Communism Peak, so we left our car behind there, down—in Krasnodar Region—just before the crossing."

Such disdain for planning offended Lesha. These places were dangerous, after all, nothing for a frivolous passerby to trifle with. To this day, a story is told about a seventeen-year-old girl who died in a descending avalanche.

Right above our thrill-seekers' hideout, an enormous glacier stretched up high, and if you looked closely, you could see something black frozen inside, and if you looked closer, you would be able to examine it and see that it was a human—a woman's, even a young girl's—foot. It's very possible that this was the foot of that very girl who had disappeared in the avalanche.

But those frivolous people were not destined to conceive a baby because a landslide started that night, and everyone began to run to the crevice by the glacier to take shelter there. Someone may have been hit on the head by a ricocheting rock, another's hand may have been mangled, but as it was, everyone survived. In a day's time, a rescue helicopter picked them up, and they landed right next to that fateful horse that had crushed Lesha's fingers.

A group of German tourists, however, were not so lucky. These German tourists had also started their ascent of Communism Peak together with our native thrill-seekers, but under an avalanche they remained.

After that, Lesha went back to his spiritual father at the Lavra.

"Oh," said the latter, "thank God that everything worked out, but what do you think, Lesha Mayonnaise, why did God save you? He saved you—for Himself. He has not finished taking joy in you, hasn't rejoiced in you enough yet. You should go on and begin a new life, take communion here with us, and then slowly move here. You don't have a family, and we need mayonnaise here in the monastery, too."

Lesha agreed. He stayed there three days or so, and then left, promising to return in a month or two: he would take care of his affairs and give himself over completely to God and the monastery. And then he disappeared for seven months. He didn't go to church, he didn't tie up his affairs, and instead he went off for the summer to Pleshcheevo Lake, where his friend had built himself a vacation home and bought a sailboat. At first, Lesha said to him:

"I can't go, brother, I promised to go to the monastery!"

The friend said:

"What's all this about a monastery? Do you even know what a church we have there on Pleshcheevo Lake? Well! Your monastery won't compare! There are such holy places there! You can go pray every day if you want, and in between services we'll go swimming by the sailboat."

And so what? Lesha Mayonnaise went, of course, without even sending a note to his spiritual father. Well, he thought, if I can really go to the services and take communion there, what more can he want?

But Sunday approached, and Lesha's companion said to him—look what nice fishing gear I got yesterday, want to go try it out in the morning? So Lesha thought—I'll go to church in the morning, and then we'll go fishing.

But in the morning his companion said:

"Where do you think you're going, that church is nowhere near, it's two hour's walk along the shore, and look at the time, your service has already started, you should have woken up earlier, now you'll only drag yourself there by the time it's all over. That's OK, let's go to church next time, and now we can go on the sailboat and perceive the Creator's beauty through His creation."

So that's what they did. They hoisted the sail—there was such a nice breeze blowing, the sun was sparkling, the wondrous forests swam by them all around—what a delight! Suddenly, the sky darkened, the forest trembled, the waves rose up, the wind blew and began to tear at the sail. The two companions lowered it. While they were busy with it, a furious water spout flew at them out of nowhere, seized the sailboat, and with frightening strength, lifted it thirty meters into the air and slammed it onto the lake.

Lesha's friend immediately perished, but the water spout didn't want to let Lesha go. On the contrary, it grabbed him across the body, wound him in the rope from the sailboat, and, tearing him away from the boat, it carried him over the water, and dragged him along the ground, collecting branches and bushes, and carried him on and on until it finally threw him down right next to a large wooden cross not far from the church.

And on that cross hung a board with an inscription saying that it had been erected there by Peter the Great in memory of his miraculous preservation from a storm on Pleshcheevo Lake, on which he had been tranquilly floating on his little boat. Peter had been preserved, but Lesha lay all broken, beaten up, distorted, and with ruptured organs, wrapped in the sail like a shroud at the foot of the cross.

They treated him for half a year—sewed him up, placed him in braces, taught him to eat, speak, and walk again, and finally he sent a note to his spiritual father. The latter came to Lesha in Botkin Hospital, and Lesha told him how that water spout had dragged him by force to the church and thrown him onto the cross. For he, lying in his hospital bed for six months, thought of nothing else that entire time. He understood that he was considered among the most stupid in the Lord's estimation, and for this reason, the Lord could only bring him to his senses in the simplest and crudest—and most straightforward—manner.

"Tonsure me! I want to be a monk on my deathbed."

But the hieromonk said:

"Lesha, my friend! What deathbed? God saved you to live, not to die. And if you love the extreme so much, then your place is truly in a monastery—everything there is so steep, there are such ups and down, falls, flights, ravines, water spouts, landslides, avalanches, twilit visions of girls in red shorts, bluebells on cliffs, and children's feet frozen into glaciers! The enemy of the human race arranges such situations there for the monks, that sailboats, Communism Peak, and hang gliding will seem like trifles!"

So, laughing, his spiritual father embraced Lesha, gave him holy communion, blessed him, and gave him a prayer rope. Two months, later he was already living in the monastery and giving praise to God.

❧ An Experiment ❧

This is a story that occurred to a doctor of biology, now Hieromonk Iakov, a Georgian.

He was born in Tbilisi and attended university in Moscow. He defended his thesis there as well. He was baptized in his childhood, like any Georgian, and he celebrated Pascha joyfully and splendidly, though he didn't go to church, and he treated God reverently, but from a distance. He was a natural scientist by profession, a biologist. He was surrounded by the cult of knowledge, logic, and experimentation.

But as he said to his friend, also a natural scientist, when their conversation turned to God:

"You and I are made from the same dough—what do we trust? Experience. If someone conducted an experiment that would draw the conclusion that the Creator and Provider existed, I wouldn't just believe—I would become a monk."

His friend began to ridicule him, saying that all such evidence pointing to the existence of God was appropriate only for the slightest and most limited human mind, so what was the use of belittling God with such evidence?

Our Georgian replied:

"Nevertheless, I believe in the essential laws of nature, and until I see a miracle involving the supernatural, I won't believe. Period."

No less than two years passed. Our hero was flying to an international conference in Tbilisi. It was winter, and getting dark early, and suddenly the lights went out on the plane. Everyone sat in total darkness—they could only hear the plane straining and creaking away. Next to our hero sat some jokester telling jokes.

This was one of his jokes: "There was once a ship full of all kinds of people—members of the government, rich people, artists, football players, engineers—two of every kind. Suddenly a storm hit, and the ship sank. And so they all stood before the Almighty and cried out to Him all together: 'How did this happen, there were so many of us, and everyone drowned without distinction!' 'What do you mean, without distinction? Do you know how much time it took Me to gather you all onto that one ship?'"

Suddenly something wheezed and a terrible crack resounded, as if the plane was breaking into pieces; everyone screamed, and this was the last thing our sceptic remembered: his insides felt like they were being torn apart . . .

He regained consciousness in his plane seat in deep snow. There were mountains all around him. The Caucasus peaks loomed in the distance. His first question was: where was the plane? What a strange dream! His whole body ached. He tried to get up but couldn't. Then he realized with difficulty that his seat belt was holding him down. He unbuckled it and tried to get up, when he suddenly saw: he was sitting in this seat on the edge of a cliff—thirty-two square feet in area—and there was really nowhere for him to go.

In the inside pocket of his jacket he discovered his lecture, which he was supposed to have reviewed on the plane before the lights went out. He took out a lighter and began to light the pages in the hopes that some passing plane would notice the flames and save him, but the paper burned up instantly, and his hands were so stiff with cold that he didn't even feel the burns. It was good that it had been cold on the plane, and that he had taken a throw blanket out of his suitcase, one given to him by his Georgian grandmother, and had wrapped himself up in it. He now sat wrapped in it. She had given it to him just for this purpose: "Darling, it's always cold on those high flights, you just wrap yourself up in this throw blanket, doze off a little—how pleasant it will be for you!"

So he burned it all; he burned his lecture page by page without even thinking twice; what to do next? Then it hit him: his plane had crashed! It had fallen from a height of thousands of meters! It had fallen and crashed into smithereens—without leaving a trace. Everyone had died, and he was alive. There he was, sitting in a chair on a mountain precipice, wrapped in his grandmother's throw blanket, and clicking away with his lighter.

Then he thought: but that doesn't happen! That can't have happened according to the laws of nature. And if that can't have happened, then he must also have been dashed to pieces along with everyone else, and now he was sitting like this after death, alone, in a strange and unusual place, in this vast snowy desert, where no human foot had stepped since the time of the world's creation! Could he be in hell? Yes, even that thought occurred to him.

And then he understood: either of those scenarios, i.e., any possible scenario, would be contrary to the laws of nature, in contradiction to all biological science. And if he had fallen to his death and was still alive, if the plane had crashed and he had survived, then this could only mean that God existed; and if he had survived, then it was for something, not just randomly. And if it was for something, then someone would definitely find him soon, before he froze to death. And if they would find him, then he would immediately become a monk and would serve God exclusively as he had promised.

He cried out from his ledge: "Lord, save me one more time! I know that You exist! Save me, so that I may serve You!"

So he sat and screamed, and finally burned his last piece of paper; then he took off his throw blanket and was ready to burn that—he even tried to, but then understood that it wouldn't burn, it would just slowly smolder. Suddenly, a helicopter appeared from behind the cliff, and he began to wave his blanket with all his strength. He waved and yelled: "Lord, have mercy! Lord, have mercy!" until he was noticed. This is exactly how it happened.

And then he went to a distant monastery and became Hieromonk Iakov. Every day, he offers a solemn prayer for those who died that day on the plane—especially the jokester who had told his last joke. In spite of its cynicism in that tragic situation, in calm times that joke can very well be read as a parable.

❧ *Quid Pro Quo* ❧

The path to monasticism for the now Archimandrite Gideon was completely different.

He was from a family of Party members; he himself followed the path of the Young Communists, and quite successfully began to climb the political establishment ladder, climbing ever higher. By age thirty, he was already an important authority, an instructor in a large regional center. He had everything under his belt—an attractive exterior, athletic victories, social connections. His ideological purity and Party reputation were so immaculate that he had already managed to travel throughout all of Europe, even the capitalist parts, on Young Communist business, and was accepted to the Moscow Higher Party School with distinction.

When he was scheduled to depart from his regional center to study in Moscow, he had a strange vision in the early hours of the morning. It seemed like he was lying in his own bed, and the Mother of God Herself came to him and said:

"Your path lies in monasticism. Tomorrow you must go not to Moscow, but to the local bishop to ask him to baptize you and tonsure you a monk."

So the Mother of God said to him while he was in a light sleep and then She disappeared.

He sat up in his bed until morning, marveling at these hitherto unheard of words. Why must he immediately enter monasticism? He could just as well look into the Church little by little, and ask the priest to baptize him at home. He could do it in secret! He had heard of this happening among members of the Regional Committee. He could be a secret Christian. He would say something about Communism, crossing his fingers behind his back in the meanwhile, so he would really be saying the complete opposite! Hallelujah!

On the other hand—this was no light matter. The Mother of God Herself told this to him!

He jumped out of bed, pulled on his shirt and slacks, and rushed off to the local bishop in his quarters.

He knocked and knocked on the gate, and finally, a sleepy novice came out, saw him, and stared, recognizing him for the authority figure that he was.

The other kept knocking:

"Let me in to see the bishop!" he yelled, all worked up and red in the face.

But the sleepy novice decided that he had come there without warning at an untimely hour and was demanding to see the bishop with the intent of arresting him; not only did he not open the door, but he leaned against it from the inside, shouting:

"*Vladyka*, run! Someone's come to arrest you!"

The bishop came down and ordered him to open the door. He and the authority figure went off in private, and finally the bishop said to him:

"I won't baptize you myself, as you are a noticeable figure in town and won't be able to escape scandal. But I have a quiet parish where monks serve—it's practically a little monastery, a skete. We'll take you there, baptize you, and then you can decide for yourself what to do."

So it happened. He spent the entire day in refuge with the bishop, hiding in his cell. Then, under cover of night, the bishop took him to the skete and handed him over to two hieromonks. They baptized him, and he remained there.

But on that same day that he spent hiding at the bishop's, he was missed: where had our responsible worker gone? He had both disappeared from the town and not arrived in Moscow. They were exhausted searching for him. Then a dark rumor spread that the monks had kidnapped him and were holding him in a bishop's cellar. The police even came to the bishop's house to look for him!

But he was already reading "Holy God" in full force, tugging at his prayer rope, making prostrations in his black cassock among the trees. There he was tonsured with the name Gideon. Only then did he decide to come to terms with the law and appear before the authorities. By means of mutual trade-offs they agreed that the Party members would leave him alone if he promised to bury everything that he knew about the life of the political establishment. For he knew much that was not proper for a person outside the "system" to know. So they reached an agreement: quid pro quo.

I saw him when I came to that little monastery, while he was being sheltered there first and then tonsured. Late in the evening my husband and I went outside to breathe the fresh air, when suddenly two figures in cassocks went jogging past us. Novices, we thought, rushing on monastery affairs—one athletic, and the other not very, because he was very plump. We walked on a little, and saw them running back already. One ran lightly and nimbly, while the other ran with great difficulty and shortness of breath. We stopped under a pine tree and saw them running by again—the one like a young deer and the other like a seal: shlep-shlep, ready to drop.

"What is this wonder?" we thought and went to the monastery guest-house to sleep. In the morning we asked a hieromonk acquaintance of ours:

"Who is it that runs around the monastery here at night?"

"Ah," he nodded knowingly, "since you saw him yourself, I will tell you. That is our new brother Gideon, who has taken to helping our father superior, because he is terribly overweight. He feeds him greens and makes him run along the monastery walls while everyone is asleep."

And truly, I recently saw this father superior. He was unrecognizable. Thin, fit, standing upright. Fr Gideon had labored to his credit.

❧ *Temptation* ❧

Once we were sitting at home with some monks drinking tea and talking about this and that. Our conversation turned to temptations.

"I still think that a car will always be a temptation for a man," said one of them.

"That's true," I followed. "I know a story of a guy who left his family to avoid parting with his car."

"No! Tell us!"

"I had a friend who liked someone else's husband very much. They worked together, and started having an affair, which the man simply considered a fling. He planned to end it before his wife found out about it, but then he got into an accident—he was fine, but his car was totaled. He was terribly upset—anyone who's gotten used to sitting behind the wheel for many years can understand a man who must suddenly get around on public transportation. And at that difficult time, his lady friend bought him a new car and gave it to her beloved for his own general use: here you go, dear, enjoy it! But how could he use it if he was planning to cut ties with his mistress? So he chose to continue their relationship.

"Suddenly his wife discovered everything. 'What's this?' she yelled. 'How could you? You must choose—her or me!' 'Of course you,' he thought, 'a wife is a wife!' But as soon as he realized that he would have to return the car and switch to riding the trolley, everything inside him froze. His wife found out that he hadn't broken things off with his lover, and filed for divorce."

"I know a similar story. But this one involves monks," said one of the brothers. "For a monk, a car is a temptation cubed. It is somewhat more than just a possession. Quite a cautionary tale—shall I tell it?"

Everyone nodded:

"Go on, go on, get on with it!"

"Well, this was how it happened. In the eighties, the monks at Holy Trinity Lavra formed a connection with someone in the local highway patrol at the time. A high-ranking police chief had come to the faith and offered to help the monks with something that was in his power: to teach them to drive and get their licenses. Many did get their licenses at that time, including our friend Antonii. He got his license, but had no car and no prospect of getting one. Where could he get one? The monks lived in the Lavra, everything was provided and issued for them, and money was only given to them for medical treatment. But when a person has a license, they naturally want to be able to drive. As they say, your pleasure becomes your temptation. And that temptation comes back to hurt you. So this story is about just that.

"At the Lavra, Hieromonk Antonii had a friend from seminary days, Fr Nikifor. They had shared a desk and were spiritual and monastic brothers. They were tonsured on the same day, one with the name Antonii, the other with the name Nikifor. One was ordained a priest in September, the other in October. One got his driver's license in March, the other in April. But Fr Antonii was to remain in the Lavra, while Fr Nikifor was assigned to a village parish in the Vladimir Diocese.

"So what? Is distance a true impediment in monastic friendship? Their strong connection continued: they sometimes met at their father confessor's, Elder Sisoi, or they visited each other, or they visited holy places together.

"Fr Nikifor had another spiritual friend, or rather sister—Vassa Fro-lovna—also a spiritual child of the father confessor Elder Sisoi. At the same time, she was not in the truest sense a friend, as Fr Nikifor was very young, and this Vassa Frolovna was a grandmother already: she had a daughter and a granddaughter, so yes, she was an old woman—if not old, then certainly getting on in years. A nice, old matron. She lived with her daughter and granddaughter in Moscow in their own apartment that they had obtained some time ago through the prayers of Elder Sisoi.

"When Fr Nikifor was in Moscow, he would stay with them. She also visited him at his parish—either by herself or with her family in the sum-mer months. She would bring him some cheese, Lenten cod sausages and marshmallow candies. She would come and clean his place, prepare him some food, lead the kliros, and sing, since there was nobody to sing there in that remote countryside. She had been a singer in a Moscow church, so she knew the services and could read, and this was such a help to him that he set aside a little room for her in his small priest's house.

"Then this Vassa purchased a car under her name. But no matter how hard she tried, she could not learn how to drive it. She would sit behind the wheel and start to push back against the seat, clutch at the wheel, and worst of all, squint and squeal in terror. So she lent it to Fr Nikifor for his use, and he began to rush around in this car: from Moscow to his parish to the Lavra to Moscow to his parish.

"What of it? His parish was made up of five old women who only attended on Sundays and feast days, and the rest of the week he would sit alone in that remote country wilderness, waiting for some old lady to repose in the Lord.

"No, it was good, of course—more chaste than any skete, if you had a taste for ascetic life and unceasing prayer. But Fr Nikifor had not yet matured enough for that—he was himself from a large family, had been tonsured into a large, social monastery with many brethren, with whom he could have spiritually inspiring monastic discussions after dinner, and it became somewhat dreary for him in that shabby village.

"Moreover, his little church house was terrible—all slanting to one side and full of holes. He sat there for a while, sat some more, skimmed through the classic monastic text *The Ladder*, and was seized with such melancholy, that he could almost cry from despair, or drink himself senseless, or run away toward the bright lights of the city without looking back. What a temptation! So he did start running—he would go out, get into his car, and in two or three hours, he would be in Moscow walking around on Vassa Frolovna's carpet in his socks. But they also lived as a spiritual family—he would give her money for household purchases, they would pickle cucumbers together, plant potatoes, can preserves for the winter, and even make apple cider.

"And in the summertime, when someone would stop by the little church house, they would find Vassa there running around barefoot in her dressing gown, fussing about and tightening up jar lids: 'Oh,' she would say in embarrassment, 'how stupid of me,' and shamefacedly point at her bare feet. This dismayed many people and set tongues wagging, especially when they would exit the little church house together and walk to the car—to go to Moscow or the river—and Fr Nikifor would first open Vassa's door with his key, and when she would take her seat as if it was a magnificent throne, he would carefully shut her door.

"This Vassa Frolovna little by little began to wind up Fr Nikifor and goad him on—why was it, say, that the village bailiff's wife gave him half a penny for serving molebens, why was he paid such trifles for his services, and why was he paid for a funeral as if it was a handout?

"He would simply wave her away and laugh her off: look for yourself, am I a monk or not, did I take an oath of poverty or not? It would be another matter if I had a family, but I wouldn't ask for more money for my own sake . . . and so on and so forth.

"At this, that Vassa would flare up in anger—what do you mean, if you had a family? What are my daughter and granddaughter to you—not family? You live in our house, you drive around in our Lada, but apparently we are strangers to you!

"Well, Fr Nikifor was not a child, of course. He saw how strongly the car was tying him down, and he would give it up with the greatest of joy, because it presented a great temptation and enticement for him. But he had already grown attached to it—to that little purple car, to that steering wheel, firm and obedient—as to a bosom friend. He had grown to love flying about in it on happy highways leading to unknown places, shifting gears and attaining every goal. He had grown to love pressing down on the gas pedal, flashing the headlights in greeting at oncoming cars, and busily give it a splash with water from an off-road pond. But he didn't have enough money to simply buy it from Vassa Frolovna!

"But Vassa Frolovna had already put two and two together and had planned it all out, saying to herself: 'The most important thing is to keep your priest by your side.'

"This Vassa Frolovna also had a sister—a secret nun named Fotiniia who had been tonsured with the blessing of Elder Sisoi. There was another sister still, but she had married a prosperous German and had gone off to Germany.

"As for Fotiniia, the nun by secret tonsure, she was younger than Vassa Frolovna and more presentable; she sang better, was the choir conductor in a large Moscow church, and always went out to the middle of the church to read the Epistle. So this Fotiniia began to visit Fr Antonii at the Lavra. What of it? She was a secret nun, and a spiritual child of Elder Sisoi to boot, as well as the sister of his closest friend's parishioner, companion in prayer, and helper. Moreover, Fotiniia had at one time also, by the prayers of the elder, moved to Moscow from the country and had also gotten an apartment: she had looked after an old lady who then passed away, and Fotiniia set down firm roots there and even put up Elder Sisoi when he traveled to Moscow.

"He also received his spiritual children there; even Fr Antonii visited him in Fotiniia's apartment more than a few times. So that became the custom: Fr Antonii would come to Moscow on leave or on monastery affairs, and Fotiniia would happily invite him in, assigning a room to him, saying, Fr Antonii, this is your little cell, I won't let anyone else inside, and here is a key to the apartment. Sometimes Fr Nikifor would come there with Vassa Frolovna, or Fr Antonii and Fotiniia would take Vassa's car and come visit

Fr Nikifor's parish. In short—on the one hand, it was a monastic brother-hood and an innocent affair; on the other hand, strangely enough, a sort of family life had begun to form among them.

"And then, to add to the mix, the sister in Germany finally brought the sisters some money for material support. So Fotiniia Frolovna took that money and bought herself the best available Lada at the time—in metallic silver—and began singing sweetly:

"'Fr Antonii, I don't know how to drive a car, and I'm afraid to, this is not a woman's job, so here are the papers for the car, why don't you sit behind the wheel and use it as much as you'd like?'

"Then what? Fr Antonii took the wretched car, foreseeing everything, but still taking it. He was sick with the desire to drive along his native roads, to take a spin over to Elder Sisoi, to visit his brothers in different monasteries. He loved the smell of gasoline, the rustle of the tires on the asphalt, the wind through the open window.

"Thus he and Fr Nikifor developed a sort of symmetry: both monks, both in their own cars, both with their respective sister, one of whom was a singer and the other a conductor. But as soon as Fr Nikifor gave in to temptation and began to drive around on those wheels, the Lord visited him and marked him with eczema on his leg. Driving along on the road, his entire body itched and burned until his eyes were popping out of his head. Fr Nikifor began to develop gastrointestinal problems, and both sisters, it turned out, suffered from migraines and an ailing pancreas.

"And so, one day over a cup of tea, Fotiniia Frolovna told them, rather announced to them in a victorious tone of voice, that a new and extremely effective method of treatment for all illnesses through physical cleansing had been discovered.

"'As it turns out, our bodies have all been poisoned by harmful chemicals that are very destructive for the tissues, for which reason it is necessary for our recovery to extract from our bodies anything chemically harmful. Many of my singers have already tried this method on themselves, and it helped them, added to their strength, increased their muscle tone, and purified their blood, and now even the readers, deacons, and priests are willing to submit themselves to the treatment.'

"'But what is this treatment?' asked Fr Nikifor.

"'On the eve of the treatment, after taking a cleansing enema, you must drink four glasses of warm boiled water. Repeat in the morning. You mustn't eat all day. The next day, you must drink a tablespoon of olive oil and keep your strength up by drinking a glass of juice—potato, carrot, or beet. Cabbage juice is also allowed. You could also try burdock root juice if it is the right time of year, or sorrel juice; also celery. And repeat this every day. Then you may with confidence move on to applesauce. They say it makes eczema vanish as if by magic!'

"What happened next? Fr Antonii and Fr Nikifor, pure-hearted and sincere people that they were, believed her. The next day they assembled a group of monks close to them and with a similar mentality who were suffering from all sorts of ailments—monks are always sick with something, that is how the Lord helps them to be humble and to fight against temptations of the flesh—and shared the news with them of this miraculous, albeit difficult, method. The Great Lent feel of the treatment—a diet of completely raw foods—appealed to them all.

"They resolved to invite Fotiniia Frolovna to the monastery—the guesthouse keeper even set aside a room for her—and they all designated her as no less than an experienced and enlightened medic; they referred to her as 'doctor,' some even as 'professor' . . .

"In several days, Fotiniia Frolovna came to the monastery along with her heating pads, enemas, and juicers, and instructed the monks for a long time. The monastery supplied the olive oil, as well as the necessary vegetables. This cleansing trend continued over the course of several months—it was reminiscent of some sort of epidemic that took hold of more and more new patients. The monks walked around with a strange glassy gleam in their eyes and expressions that suggested they were completely cut off from reality, and shared their sensations with each fellow brother in whispers. Fotiniia Frolovna was now considered an indisputable authority: some even tried to ingratiate themselves with her, and in her voice appeared intonations of command.

"Vassa Frolovna, however, found no place for herself in this picture. So she took Fr Nikifor out of the monastery, where he had come specifically for his time of leave in order to give his body over to the full cleansing process, and ordered him to forget about this charlatan method of her sister's.

"'We'll find another method,' she said. And find another one she did, and soon.

"She went down to the cellar of the little priestly house, where all her picklings and conserves were stored, when suddenly the ground gave way beneath her feet and she found herself in an underground hole. In her fear she began to feel her way around the soil and stumbled across a little chest. She and Fr Nikifor took the little chest out and discovered that it was full to the brim with some sort of old, perhaps ancient, coins. Vassa Frolovna even bit them to see what sort of metal it was, but she couldn't identify it. They wanted to give the treasure trove to the government, but Vassa Frolovna placed a coin on her ailing head, as she was tormented by a migraine, and the headache vanished. So she and Fr Nikifor took to sitting down every night and treating themselves with the coins—it was good to place them on the eyes, or on the forehead, or on the small of your back—everything worked.

"Fr Nikifor told Fr Antonii about this and offered for him to make use of the coins as well—to place one on his eczema under a bandage, but Fr Antonii finally came to his senses. He understood that this was all just a temptation. A classic temptation, just as it was described in the writings of the holy fathers! He closed up the monastery clinic and sent Fotiniia Frolovna home, despite all her protests and efforts to set the other monks desiring to continue the treatment against him. He understood that it was time to somehow escape from the bondage of these sisters. He prayed at the relics of St Sergius, sat in his car, and drove to Fotiniia Frolovna's.

"'Mother Fotiniia, may the Lord save you, you gave me so much joy and relief with this car; I want to thank you also for sheltering me in your home, but it's time for me to know my own worth. Here you go, I'm returning all your keys, the documents, the proxy.'

"She was taken by surprise, began to scold him, and then almost broke down in tears. He put all the items on a little table in the hallway and ran off to the train station. Well, he thought, thank God, he got off easy.

"But it turned out otherwise. It's not so easy to get rid of temptation.

"Some time later, a parishioner who had been confessing to him for several years came to him and said:

"'Fr Antonii, I just inherited a little Finnish-style house in Semkhoz from my parents. I already have a *dacha* there, so I have no need of that house—let me donate it to you. Please take it as a gift. From the bottom of my heart. The only thing is there are no conveniences there—the toilet is outside, though it's a large plot all covered with trees.'

"He filled out a gift deed and made everything official.

"Fr Antonii had dreamed of just such a secluded little house for a long time—somewhere to hide from the public eye, lead an ascetic life for a while, pray to the Lord in total peace, and think of life, death, and everything else ...

"He went there—it was a pleasant little house, two steps from the Lavra—he even did a few renovations there, but left the toilet outside—the simpler the better ... The monastic brethren began to visit—to rest and pray a little. Soon everyone knew about Fr Antonii's little 'hacienda.'

"But he decided to house one of his parishioners there, who had just been kicked out of the house by her drunkard husband, leaving her to wander around the train stations with her little son. She lived there for a month, then another month, then a third. Some of the brothers began to complain: it was such a nice little place for solitude and prayer, but you had to go and put that lady there with her son! Now we have nowhere to take some time out.

"And so, one night, this resident came out into the garden—who knows why—to admire the moon, perhaps, or to use the toilet, and she saw a metallic grey Lada driving up to the little house. A woman in a dark headscarf and long skirt climbed out, opened the trunk, took out a canister of gasoline, and began to douse the wooden wall. Then she struck a match. The house immediately lit on fire, the woman jumped into her car and drove off, the parishioner rushed into the burning house and grabbed her son, and before their very eyes everything burned to a crisp within twenty minutes.

"After that, the eczema on Fr Antonii's leg developed into psoriasis when he recognized the arsonist by her description."

"Well, and how did it all end? Did this Fotiniia Frolovna, Lord save her, finally leave him alone?" one of the monks asked.

"Yes, it all ended well! Everything ended as it should. Fr Antonii gained some good spiritual experience, and began to avoid any and all possessions, to stay away from all property, fixed or movable. For with such property, a monk finds himself in 'a chicken or an egg' situation—it's unclear what came first. He may see it one way, but then it turns out to the contrary. Who chases whom, the mouse or the cat? Does life lead to death or death to life?"

Such was the cautionary tale that I once heard from one of our neighborly monks.

∾ Confession to the Prison Guard ∾

Once we went on a pilgrimage with Andrei Donatovich Sinyavsky and Maria Vasil'evna Rozanova: first to Pechory, home of the beautiful and famous Pskov Caves Monastery of the Dormition, then to the childhood home of Maria Rozanova. There, as it turned out, my husband and I had a friend who was also the diocesan bishop. He put us up with the Sinyavskys in the guesthouse, and invited us to join him at his residence in the evening to eat.

It was a wonderful evening; Andrei Donatovich and the bishop immediately fell into conversation, while the rest of us listened, as we dined exquisitely, pairing the food with sips of both juice and fine wine.

"I have a question. What will you say to this?" Andrei Donatovich suddenly remembered. "When I was serving my time in the concentration camp, there were many religious prisoners there, or those who had been convicted under the 'religious clause.' They prayed, fasted, sang psalms, read the Gospel and this had an effect on one of the prisoners—he suddenly came to the Faith. And how! He became all directed toward God. He desired to confess and repent. He was serving time for theft, although in reality he had killed a man. But this crime had not been discovered, and the murderer had not been found.

"And so he came to the prison guard and told him everything with tears of repentance. They looked through the files, found that case, put him on trial, and gave him the death sentence. So my question is—how do I say it—to the Lord God Himself: how is it, in His providential plan, that a person repented of his sins, and was shot for it? It bothers me. What are your thoughts?"

The bishop thought, looked heavenward, and began to answer in a quiet voice, almost as if he was talking to himself:

"I had an acquaintance—a hieromonk. He served at a village parish, and in between services he would drive to Moscow in his car. He began to be pestered by a traffic cop who always stood at the turn from the village where that hieromonk served, on the highway leading to the city.

"Every time the hieromonk would drive to Moscow after the Sunday Liturgy, this traffic cop would stop him and badger him. Well, the priest would give him some money, and he would let him go in peace. But then an elder told him that it wasn't right to corrupt the police with bribes like that. And he decided not to give the cop any more money.

"One Sunday after Liturgy, he drove off as usual to Moscow. He had had a good morning of serving, praying, and partaking of holy communion, and had even consumed all the Gifts from the chalice, as he had served without a deacon. He drank a cup of tea for the road, and set off.

"Then the traffic cop stopped him, waving his baton. The hieromonk rolled down his window and looked out. The cop kept waiting for him to put a crisp bill into his hand. But he held on to his steering wheel, looking out through his window and appearing disinterested.

"The traffic cop grew nervous.

"'You . . . broke the law . . .'

"'What? Where?' the hieromonk said in surprise.

"'Why do you have tires that belong on a Tatra?' the cop finally came up with something.

"'Fine,' agreed the hieromonk. 'But you must write on the ticket: for having tires like on a Tatra . . .'

"'Why?' the cop asked suspiciously.

"'So that I can show your superior (here he provided the name) at the Lavra, it was he who gave me my license.'

"'That's fine,' the cop was taken aback. 'Just keep driving.'

"The traffic cop let him go, but held a grudge against him. He found out that when they give communion, these 'pops' always drink the wine. So the next time, he kept an eye out for him.

"Our hieromonk stopped and rolled down the window:

"'What now?'

"'Did you drink today?' the cop asked triumphantly.

"'No, I didn't drink, I consumed.'

"'Aha,' his tormentor exclaimed spitefully. 'Well then, hand over your license.'

"He suspended his license for a whole year and even drew up a report so that everything would be followed to the letter. He left nothing to be contested.

"The sorrowful hieromonk came without a car to the Lavra. He met me and told me the story, then plied me with questions:

"'*Vladyka*, where was I in the wrong? The commandments tell you not to bear false witness, not to lie! So I told him the truth! It turns out that I must suffer for telling the truth?'

"And I said to him:

"'Oh, that tempter-traffic cop of yours had you wound around his little finger. You should have been more aware of whom you were confessing to. Were you ever taught to confess to a traffic cop? In addition, did you really drink? Did you really consume alcohol? It was the blood of Christ!' And that, I think, is what happened with your repentant criminal," sighed the bishop, looking at Sinyavsky, and then adding with feeling, "Why did he go and confess to the prison guard? So in the providential plan he chose the wrong man for his confession: don't confess to the prison guard, or the traffic cop, or the tempter, or the enemy of mankind. It is only written: 'O give thanks unto the Lord, for He is good, for His mercy endureth for ever!' (Ps 135:1)."

❧ *One Wave after Another* ❧

In 1988, when church buildings were slowly being returned to the Church, a bishop that we knew, and for whom my husband was gathering materials about the history of the Vladimir Diocese, proposed to ordain my husband as a deacon and send him to serve in Murom, where the only Orthodox church had just been reopened.

If the offer had come four years earlier or six years later, he would have immediately accepted. But we were experiencing very difficult times for our family then, and it seemed impossible to move the entire family, including our school-age children. Thus my husband declined.

And so, when in 1995 he was ordained to the diaconate and then to the priesthood and began to serve in the Church of the Holy Martyr Tatiana, he received a letter from Murom. Inside the envelope lay a photograph of the church. On the other side was written: "This church was the last to be shut down in 1937. There served Deacon Vigilianskii, who was shot by the godless authorities. In 1988, the church was reopened, and the Divine Liturgy has been served there since that time."

This was such providential and symbolic news: the last clergy member to serve there before its closing was the New Martyr Vigilianskii, and the first to serve there after its reopening might have been Vigilianskii also, i.e., my husband. This would have restored the continuity of time, connected the break in the chain, one wave after another . . . It would have been a story taken straight out of the lives of the saints.

But things didn't turn out so dramatically, beautifully, literally, and . . . implausibly. That unity of place didn't happen: the one served there, the other serves here.

Even the bishop who had proposed ordination to my husband and the assignment in Murom didn't know the last name of the last Murom clergy member then. He had made the offer driven not so much by human logic and forethought as by some other impulse and current.

And so, I make so bold as to express my opinion that it was divine providence at work here, creating mysterious dramatic intrigue, whispering and indicating to the bishop, leading and prodding my husband toward something, being potentially present there, so that we would—albeit after the fact—discover its workings in amazed and joyful recognition.

❧ The Sound of Trumpets ❧

There lived in Holy Trinity Monastery a hierodeacon named Potapii, a man of mighty build and towering height. But his exceptional voice made the biggest impression—this he treasured, nurtured, and cared for very much.

He could often be seen on Afon Hill, where he walked before the service, exercising his vocal chords and slowly warming up his voice. The wind carried abroad his delightful bass cadences: "A-a-a! A-u-a! I-u-e-o-a-y-e-iu!" Not only were they broadcasted—these "sounds retreating into velvet"[1]— but they were palpable, almost tangible.

Soon he was noticed by the ruling bishop himself, Bishop Varnava, who made him his protodeacon, took him away to his diocesan center of Emsk, and placed him in a small monastery located right in the city center. They often went around the diocese together, and Fr Potapii would invariably lift the spirits of the praying congregations with his first invocation, when his bass so majestically, severely, and composedly presented that first "Arise!"

But in between the services and trips, when he sat in his cell, the large Fr Potapii felt unbearably cramped and oppressed in that little monastery where the bishop had assigned him. What's more, this little monastery did not belong to the monastery brethren at all, since there was also a museum there that considered itself the master of both the church and monastery buildings. The museum workers were very hostile and even aggressive toward the small body of monks who timidly backed into their corners. Potapii didn't even have a monastery garden into which he could retreat in order to try out his voice properly: nowhere to do his exercises, starting with the hollow grumble of "Bless, Master," continuing on to the hollow—since it was not possible to go any lower—bass intonation of "Bre-e-e-ethre-e-e-en," and spreading further in breadth and height, ending with the high bellow of "We shall be-e-e-e with the Lo-o-ord!"

At this moment, those ever-present museum workers would jump out and, dramatically plugging their ears, drive him back to the monastery house. "My blood froze in my veins from your howling!" the directress would cry out, offended. "And my milk turned. It's all curdled now!" added the cashier, screwing up her lips.

In a word, things were bad for Potapii there. He was sick at heart. They say that he was even not above flirting with "the demon alcohol."

From time to time he would call the iconographer Hierodeacon Dionisii in Holy Trinity Monastery and offer to sell him relics. These little pieces of relics could be placed in specially made reliquaries that were then built into icons, making the icons much more spiritually powerful.

These could be relics of St Spyridon, or St Panteleimon the Healer, or the holy Martyr Tatiana, or even St Nicholas the Wonderworker.

"Where does he get them?" Dionisii would wonder. "He doesn't seem to go anywhere very far away. Does he cut them off his own body, or what?"

This remained a mystery.

But Dionisii always willingly bought the holy relics and wrote a corresponding icon especially for each one, then generously handed them out to his priest-acquaintances and laymen, or sold them in times of need. Potapii would come to him in the monastery and take money, a tape recorder, a projector, a cell phone, or simply a bottle of good cognac in exchange for the delivery of relics: anything that he laid his eyes on.

But then there was a rumor that things were going badly for Fr Potapii: that he had "taken advantage," "crossed the line," "had picked up a passenger," and was now being treated, not just anywhere, but in a mental hospital.

Since by "passengers" the monks of Holy Trinity Monastery meant demons, this grim news elicited much concern among those brethren who loved Potapii.

"The psych ward will not rid you of your demons," they commented. "There you'll only take on some more passengers!"

So Dionisii set off for Emsk to visit his ailing friend.

He arrived, subdued, at the hospital surrounded on all sides by a high wall, and asked:

"Where is Protodeacon Potapii being treated?"

And—surprisingly—the severe face of the nurse softened and she began to coo and softly twitter:

"Let's go, let's go, I'll take you to him! But please don't take away our joy!"

Dionisii was surprised, and grew hesitant: did she really mean Potapii? But he submissively went after her.

They passed a few somber-looking, typical, boxy buildings, walked through the park, walked up a hill, and ended up near a tidy little two-story cottage.

"Come in, come in," the nurse welcomed Dionisii cheerfully, holding open the door. "Here we house our especially important guests, you can say our VIPs, of the sanatorium variety."

Dionisii found himself in what looked like a hunting lodge or an ethnographic retreat. From one wall, a color photograph of deer looked down on him, from another—a photograph of a hedgehog displaying a red cap mushroom on his needles. On a third wall hung an oil painting vibrantly depicting ears of corn. There was a preserved crocodile with its chops opened wide on the bureau next to the television, a tapestry hanging over the soft straw-colored couch reminiscent of illustrations of Papa Carlo's hearth,[2] and Ukrainian-embroidered decorative hand towels on the table, windowsill, and television.

Shuffling along the floor in soft white slippers and dressed in a white velour robe, Fr Potapii came in through the side door.

The nurse grew abashed and left them alone together.

"Yes," said Potapii, "yes, yes! See what a golden place this is? A mental hospital and sanatorium in one. This is where I've been hiding. Slippers, a robe. Three meals a day. Just don't tell anyone in our monastery, or the brethren will all rush over here tomorrow! There will be a flood, it will be full to the brim, you won't be able to push your way through!"

"But why did they put you here? I never thought that you would be in a mental hospital . . ."

"It was all *Vladyka*, he petitioned for me a little—said that I was his protodeacon, that they should treasure me as the apple of his eye. Sometimes I sing for them here. They prefer romances. So I give them romances. 'The night is still, the desert hearkens to the Lord . . .' And sometimes I prophesize."

"You know how to?" chuckled Dionisii.

"It's a simple matter. Singing is more difficult. Some nurse or nanny will ask me to, so what am I supposed to do? So I tell her: 'You have sorrow in your heart,' 'You often think that you are undervalued,' or 'You are capable of much more.' And then I immediately say something about the future."

"What do you say about the future?"

"'You are now at the crossroads of your journey.' 'Soon you will meet a person who will influence your life.' 'You are on the threshold of a new period in your life.' And that's enough for them! And that's how it is. Just try and object!"

"But what happened to you?" Dionisii threw his glance over the walls with the deer and the hearth. "What was it, a passenger?"

"No, no," he winced. "There, in the museum, they noticed something missing: something disappeared from their storage room. Nothing but a trifle for them. They grabbed the guard—a good fellow. And he had sworn to me that there, in those museum storerooms, all those things had been lying for years unneeded, in the dust! Like a dog in the manger! They just hid it from the public eye and were happy with themselves! The guard went to jail, and I came here, farther from sin!"

"I see," Dionisii grew serious, having come to a realization. He sat with Potapii for a while and then hurried off home.

Back in his cell, he took what was left of the relics of the Great Martyr Pantelcimon and drove to the museum where Potapii's monastery was located.

He came to the director, and unwrapping everything, carefully laid it on her table—all the dark, tiny little splinters.

"Here—I am returning them to you!"

"What is this?" She fixed her gaze on him with disgust and wonder. "What is this dust?"

"The relics of the holy Great Martyr Pantelcimon," he replied.

"We're not taking that!" she replied firmly.

"But it was stolen from you!" he exclaimed.

"Young man," she shook her head with dignity, "pardon me, but you are offering us some sort of rubbish. If you must know, what was stolen from us was museum treasures—a cutlass from the time of Admiral Ushakov, a ring with the seal of Emperor Paul I, a shepherd statuette belonging to the family of Count Sheremetiev . . ."

Dionisii wrapped up the relics again, put them in the chest pocket of his cassock, and went out into the monastery courtyard.

She also came out almost immediately after him. She sat down behind her driver, who started the engine. Dionisii, walking past, suddenly decided to play a prank: he had been very offended by her "dirt" and "rubbish."

He bent down to her open window and asked:

"Are you the only passenger here or are there more?"

Before the car drove off, she managed to reply, haughtily leaning against the back of her seat:

"I am the only passenger here," and waving her hand, she gave her driver the signal to drive on.

Fr Potapii soon left the hospital and wrote the bishop a petition to return him to his native Holy Trinity Monastery, but he still promised to serve the bishop wherever and whenever he was needed.

Quite soon he could again be observed walking up and down Afon Hill and trying out his voice.

"A! A! A!" At first the low notes resounded with a refined huskiness, then amid the guttural grumbling the following words could be identified: "Sacrifice, master," "Pierce, master"[3] And then a great growl ending in a real, thundering roar at the words "Lord have mercy!"

The wind carried this all over the monastery, and the sound seemed to linger in the hollows, like the smell of good Athonite incense prepared without any added fragrances.

As for Dionisii, he wrote an icon to the Healer Panteleimon, made a reliquary for it, laid the relics inside, and gave this icon to me. Even now it shines in my home like a window into the heavenly kingdom.

Fr Potapii's supply of relics dried up. How many times did Dionisii ask him, seeing him on Afon Hill:

"Sweep up all the corners! Let me have someone's, anyone's . . ."

But Potapii would just carefully place his fingers on his throat and draw forth the sound of trumpets:

"Let us Att-e-e-end! Wi-i-isdo-o-o-om!"[4]

❧ *"Our Boys" and "the Germans"* ❧

My husband worked for a while in the literary department of the journal *Ogonek*. This was during the times when censorship was almost completely lifted, and the journal began to receive a stream of whistle-blower materials revealing the true nature of the Soviet regime. In those days, my husband received a call from the writer Evgenii Popov, who asked him to accept a meeting with a certain KGB agent who would like to make a confession of his past activities.

"You see," said Popov, "in the late seventies he ran Hotel Metropol and analyzed the wiretapping records from Evgenia Ginzburg's apartment, where her almanac was being prepared for publication. And now this guy tells me, you see, that among all the speakers on the tapes I elicited the most human sympathy from him, so now he would like to admit his guilt to me and in general to unburden himself. But as soon as I recall what we chatted about in that apartment, drinking and having a good time, and what he heard then, I feel sick to my stomach, and he himself is so revolting to me, so revolting, that I don't want to meet with him under any circumstances."

All right. My husband invited this KGB agent (let's call him Ch.) to talk, and he came to see him at the magazine offices with an article in which he denounced the activity directed against the people by his organization. While my husband corrected the style, underlined the unclear sections, and eliminated overgeneralizations, they began to talk. My husband, who in his youth and young adult years had had his share of trials at the hands of Ch.'s colleagues, began to ask him questions. So they sat across from each other: Ch.—tense, trying to stuff his hands into his armpits and his feet farther under the table, and my husband—carelessly sprawled out in his office armchair and tapping the table with his pencil. For a moment, my husband imagined that in past days they could have sat in the exact same attitudes, but in reversed positions—Ch. in the armchair and my husband shrinking back in his chair, with Ch. asking the questions:

"Well, well, can you give me more details? And when did you intercept Popov's conversations? And what was the goal of 'Operation Metropol?' Who was your informant in the case? You are not being completely honest, and you're avoiding giving me a direct answer . . . I am interested in everything—the reports, contacts, what provocative measures you took . . . How did you personally become an employee of the regime?"

In short, my husband discovered much about his interlocutor: he had served at the front, had gone through Stalingrad, had been injured, and then, after the hospital and the war, had finished law school, become a lawyer, and from there had gone on to work for the authorities. His article soon appeared in the *Ogonek* and caused an uproar. It was entitled "The Steel Trap of the Party" or something like that.

But then, Ch.'s former colleagues ("former" because he was already retired) did not forgive him. They wrote a severe response, called him a "Judas," "loosed" him from access to the department medical center, and even, I think, took away his food tokens, which were considerably important to him as it was 1989, and all of Moscow lived on these orders, tokens, and food stamps. So poor Ch., finding himself estranged, suffered. He even began to come by the Church of Metropolitan Philip that had just opened at the time. He wanted to change his entire life so much that he decided to get baptized and even asked my husband to help him do this.

At that time, several other people had already approached my husband with the same request: the wife of the Russian ambassador in Germany, my classmate along with his children, the daughter and grandson of a People's Artist of the USSR; Zhenya Popov himself dreamed of baptizing his newborn son Vasenka, and we were planning to go to the Church of the Transfiguration in Peredelkino, where they performed the mystery without abbreviation and by full immersion, as was proper. So we invited Ch. there as well, to baptize them all together.

True, as soon as Popov found out that Ch. was going to be there, he immediately backed out:

"To baptize my Vasenka in the same font as that devil—no, I'm not ready to do that. Let's separate them—Vasenka tomorrow, Ch. at some other time."

So Vasenka was baptized alone in a small font, and several days later a varied assembly of catechumens were baptized in the company of their godmothers and godfathers.

"Keep in mind," warned my husband on the eve of the baptism, turning to Ch., "great temptations await you. The evil one will try to place obstacles on your path to salvation, but you must be ready and bravely continue to move toward your goal."

"What kind of obstacles can there be?" Ch. flippantly waved him away.

"Well, at the very least, you can oversleep or become ill, your water pipe can burst, your key can get stuck in the lock, you can get stuck in the elevator or twist your ankle, the train could be canceled. Or you will wake up tomorrow morning and suddenly think: 'What am I doing, am I losing it in my old age? What is this fantasy? What have I stuck my nose into? I lived just fine for sixty years without baptism, and now what is this strange behavior?' You'll turn over onto your other side and go back to sleep."

"No," Ch. shook his head. "That can't be. I will definitely come."

They agreed to meet at an appointed time at the commuter train. And sure enough, when we reached the platform, Ch. was already standing at the train. But he looked scared and subdued.

"What happened?"

"This," and he showed us his right arm hanging lifelessly by his side, "my arm is numb. I can't lift it or move it. I think I may have had a minor stroke at night. What should I do? I can't even cross myself!"

He tried to take it with his left hand and place the sign of the cross over himself, but it wouldn't obey him.

"It's all right," my husband cheered him up, "you can cross yourself with your left hand."

"A temptation, just like you warned me," muttered Ch. as he sat down inside the train.

We finally reached Peredelkino. Several hieromonks who were near and dear to us served there at the Church of the Transfiguration, along with the abbot, who was also a friend.

Not anticipating any complications, our friendly group of neophytes awaiting holy baptism moved forward to the church. But it wasn't to be so easy. Just the previous night the warden had gotten into an argument with the abbot, and had taken off who knows where early that morning, taking with him the keys to the locked baptistery.

"I would baptize you all," the abbot shrugged his shoulders, "but I don't have any spare keys, and it's unclear when the warden will return. If you want, we can wait, or come another time."

My husband gazed at the significantly sized flock of varying ages and races that stood in the church courtyard, awaiting their birth into life eternal, glanced over the focused and stroke-ridden Ch. with his limp arm, and understood that it would be much more difficult to gather everyone together again the next time. So he said:

"Let's go take a walk for an hour—we'll go to the grave of Pasternak, Tchaikovsky, and by then the warden will return!"

Splitting up into small groups, everyone amicably followed him.

"Let me tell you in the meantime about my time working in the NTS,"[1] offered Ch., finding himself paired with my husband on the pathway. He was expressing his gratitude in the form of sincerity; he was also convinced that his stories in one way or another were parts of one great history.

My husband nodded.

"Well, I was brought in—I had specially traveled to Germany with false documents and had met with their representative there . . . I became such an authority there that in the end I began to head the organization and began to break it down from the inside by inserting my own people. At one time there was almost nobody left except our people, and they all worked for us: it became a sort of branch of the KGB. And to those people who were not connected to us, we would give all sorts of phony assignments—we would set them up to work at a Soviet plant or factory, or even send them to the Public Housing and Utilities Unit to get some sort of list of residents and employees . . . So they imitated work but were really performing a farce. Such were our victories. Soon it was time to close down the operation, and I wrote a report to the command, which had just recently changed: Andropov[2] had come into power. Everything was written up in the report—the mission had been accomplished, and the NTS no longer existed, since it was entirely made up of our own people. And then what? Once in office, Andropov delivered a lecture to a secret assembly of the KGB, and we heard the following: 'At the moment, the NTS presents a real danger to us' 'What, has he gone mad?' I exclaimed. 'What danger?' But my director told me, 'You just sit there and be quiet. Are you unwell or something?'

"And sure enough—just after this secret lecture, rumors began to spread among enemy circles that the KGB was mobilizing its powers and resources in a battle against anti-Soviet organizations, including the NTS. At this, the

CIA became involved: they directed a flow of funds to our boys in the NTS, since the Soviets were so scared of it; from their end, the KGB increased our financial support, and so a snowball was sent rolling down the hill, growing larger and larger at every turn: titles, ranks, promotions, awards ... These were the games we were forced to play," sighed Ch.

In the meantime, it was time to return to the church. We arrived, and the warden had indeed returned, but was still angry at the abbot. My husband went off to discuss it with the abbot. Then the warden said:

"Well, all right, I'll open the baptistery for you. But this is the problem: our hot water's been turned off. And the font, inasmuch as you plan to be baptized with full immersion, will not only take two hours to fill up, but the water will be freezing cold spring water. Who would dare to dunk himself into such water?"

Very well. My husband took all the catechumens to the holy spring, having explained to them that we would have to wait a little longer while the font was being filled up. He didn't dare tell them about the ice cold water: for man is weak and afraid. What if his charges would get frightened, refuse to be baptized, and go home? As for waiting—why not wait? It was May, the lilacs were blooming, the apple and cherries were blossoming, dandelions were flaming in the young grass, the sun was warm but not hot. They went by way of the old cemetery and Pasternak's field to the holy spring. Ch. scooped some water with his left hand and washed his face. His right hand still hung lifeless and dangling by his side. Not in vain did he roam the spring fields and ravines after my husband, sharing his inside information with him in the fear that "there won't be any time left" and desiring no matter what to be baptized unto forgiveness of sins; then, whatever came next would not be so frightening.

We came back to the church once again. The priest was already awaiting us in his *epitrachelion*—the font would be full at any moment. Not a word was said about the ice-cold water.

And so the blessed hour was upon us. The priest led everyone inside and baptized the infants in the small font, into which two kettles-full of boiled water had been poured. The adults he sent in their baptismal gowns down the stairs into the large ice-cold font, and standing at the edge, dunked each person's head three times: "In the name of the Father, amen; the Son, amen;

and the Holy Spirit, amen," so that none of them would remain merely "sprinkled"[3] but be loyal children of the Church.

Everyone left the baptistery with faces transformed and a certain mysterious, unearthly light in their eyes. Then Ch. suddenly lifted up his right hand as if nothing was wrong with it and made the sign of the cross over himself.

"Your arm . . . it's working!" my husband exclaimed in surprise.

"Oh yes? I'd forgotten all about it!" he broke out into a smile.

"How was the water?"

"What of it? It was clean!"

"But it was ice-cold spring water!"

"Really?" all the newly baptized were surprised. "Was it really ice cold? We didn't feel it!"

"It was good water!"

"Just fine!"

So my husband asked the warden:

"So the hot water was turned on after all?"

"No, we still only have cold water . . ."

With that, we departed, wondering and rejoicing the entire journey.

Ch. became a model parishioner. Every time he saw me in church, he meaningfully raised his right hand to his face and carefully made the sign of the cross. I felt sorry that Zhenya Popov didn't want to baptize his Vasen'ka together with Ch. that time. What a touching and symbolic Christian picture that would have been: "the calf and the young lion . . . together" (Isa 11:6)!

Soon, Ch. died and was given a Christian burial. There, he will be met by the Lord, Who Himself, without regarding the faces, will divide the sheep from the goats. Everyone will be mixed together and divided: the former will stand at His right hand, and the latter at His left—NTS, KGB, CIA, "our boys" and "the Germans," Party members and non-Party members, the Reds and the Whites, the black, yellow, orange, green, pink, and blue . . . and somewhere amongst them—all of us.

❧ *Five Months of Love* ❧

I n September 1996, my husband received a telephone call from Maria Vasilievna Rozanova in Paris—she was the wife of the writer Andrei Sinyavsky. She told him that Sinyavsky was dying, he was completely paralyzed, including his brain, and all he wanted was for Fr Vladimir to confess and commune him before death.

"Hurry," added Maria Vasilievna, "they say he has days, if not hours."

We were friends with the Sinyavskys, and Andrei Donatovich's illness was a huge blow to us. Fr Vladimir would have been happy to rush off right away and fly to his dying friend's side, but how? He had just returned from vacation, from which his superior impatiently awaited his return, as he had had to serve all that time in the church alone, so it was unlikely that he would be allowed to leave again. That was one thing. He had no French visa—that was another thing. And no ticket to France—three. And four　he literally had no money to buy the ticket.

So my husband told Maria Vasilievna:

"It's impossible."

And then immediately added:

"Wait for me. I'll administer holy unction, too."

Then he hung up the phone in total disbelief at himself.

Moreover, we had been expecting a visit from our friend, Andrei Chernov, from the Literature Institute, since the previous night. Soon he appeared on our doorstep, leading behind him an unknown, modest-looking, and not very remarkable person.

It turned out that this was a recently established banker who wanted to donate a small sum, namely 500 dollars, to some good cause. That is why he asked Chernov to bring him to a priest, so that he could help him decide what to do with the money.

Fr Vladimir told him about the dying Sinyavsky, who was in need of his final communion, and the recently established banker happily placed the money on the table:

"I knew that you would advise me to spend it on something worthy!"

So the money for Fr Vladimir's flight was found.

While he was talking to the banker, I got a call from another of my friends from the institute, now the chief editor of the magazine *Stas*, who asked me to quickly write an article about Akhmatova[1] for the latest issue.

"I'll pay you in advance without waiting for the magazine release, just as soon as you bring me the article."

The next day I brought him the article that I had written overnight, and he handed me three hundred-dollar bills. So it turned out that we had enough money for my ticket, too, since I also wanted to bid farewell to the beloved writer. Moreover, Fr Vladimir always felt somewhat helpless in France, as he didn't speak French, so it was better for me to be by his side.

By the way, this was the only time that I was paid so much money for an article and that I was given the payment immediately, before the issue was released.

Happily, the attaché on cultural affairs at the French embassy at the time was a wonderful man with a Russian background—Alesha Berulovich—and his assistant, Annique Pousselle, was a friend of ours. When they learned about the dying Sinyavsky, she helped us get visas that same day; we booked our tickets; now all that remained was the matter of the church rector, Fr Maksim. The situation could even arise that in spite of his sincere desire to release Fr Vladimir, he would not be able to: services must continue at the church, and if Fr Maksim had a lecture at the academy, and if Fr Vladimir would just leave, there would be no one left to serve. My husband understood this very well and thus called his rector with some trepidation. But he unexpectedly and calmly said:

"Of course you must go."

In short, if it pleases God, He will do the impossible: three days after Maria Vasilievna's call, we were already sitting in her home on Rue Fontenay-aux-Roses.

"Sinyavsky is very bad," she said. "Every day there's something new—his leg will grow numb, or his hand—the tumor keeps growing and pressing on his brain. The doctors here consulted together and gave him no more than several days to live. In addition to it all, he has caught a bad cold: he slept with the window open last night, his blanket fell onto the floor, and he couldn't pick it up. But I beg of you—don't tell him that he is dying. When he heard that you would administer holy unction, he became terrified—don't you receive unction before death? He even made me read about it in the encyclopedia, though it does say there that it's done for healing."

"For healing of soul and body," confirmed my husband.

Fr Vladimir went upstairs to Andrei Donatovich's office, which was on the second floor, and they had a long discussion there, after which Andrei Donatovich received confession and holy unction, and we set off to Fr Nikolai Ozolin, a priest who served and taught at the St Sergius Theological Institute, to ask him to prepare the Holy Gifts the following day.

While we walked to the institute, a terrible pulsating sound began to echo all around us: buk-buk-buk-buk, and it grew louder and louder; then strange-looking young people began to cross our path, jumping up and down with horns on their heads. The horns were attached to their heads or constructed out of their own hair, and vile-looking tails dragged behind them from between their legs. These jumping and writhing people kept increasing more and more in number, until a crowd covered the entire street, and in the midst rode a bus from which issued that "buk-buk-buk" noise increasing to impossibly loud pitches. It turned out that this was a protest against the arrival of the Pope of Rome in France, and so all hell had broken loose. The faces of the protesters were smeared with black grime, and they grimaced and jumped up and down, holding up two fingers in the sign of the letter "V" for "victoire." Victory.

"They are demons," we guessed, pressing against the houses to avoid being trampled.

Finally, we reached Fr Nikolai, and he promised to give us the Holy Gifts the next morning after Liturgy for Sinyavsky.

Walking along a narrow Paris street on our way home, we ran into our friend, Professor Krotovskii, and his wife. Professor Krotovskii was a God-given doctor who had been performing surgical wonders for many years, saving people from death or disability. He was deeply saddened when he heard about Sinyavsky, and offered to personally examine his X-rays and test results—maybe the Parisian doctors were overexaggerating? What if there was still some hope? Perhaps it wasn't as bad as we thought . . .

So we went to Maria Vasilievna's home together with the Krotovskiis. But alas! As soon as he looked at the X-rays and studied the papers, his expression fell and he said:

"It's even worse than I expected . . . It really is a matter of hours, not even days."

The next day, Fr Vladimir communed Andrei Donatovich, and we flew back to Moscow. Two days later Maria Vasilievna called us and asked Fr Vladimir to come to the phone.

"That's it," we thought. "Memory eternal!"

However, Maria Vasilievna directed their conversation in an entirely different direction.

"Vigilianskii," she said quite playfully, "guess who is sitting in front of me at this very moment and drinking tea?"

"I don't know, Maria Vasilievna, it could be anyone, from Gorbachev to Limonov."

"But it isn't," she boldly replied. "In front of me is sitting . . . Sinyavsky. He came down from the second floor by himself today and is now sitting here before my very eyes! But that's not all—they took new X-rays of his head, and there was no tumor there! The doctors can't understand it themselves!"

Over the next five months, Andrei Donatovich would come down to the kitchen in the same manner to drink tea; he would work on his latest novel, meet with friends, bidding farewell to this life and preparing himself for the next one. Fr Nikolai Ozolin came to him several times with the Holy Gifts and communed him.

Fr Vladimir told him:

"You will live for as long as you have the desire to be with God."

And he shrank from his own boldness at saying these words to a dying man.

Andrei Sinyavsky died on February 25, 1997.

A very naïve man, upon hearing the story of these five months, exclaimed:

"But why so little time?"

In reality, it was neither too little nor too long. It was the exact time that God needed to take him—humble, meek, ready, fully matured, like an exquisite fruit—to His eternal abode.

Fr Vladimir, also, grew in his faith in the miraculous power of the Church Mysteries, that cured, healed, and gladdened the heart of the suffering man.

❧ *Mysteries beyond the Grave* ❧

In the Gospel parable of the rich man and Lazarus, the possibility of communication between the living and the dead is refered to directly by Abraham himself, who says from his resting place in the "bosom of Abraham": "Between us and you there is a great gulf fixed, so that those who want to pass from here to you cannot, nor can those from there pass to us" (Lk 16:26).

And yet miraculous events occur from time to time. Countless incredible stories witnessing to just how fine, even transparent, the line is which divides this world from the next have been collected in the book *Eternal Mysteries Beyond the Grave,* by Archimandrite Panteleimon.[1] Or in the book *From the Mysterious Realm,* Archpriest Grigorii D'iachenko related to us the multitude of strange reports of the dead giving the living, whom they continued to love, fateful signs. They warn them of danger, or ask help for themselves, or simply send messages of love! Brother has appeared to brother to inform him of his death, son has appeared to mother to warn her of her own impending journey to the next world, and the deceased husband has appeared to his wife to ask for her fervent prayer.

And what these things were, are, and will be—whether it is the ability to see on the part of the living or the angels bringing comfort to those in mourning—God knows! But these instances also took place with people close to me, people very near to me.

Maria Vasilievna Rozanova and her husband Andrei Sinyavsky spent almost fifty years together. Of course, Maria Vasilievna thought the whole world of him, so great was her love for him. And then he died . . .

His funeral took place, and she buried him in the cemetery at Fontenay-aux-Roses, not far from their house.

Winter passed and spring came. The snow melted, the rivers swelled, the birds began to sing, the fountains gushed out with golden fish sparkling in their waters, but Maria Vasilievna had no peace at heart, she was disturbed—Sinyavsky was appearing to her in her sleep almost every night looking unwell, uneasy: things were clearly not going well for him and he was in torment, asking something of her.

Maria Vasilievna couldn't bear it any longer—she went to the cemetery, taking with her as translator a Russian parishioner who was an old friend.

They came to the cemetery manager, and Maria Vasilievna began to insist that her husband's body be exhumed, because she had to make sure that everything was alright.

But the funeral director simply shrugged his shoulders: this was such a complicated procedure! And what was she expecting to see? Moreover, madame herself had wanted her husband to be buried in the ground instead of in a crypt. It was especially difficult to dig up graves in the spring: if the groundwater rose, it would be impossible to dig through that slush!

But Maria Vasilievna was adamant:

"I can feel that Sinyavsky is not doing well down there! Something bad happened to him . . . He wouldn't come to me in such agitation for no reason!"

What could they do? This cemetery manager sighed, sighed some more, shook his head, clicked his tongue, but there was nothing to be done, so he appointed the day of exhumation. The gravediggers crowded together at the grave of the Russian writer, and next to them stood the loyal Maria Vasilievna with her friend.

"Madame, kindly step back—this sight is not for the faint of heart!" The cemetery manager entreated her. "The gravediggers will see themselves if something is not right. There's no need for you to look inside."

"Well, I like that!" fretted Maria Vasilievna. "Did I spend half a century with my husband only to desert him in a difficult moment! Dig on, please."

The gravediggers took to the earth with their shovels, and had already gone far down when Maria Vasilievna heard the exclamation—timid and quiet at first but growing more and more in number and volume: "Police! Police!"

She glanced down into the dug-up grave and was horrified: the ground-water had washed over the grave so much that the lid was not only moved to the side but had cracked, showing the interior lining . . .

"Well, there we have it!" said Maria Vasilievna. "He didn't come to me in vain! That's how wretched he was down there!"

The police came, extracted the coffin, placed the body in a new one, and reburied him, this time in a crypt. After that, Andrei Donatovich stopped appearing to his beloved wife in her dreams. She understood this to mean that he was finally at rest and settled in a dry place, "in a place of light, in a place of green pasture, in a place of repose," a place "whence all sickness, sorrow, and sighing are fled away."[2]

One wants to repeat again and again in response to this, being filled with the meaning of the words: truly "He is not the God of the dead, but the God of the living!" (Mk 12:27).

❧ *Augustine* ❧

I've already written an entire poem about this. And the abbot of Sreten-sky Monastery, Bishop Tikhon, who was one of the players in this story, wrote about it in his memoirs. Nonetheless, I would like to return to this subject once more and tell it how I witnessed it.

Once I came to my father confessor in the monastery. He saw me and was dismayed:

"What, you're here? I've just sent a young monk to see you. He is an ascetic from the Caucasus Mountains. Please help him, he doesn't have a passport, and without any documents they won't take him into the monastery. He's already been to the Lavra, and then wanted to stay here, but there's no way! Think of some way to make him legal! His name is Augustine. He's a person with a very developed spiritual life. I myself asked to be remembered in his anchorite prayers."

The word of my father confessor was law to me. So I returned home to save this young monk. I arrived to see him already sitting in our kitchen, drinking tea with my children, surrounded by several men in cassocks—

priests and hieromonks—awaiting his stories about the ascetics of the Caucasus Mountains.

This was his story.

When he was seven years old, he was sent from Moscow with his mother to the Caucasus Mountains, where they began their ascetic journey under the direction of a certain spiritual ascetic elder. This elder tonsured the mother, then tonsured the boy, and they lived under God's protection, in fervent prayer, and by the work of their hands—they planted a garden, kept bees, had goats, cows, and even cats. When Augustine turned sixteen and it was high time for him to get his passport, the elder didn't give him his blessing and said that he himself had destroyed his own passport—a document of the antichrist—a long time ago. Then Augustine's mother also destroyed hers. She just took it and burned it. This was the tradition among the Caucasus ascetics, for they saw in the hammer-and-sickle-inscribed Soviet passport the mark of the antichrist.

The elder soon peacefully reposed in the Lord, and they remained completely alone, but continued to live as they had in the elder's presence—by prayers, fasting, and work.

The problem was that no matter how precipitous were the paths leading to their humble cell, they still came across certain wandering monks, pilgrims, hunters, vagabonds, and criminals there. They were also susceptible to cutthroats—Islamized Greeks who would steal a goat or a jar of honey or take off with all the potatoes.

And suddenly the following tragic story took place: one of these Greeks was shot, and it was suspected that the murderer was a hunter who at times stopped by the hut of Augustine and his mother. There the other Greeks went in order to catch him and kill him, but he had already gone somewhere else on his own. Augustine was fixing a bridge over a ravine, and his mother was alone. They began to torture her to find out where the hunter went and when he would return, and even threatened to rape her if she didn't tell them. The old nun was so shaken by their threats that she cried out:

"Better burn me alive than to do that to me!"

And so one of them poked her with a burning torch, apparently as a warning, because when she suddenly caught on fire, they got scared and tried to extinguish the fire. But as she had many layers wrapped and wound around her—her cassock, *ryassa*—the fire grew in intensity, and there was no water nearby, so they ran away in terror.

Augustine sensed that something was wrong—a distinct and nagging thought led him to abandon his unfinished work and return home. He saw from a distance the four criminals hurriedly descending the path leading from the hut and recognized the evildoers. But they also noticed him. He found his mother still alive: she was writhing on the floor near death, but she managed to bless him and order him to flee that place.

This was a true story—I not only heard it from Augustine in my kitchen, but also read about it in the book *In the Caucasus Mountains*.

And so, he buried his mother, came down from the mountains, set off for Sukhumi, and went straight to the church, where some nuns that he knew were laboring. He lived with them for several days, and then they told him:

"It's not safe for you to stay here. They're looking for you. Several severe-looking men have already come here and were studying you and asking about you. Here is some money for you: go to the Holy Trinity Lavra of St Sergius. There are still elders there to this very day."

He did as they told him. He arrived at the Lavra, came to Elder Kirill and Elder Naum, and they said to him:

"They won't admit you here to the monastery without a passport. The authorities watch us like hawks. Go to the Pskov Caves Monastery, they are more lax there. Maybe they will take you."

He did so. He stayed with one of the Pechory elders and with my father confessor, and met some of the other monks. The elder tried to talk to the Father Superior about him—this and that, such a kind novice, no passport. But the Father Superior—at the time it was Archimandrite Gabriel—categorically refused. What could he do? My father confessor felt sorry for him and sent him to Moscow to us: perhaps we could think of something in our capital city.

And so, when Augustine got settled in our home, a multitude of believers began to throng to him as an ascetic from the Caucasus Mountains. There were among them monks from the Lavra, Moscow priests, and simply zealous laypeople longing for the angelic life.

The future abbot of the Sretensky Monastery in Moscow, Bishop Tikhon, who was then Gosha Shevkunov, was also in their number. Everyone wanted to hear Augustine's stories of asceticism, draw near to his holy life, and partake in his grace.

The humble monk talked to them and told them everything, lifting his pure dovelike eyes to the pious and grateful listeners.

However, it was time to do something for him in return. The simplest way would be to go straight to the police and explain everything: here was so-and-so, who lived as a monk in the mountainous desert, where no passports are issued, which is why he never got one, so let's fix the situation. If we have to pay a fee, we'll pay a fee.

But this plan was soon nixed. It was still Soviet times, and the authorities hunted for monks who lived without passports in the impassable and inaccessible Caucasus Mountains. You had to know the paths in order to find your way there, and no one had the desire to enlighten the police in this matter. So even if Augustine had gone and surrendered himself, they would have forced him to reveal these secret pathways and show them where all the elders lived.

Moreover, he was already twenty years old and as such was in danger of criminal charges for breaking passport laws and evading military service, and could even possibly be drafted into the army, but as a monk he could not fulfill his military duty by bearing arms. So that meant going to the police was no longer an option, at least by simply walking in. But perhaps we could try to approach it from another angle, i.e., through a connection.

The only person in our acquaintance who had a connection with the Ministry of Internal Affairs was the famous mystery novelist Arkadii Vainer—he had worked for Moscow Criminal Intelligence before becoming a writer. He was my neighbor, one entrance over, was friends with my parents, and liked my poetry. I went to see him. He listened to me with obvious interest: he had apparently never dealt with such subjects before—ascetics, hermits, hunters, Islamized Greeks. It was all so exotic! But in the end he firmly said:

"No, he mustn't turn himself in under any circumstances. He will be of interest to not only the police but the committee members also. They're going to reopen all the cold cases from the Caucasus—you know how many unsolved cases they have in connection with that area—and they'll definitely find something to pin on him. You can try to go the psychiatric route—he lost his memory, his mother died, now he can't remember who, what, where, or how. They'll hold on to him for a while, then they'll release him after fixing his passport. Of course, it would be good to find a psychiatrist among your acquaintances, so that he could oversee the entire matter, otherwise they'll shoot him up and inject him with all sorts of drugs, and he will lose his memory for sure, along with any reasoning."

I did have one such psychiatrist in mind—a beacon of psychiatry who had written his dissertation on the psychological rehabilitation of astronauts. He conducted himself, even looked like, a character from a popular joke—he was constantly scratching himself, spitting, snorting, whistling, grunting, stammering, and even occasionally crossing his eyes. When he heard the story of Augustine and the idea of the famous mystery novelist to claim memory loss, he immediately rejected the plan.

"They administer such tests there now that he'll give up all the information whether he wants to or not. Then what? They'll sink their claws into him like a tasty treat and start tearing him to shreds. Look at it like this: he is a person who grew up in naturally antisocial circumstances, without a whiff of the Soviet regime or school of thought. Like Mowgli,[1] let's say. My colleagues will start examining him, writing dissertations on him, victimizing him to death, and then diagnose him with religious delusion. No, you can't send him to the psychiatrists under any circumstance."

All right. Then, perhaps, some person of high rank and importance could help us out, someone with access to the top. He could write some sort of request. I am asking for an exception to be made, in view of my service to the Fatherland . . . To whom could I personally appeal with such a request? Alla Pugacheva? Bulat Okudzhava? The astronaut Sevastyanov? The sports commentator Nikolai Ozerov, who lived a floor immediately below us? Hero of the Soviet Union Heinrich Hoffmann? Muslim Magomaev? Or better—Yevtushenko. He had been a patron in the past, always signing any petitions that I brought to him. Let him defend a poor monk this time.

So I called Yevgeny Aleksandrovich, by some miracle reaching him in Moscow—he had just returned from somewhere and was supposed to leave somewhere else at any moment, and this evening—his only evening here—he had a meeting planned with the renowned English writer, Graham Greene, in the banquet hall of the Central House of Writers. So that's where I went. I sat down right in between the two of them and began a spontaneous conversation with them. By the way, I had read Graham Greene back in school, and so I felt it in my right to just sit down like that without an invitation next to the renowned English author: I was a reader of his, after all!

Finally Yevtushenko asked:

"Well, what do you have that's so urgent?"

I told him everything.

"All right," he responded. I think he even liked that I had appealed to him on such a daring subject. "But officially, nothing will come out of it: you exaggerate my abilities."

"Then let's try the option with the false passport," I offered. "It can't be that you, a National Poet, don't know the right people."

Flattered, he even blushed a little.

"Fine," he said, glancing to the side almost conspiratorially. He covered his mouth with his fingers and mumbled through the cracks: "I'll put you in touch with my chauffeur—perhaps he'll come up with something."

"Bring me a passport under any man's name, it doesn't matter whose, and a photograph of your guy," nodded the chauffeur. "I'll give it to the proper parties, they'll take off the existing photograph and attach the new one, then forge the seal."

"And that's all?

"That's all."

"And where am I supposed to get this passport under any man's name?" He shrugged.

"That's your business—I don't know. Steal it from somebody."

I began to rack my brains to think whose passport I could steal, and do so with the least possible consequences for the owner, when the plan for Augustine's salvation changed.

The future abbot of Sretensky Monastery, Bishop Tikhon—then simply Gosha—was friends with Zurab Chavchavadze, a relative of the Catholicos-Patriarch of All Georgia Ilia. He offered to take Augustine to the Patriarch personally: after all, the Caucasus Mountains were under his canonical jurisdiction, and he could help with issuing a passport for the humble monk without any further questions.

This plan was unanimously accepted by all persons involved in Augustine's fate, and Augustine himself was supposed to depart in the near future together with Zurab and Gosha to Tbilisi. Only days remained until the salvation of Augustine would be secured.

His departure, however, was put off for a while for technical reasons: Gosha, who worked at the time for the Publications Department of the Moscow Patriarchate and stood at the fountainhead of Orthodox cinema, was appropriately shooting a film about Russia and Georgia—Orthodox sister-countries, of which Russia represented bread, and Georgia represented wine—which came together in the mystery of the Eucharist and became the Body and Blood of Christ. He was planning to shoot the section about wine in Georgia, but it was too late to film the Russian bread, i.e., stalks of wheat: the harvest had already been gathered. The only place where the wheat had not yet been harvested was in the Omsk Diocese. It was imperative to go there right away or they would miss that opportunity as well: nothing but a snowy field would be left. So Gosha flew there.

In the meantime, the uncertainty and anticipation was eating away at Augustine, who became more and more distressed. It increasingly seemed to him that he was being driven into a corner from every side. I expressed my surprise at his uncertainty in reading the Psalter, for example, when his reading of the Six Psalms was as smooth as butter; or when my husband became perplexed that in spite of his spending the first seven years of his life in Moscow, he didn't remember either any street names or any metro stations. Moreover, we couldn't understand why he spoke with a Rostov accent. That upset Augustine. But my husband came to his rescue himself:

"Perhaps your elder spoke with that accent? Was he from the south of Russia originally?"

"Yes, yes," the other said happily. "That's exactly where he was from. And I simply mimicked him. He was from the Rostov area."

Then our friend—a hieromonk from the Lavra, a future archbishop, who visited us in order to hear the stories of asceticism—began to share his suspicions with us: what if this Augustine was actually an errand boy sent in an operation by the Secret Service to find out if the Church had any channels for preparing false passports?

All these vibes filled the air, and even Augustine fell into an agitated, depressed state and hung out on the balcony all day, which he was categorically forbidden to do—he could have been observed in his cassock, then someone could come by and ask: "Who was that? What kind of a priest is he? Your documents, please?" Our house was, after all, under special observation, because across from us lived the political refugee Luis Corvalan, and in our immediate proximity was located the window of a Greek billionaire's daughter, Christina Onassis, who had married a Soviet citizen.

Not only did Augustine hang out on the balcony, but he also loudly commented on the passersby. He saw a young woman in white trousers in the neighboring entryway and barked:

"What a cow!"

He looked into the unshuttered window of an American millionaire's daughter and yelled:

"How shameless! She's walking around naked!"

He also noticed a certain love triangle unfolding right underneath our balcony: a bald man would roll up to the entry doors in his car and let a young girl out. They would kiss and he would drive off. As soon as he was out of sight, a young guy would appear on his motorcycle. The same girl would give him a kiss on the cheek, jump onto the motorcycle, and they would disappear in a trail of dust until the middle of the night. Then, the next day, the bald man would again drive up in his car, and the girl, as if nothing was going on, as if there was no such man on the motorcycle, would hop into his car!

These womanly wiles tormented Augustine! He would wear himself out standing guard on the balcony. He even began to throw clumps of soil from the flowerpots onto the girl so that she would come to her senses. And who knows what our monk, outraged to the core, would have decided to do next had not my husband distracted him from the matter.

For he decided, while there was still time, to drive Augustine to a pious elder. This would allow him to be spiritually strengthened for the upcoming journey, to pray, confess to him, receive his blessing, and set off for his new life with renewed strength.

Elder Seraphim (Tiapochkin) had, alas, already passed away, but his spiritual father, also an elder, Schema-Archimandrite Grigorii, lived in that same Belgorod Diocese, in the village of Pokrovka.

At one time in the past, my husband, then just Volodia, had gone to Pokrovka: our father confessor had painted the frescoes in the church there. My husband had gone to visit him there. But there was nobody in the church, and he walked into the priest's house—it was empty. Then he went through to the innermost room, assuming that someone might be there. But he didn't see anyone there either. He was about to turn around to leave, when he heard:

"Fr Vladimir, what are you doing, walking in like that without saying a prayer?"

He looked around and suddenly saw a little dried-up old man sitting on the couch. It was Schema-Archimandrite Grigorii. My husband decided that he had called him "Father" in some sort of spiritual delusion, but he was astounded and baffled by the fact that he had called him by his name upon seeing him for the first time . . .

So he and Augustine went to this wonderful Elder Grigorii. They arrived, and my husband said:

"Here, Fr Grigorii, I've brought you a monk. He came down from the Caucasus Mountains, where it's not the custom for them to have Soviet documents. But here a passport is needed everywhere, they won't even take him into a monastery without it."

The elder looked at Augustine and simply waved his hand:

"He's no monk!"

Augustine smiled uneasily and became nervous, but my husband simply assumed that the elder had spoken in that way out of monastic etiquette. Well, in the lives of the saints, for example, this happened to the desert dwellers. Let's say that a Father of great spiritual stature was dying, and he would say to himself: "I'm no monk! I haven't even gotten started!"

So the elder was humbling Augustine in the same manner. He knew better than anyone how best to discipline a young monk.

Then Fr Grigorii added:

"He doesn't observe the monastic oath, he doesn't keep the monastic rule. He's an impostor—that's what! He threw someone else's cassock onto himself, pulled on someone else's *ryassa*—there you have it!"

My husband nodded knowingly, but Augustine squirmed where he stood.

"Well, we're thinking of sending him to the Georgian Patriarch. Give us your blessing to do this!" my husband entreated him.

"To the Georgian Patriarch?" the elder was amazed. "Why on earth would he give himself up to the Patriarch? It's useless!"

"It won't work?" asked my husband in fear.

"Useless!" the elder waved his hand again.

"What are we to do?"

"Why waste your time, hand him over to the police and have done with it. When you leave Pokrovka for Belgorod, the first policeman you see, go ahead and hand over your monk to him."

"Well," thought my husband, "the elder's gone mad!"

"But they'll throw him in prison!"

"All the better," Fr Grigorii nodded his head in approval. "Good riddance!"

Shocked, my husband did not, of course, hand Augustine over to any policeman, but brought him back safe and sound to our home in Moscow. But he remained deeply concerned.

In the meantime, the future abbot of Sretensky Monastery, still Gosha at the time, had successfully, if belatedly, filmed the fields of wheat and was now on his way to the airport to fly to Moscow, accompanied by the subdeacon of the Bishop of Omsk. The flight was delayed, and the young subdeacon was noticeably unsure of whether or not to leave the Moscow guest, to whom his bishop had assigned him, on his own. So, walking around the departures area, they came up to a fateful desk on which was written the word "Wanted." It was accompanied by photographs of criminals.

"By the way," the subdeacon suddenly livened up, seizing the opportunity to start a conversation, "there was a con artist here. He set himself up to work as a reader in our church, and then robbed both the church and the priest who had taken him in. He took the Gospel in its cover with precious stones, the censer, money from the church collection box, and the priest's cassock and documents: his passport, birth certificate, seminary diploma. Recently one of our people saw him in the Lavra itself! He was apparently walking around there in a cassock and passing himself off as Monk Augustine. What wonders!"

That day, we had gathered together to see Augustine off—Zurab Chavchavadze came, and we were waiting for Gosha, who had just arrived from Omsk. He came, looking very mysterious, and right away took off with my husband to the store:

"Let's go buy something, there's nothing to eat here!"

"We have everything we need. Why?"

He led him away. It turned out to be a maneuver: he just wanted to tell him everything that he had discovered without raising Augustine's suspicions.

"We need to take him away from the house under some plausible pretext and search his things: what if he has a gun, you never know!"

My husband called our friend, a hieromonk from the Lavra, a future archbishop, and asked his help. He had the monastery car and was able to come fairly quickly. He immediately understood his task.

"I've been asked to examine some icons—to check if they're genuinely old or a forgery. Do you want to come with me?" he asked Augustine, and they left together.

In the meantime, we dug through the belongings of our monk and, sure enough, found the stolen passport of the Omsk priest, his birth certificate, diploma, cross, Gospel in its valuable cover—in short, the thief had been discovered and caught red-handed.

When the future archbishop returned, the future abbot of Sretensky Monastery called everyone together in the room, locked the door, and began his speech so intriguingly, with such dramatic flair and masterful presentation of the storyline, that he created a perfect atmosphere for the moment of truth and the promise of exposure and catharsis.

Augustine sat, tense and red in the face.

"Well, now it's your turn to tell us everything, Serezha," the future bishop turned to him.

It turned out that he was not a monk and not named Augustine, but was simply called Serezha. He had served in the army and worked in the storage depot, and the military instructor who was his supervisor was a thief. Suddenly an inspection was announced, so Serezha got scared and ran away. He was serving somewhere in the south of Russia. Where could he go? It was clear that he had to go as far away as possible, into the mountains. There he met a pilgrim, and together they reached the elders in the Caucasus, where a young novice was also laboring with them; so he took the latter's story for himself. The only difference was that the novice was called Daniil, not Augustine.

I have already mentioned that the book *In the Caucasus Mountains* had recently come out, in which you could read about both Daniil and his mother, set on fire by the criminals. So the story itself was, I repeat, true. Only Augustine, who had adopted the story for himself, was a fake.

Serezha lived there with the monks, and grew to love them very much after living with them, but nevertheless they asked him to leave them: he didn't like to work, talked too much, ate with a healthy appetite, and was, in general, "of another spirit." In short, he was a burden to them. They gave him a letter to the nuns of the Sukhumi church: they bought him a ticket, and he reached Omsk and immediately went to the church.

The priest there took him in as his acolyte and gave him a place to live, while the local bishop promised to help him obtain a passport—Serezha had told him that his passport had been stolen. Then he tonsured him a reader.

But a singer in that church, who developed a passionate attraction to the young acolyte, ruined everything. She would attach herself to him, grab him by the hand, give him presents. Serezha would simply give away her presents—either to the priest or to the other singers. This was discovered and she was terribly offended. She backed him up against a wall—against the church enclosure—when he was shaking out the dust from the carpets there:

"Are you going to marry me or not?"

He said:

"I don't want to marry—I'm going to be a monk!"

And she began to wail her heart out.

At that, the prosphora baker, the gardener, the warden, the priest himself all jumped out.

And she kept tearing her hair and crying out:

"He's ruined and defiled me, he promised to fix everything with an honorable marriage, I'm going to have a child from him now, and he's hiding in the bushes: I don't know you, he says, or your child. He's used me and refused me!"

The priest was a pure, chaste man, and when he heard these words, his expression darkened; he took Serezha firmly by the elbow and said to him:

"Marry her! If you don't, I'll lay such a heavy penance on you, then chase you out of the church as the shameless person that you are. I'll tell the bishop not to give you a passport, too!"

Everyone stood around him and scolded him for all he was worth. The girl kept on screaming like mad.

Serezha took serious offense. He returned to the cell where he lived in the priest's house, and decided to punish them. He took his new cassock and *ryassa*, took the Gospel in its precious cover, took the church censer. Then he realized suddenly—he didn't have a cent to his name. He worked in the church for free, lived with the priest with all his expenses paid, and ate in the church refectory. How was he supposed to get anywhere? So he came up with an idea: he wouldn't steal the money, but simply take what he had earned, his hard-earned wages. He entered the church, robbed the collection boxes, left, and that was the last they saw of him.

Thereby he continued on his way to the Lavra, but he thought better of bringing the priest's passport into the matter. From the Lavra, as we remember, he was sent to Pechory, and from there to us in Moscow.

The future abbot of Sretensky Monastery drove the stolen goods to Omsk and returned them to the priest, convincing him to withdraw his report to the police. Before leaving, he came to our house and handed the false Augustine a book:

"Here, read!"

The book was *Crime and Punishment*.

Then the future archbishop came to our house and confessed the thief and liar. Afterwards, the latter went to surrender himself to the police.

The only condition that we gave him was the following: he should under no circumstances tell them about his time in the Caucasus Mountains. If they ask him where he had been, he should say—in Omsk, in the Lavra, in Pechory, but that most of his time was spent in Moscow, and we would confirm this.

Later, we were visited by investigators from the Military Prosecutor's offices in order to compare findings, but everything matched up: we confirmed that when he had really been hiding in the Caucasus Mountains, he actually spent that time at our house in Moscow. We spoke in his favor. The investigators admitted that during the course of the investigation, he behaved in an exemplary manner and repeated the entire time that he wanted to become a monk. Even his military command wasn't interested in charging him with desertion; they weren't after his blood. So he was given a short sentence in a penal colony, from which he was then released early on probation for exemplary conduct.

He returned to the free world and soon became a monk.

"When I was serving my sentence, I suffered most from the fact that my cassock had been taken off me," he admitted. "I felt like Adam and Eve after the fall—naked."

In the meantime, Schema-Archimandrite Gavriil, who had unmasked him at first glance, departed for his heavenly dwelling place. A recently released book—an enormous volume—called *The Last Russian Elders* finished with a chapter dedicated to him.

❧ *The Lord Gave and the Lord Took Away*[1] ❧

Monk Vlasii labored at Holy Trinity Monastery. No longer young, he was overweight and simultaneously grey and balding: he had long and sparse strands of grey hair around a circular bald spot on the back of his head. In appearance and by expression, he resembled some sort of forest creature or, God forgive me, water troll. He had a potato nose and small, shrewd eyes peering out from under shaggy eyebrows; he was sharp-tongued and sarcastic, and had a fighting spirit. He would give his abbot ten responses to one comment.

He was actually physically similar to the abbot; like brothers, they resembled each other so much that they were often mistaken for each other. For this reason, the abbot grew to dislike Vlasii very much: he kept constant watch for a chance to be rid of him. And as we know, where the human will is inclined to do evil, all the evil one has to do is give the person an opportunity.

Soon that opportunity presented itself. There was a murder in the vicinity of the monastery. Witnesses recreated a sketch and came to the monastery with this image for identification. The abbot looked and looked at the blurry image and said:

"Oh, that's our monk, Vlasii."

"Where can we find him?"

"At the *banya*. It's bathing day today."

And so the policemen rushed into the *banya* and took the poor, naked, and steaming Vlasii right off the heated bench where he was luxuriously lashing himself with twigs.[2] He barely had a chance to cover his nakedness before they clapped the handcuffs on him and dragged him off to prison like a seasoned criminal in front of the whole monastery.

Well, of course, soon everything came to light—it was obviously not him in the sketch, the witnesses didn't recognize him, he had an alibi, and he had never seen the murder victim in his entire life. He was released. He returned to the monastery, but the abbot refused to receive him. He gave the excuse that Vlasii had started a rumor that the abbot gave him up to go to jail because he had recognized his own self in the sketch.

What could he do? Dejected, Monk Vlasii set off for Moscow, where he had some friends who had taken pilgrimages to Holy Trinity Monastery. He came to us and moved in with us for good—all bent out of shape, tattered, homeless, toothless. He sat with his feathers ruffled for days on end, depressed, reliving his injury.

I decided to distract him and took him to see my friend, the writer and traveler Gennadii Snegirev. We went over and saw another somber-looking person sitting in his kitchen, also in deep depression, almost in tears. One thing led to another, and soon we got to the bottom of the gloomy man's deep sadness.

This happened in the early nineties, when private business was just being developed, and there was much uncertainty in it, many dark and even criminal moments. But so far the business of our gloomy person, named Riurik, had been going well. Then, he took all his money—whatever he had, whatever he had borrowed with high interest from the bank, and whatever he had borrowed from very serious people—and dumped it into an enormous batch of computers. They arrived by train from abroad. In theory, everything was secured and paid for in advance—the railroad workers, the border patrol, and the customs officers. But suddenly, it all fell through: there was an inspection and all the goods were seized. Riurik was ruined.

"I'm a dead man!" he stated again and again. "They're going to kill me!"

"They won't kill you!" Vlasii waved his hand. "I'll pray for you, and everything will be restored to you and multiplied."

What happened next? They parted ways that evening, and in several days some official personages called our businessman and presented their apologies to him: this and that, there had been a misunderstanding, please accept your goods whole and undamaged. And sure enough, Riurik got his computers, earned enormous sums of money from them, settled his debts with the bank and creditors, and made enormous and rapid progress in his material well-being.

Since that time, he considered the simple monk Vlasii to be a holy elder who, no matter what he asked of the Lord, the Lord fulfilled it for him. He took Vlasii into his home in Rublevka, gave him food and drink, new clothing, new teeth, all but calling him "Your Reverence." He felt just like a second Motovilov (a disciple of a saint) in the company of Seraphim of Sarov.

So Vlasii lived with him in luxury and comfort, teeth white as snow and of the very best quality, porcelain, like a Hollywood star's. He wore a long, black raincoat made of the softest kidskin, a cashmere scarf, tinted glasses, a Swiss watch, a briefcase, and carried an English umbrella. All he needed was a cigar hanging from the corner of his mouth and a large ring on his finger . . .

Vlasii started to look like some Uncle Sam from abroad: the owner of factories, newspapers, ships, or a mafia boss, a "godfather." But Vlasii himself lost interest in it all. The more you amuse the body, the more you oppress the soul. He began to ask Riurik to let him go back to the monastery, to freedom, to liberty.

But Riurik just said:

"They'll only hurt you there again, and it would be difficult for me to reach you. I had better buy you an apartment in Emsk—it's not far from your dear Holy Trinity Monastery and just an hour's flight from Moscow."

He bought him a glamorous apartment in the center of Emsk, in an exclusive building over the river. He furnished it with expensive furniture, filled it with all sorts of curiosities from overseas—a computer, a dishwasher, a home cinema. He set a monthly allowance for Fr Vlasii. So Fr Vlasii moved to his new spot.

But it still seemed to Riurik that he hadn't given enough to his benefactor—and yet are there any earthly treasures that could fully repay spiritual gifts? He discovered that Fr Vlasii's fiftieth birthday was approaching. He decided to organize a lavish celebration for him.

First, Riurik invited all Fr Vlasii's fellow monks from Holy Trinity Monastery, but the abbot didn't let them go. Second, he invited Vlasii's acquaintances from Moscow. Third, he invited all the "newbies" with whom Vlasii had struck up an acquaintance and friendship after moving to Emsk. These were, first of all, his neighbors from the exclusive building, who, having heard that a "miracle-worker" had moved to their neighborhood, began to turn to him "for prophecies and healings." In addition, he invited the acquaintances of the neighbors, since Monk Vlasii's fame had already spread, and he had become like a candle placed to shine in a high place.

The festivities were set to last three days. Luxury rooms in the best hotel in Emsk were booked for visitors from other cities, sleeping car train tickets were ordered, and souvenirs with icons, spiritual brochures, and postcards of Emsk churches were purchased.

A get-together of all the guests was planned for the first day, then a tour of the Emsk holy sites with entry into the churches and the singing of troparia, then a celebratory dinner at the Pena restaurant, with congratulations for the birthday boy by costumed actors. And sure enough, Peter the Great himself came out, a big, strapping fellow in a wig and tricorne, appropriately dressed in a light blue waistcoat and white tights, which he had rented at a local theater. In his wake, a strange-looking figure in curious old-fashioned clothing rolled out toward the guests already fairly tipsy. The guests tried to guess, who could this be? Was it Columbus, the discoverer of America, or Byron, because he staggered a little and even seemed to be limping, or Pushkin, because what kind of a gathering would it be without him? As it turned out, this was a certain Prince Daumantas, founder of many great cities of Russia, including Emsk.

The next day the guests were driven seventy kilometers away on a tour of the famous Holy Trinity Monastery; there, Vlasii made an appearance like royalty, offering his friends, the monks, "great consolation," which in the monastic tongue meant that he gave them several bottles of fine French cognac.

Afterwards, the guests went to a military airport attached to the local military sector, from which they were supposed to fly in a jet-propelled airplane over all of the Emsk Diocese and admire its beauty from a bird's-eye view.

The third day was left for "dessert," let's say. Everyone went to the dock "with joyful steps" and boarded a specially rented motorboat which took them to an island to see an elder. However, the elder was very old and infirm, and saw almost no one these days: this was ensured by his two female cell attendants, sharp-tongued and imposing in appearance. So the guests, having reached the elder's little house, remained standing there behind the picket fence, behind the padlocked gate.

Meanwhile, the air darkened to grey, the cold wind started to blow, a fine rain began to sprinkle down. Everyone huddled together underneath a large tree, whose crown served as a canopy at first. So they stood, hushed, pressing together, shivering with cold. And on top of it all, a fine stallion galloped over from some distant pasture. Happily clopping along, he trotted on the stones with abandon until he reached the pilgrims. Here, he stopped in amazement. He observed them with an enormous, and as everyone noticed, mischievous eye, and suddenly grabbed the purse of a lady from the city administration of Emsk with his teeth; she was participating in the birthday festivities since she was a neighbor of Vlasii in the exclusive house. He seized it and took off with it into the distance.

"My purse, my purse!" she whimpered. "It's all lost!"

In the meantime, the stallion trotted around the house of the elder, tossed the precious purse along the way, and headed back in our direction once again.

"What is this?" wailed a lady from the Emsk mayor's office, who had also managed to enter into Fr Vlasii's circle of friends. She turned her back to the stallion flying in her direction and guarded her purse with her own body.

But he nonchalantly seized the edge of a shawl dangling from her shoulder with his teeth, yanked at it, pulled it from her shoulder, and galloped away again.

"Horses are a bad omen!" Riurik anxiously commented.

"That's if you see them in your dreams," the others corrected him. "This one's not a dream."

So they continued to stand under the tree. They sensed that the celebrations were coming to an end.

Monk Vlasii's beneficence was also coming to an end.

After the celebration, when all the guests separated and parted ways, he mechanically continued his banquet—with starving artists from the theater playing the part of Peter the Great and Prince Daumantas in his victory parades, with his house neighbors, or simply with people he met at the shop. Perhaps this was why his potato nose became reddish-grey, his little eyes even smaller, and his acerbic tongue sharper. People said that his bygone glory had gone to his head and pushed him over the edge. Rumors reached Moscow that he had publicly thrashed the lady from the city administration with his belt as a disciplinary measure, and that he had threatened a representative of the local duma with the psalm of damnation: "Let the usurer consume all that he hath, and let the stranger plunder his labor" (Ps 108.11).

Alarmed by these rumors, Riurik came to check up on his beloved "little elder" and found him in the company of crazed and rowdy drunks surrounded by mayhem: scraps, leftovers, and empty bottles lay everywhere. In response to the cries of the shocked Riurik, Monk Vlasii said reasonably that even Christ ate and drank with the publicans and sinners. Everything might have been smoothed over for Vlasii this time if he hadn't decided that very moment to "take the edge off." And since Riurik was keeping close watch over him, he was forced to do this in the bathroom, and then toss the empty bottle—the incriminating evidence—out the window. But it so happened—what a temptation!—that this bottle fell directly onto Riurik's parked Mercedes, smashing his windshield and damaging the hood. And since Riurik had recently begun to drive around with bodyguards, they immediately determined the who, what, and how, and instantly reacted, breaking into the apartment and smoking Vlasii out.

Naturally, Vlasii fell from grace for good—so much so that Riurik took everything away from him at once. Worst of all, he shouted in his face so rudely, so defiantly:

"I don't need your prayers anymore! I'll take care of myself somehow! Look at how far I've gone! It's possible!"

So Vlasii departed in sackcloth and ashes—poor as a church mouse, naked he came into this world and naked he went out of it—back to where he belonged, back to the monastery.

The most surprising part was that a year or two later, Vlasii suddenly received the news that Riurik had been ruined in the end. What's more, he was under investigation, under orders not to leave town, and facing criminal prosecution.

"He's taken care of himself!" Vlasii noted. "He's gone far! What an idiot: 'The Lord gave and the Lord has taken away!' (Job 1:21)."

He sighed meaningfully, and what's more, completely good-naturedly.

❧ Halvah ❧

One day I was driving to Pskov Caves Monastery with an acquaintance—a very secular and nonchurchly lady, but one who was drawn more and more toward the spiritual life. This was during Great Lent, in the beginning of *perestroika*, when it was very difficult to fast because there were hardly any Lenten products in the stores except potatoes, cabbages, and onions. And if there were any, it was by special order and given out in exchange for tokens, and only in specific stores assigned to those particular lucky tokens.

Incidentally, in this time of half-hunger, Orthodox Dutchmen would come here to Russia to either study or train at the Academy attached to the Holy Trinity Lavra of St Sergius. Accustomed to Dutch Lenten delicacies—nuts, sugared fruits, enormous shrimp, oysters, snails, crawfish, shellfish, crab, and calamari—they became horrified when they toured our stores at the beginning of Lent, and cried out in a loud voice:

"How do you keep the fasts here? As it is, you live in hell!"

Moving on, my travel companion and I would get supplies in exchange for our writing commissions. So I always had reserves of buckwheat groats, flour, millet, and rice. Some of these I took with me to Pechory, since we were planning on stopping at the home of a wonderful, but very poor, nun, and I wanted to not only load her up with our goods, but also throw in a few fruits and vegetables.

As soon as we settled into our sleeping car, my companion woefully cried out:

"Oh no! I forgot it! I forgot it!"

"What? Your ticket, your passport?" I asked, frightened.

"No, the halvah, I left the halvah that I got from the writers' supply! I had especially prepared it to take it with me. How nice it would have been to open it up and have some right now with our tea!"

Well, it was too bad, but what could be done? I didn't have any halvah with me, either. We drank our watery tea on its own and went to bed. But she continued to complain from time to time:

"How could I forget it? It was such good, fresh halvah! I could feel how soft it was through the packaging!"

The sting of that forgotten halvah was still fresh.

Finally, we arrived in Pechory, went to church, prayed at the Liturgy, stood through the moleben, stopped by to see my father confessor, and finally went to see the nun in her cell.

I dropped the bag of produce right on her table with a thud:

"Here you go, dear *Matushka!* Please accept our gifts!"

She unhurriedly arranged the bags and bundles on her shelves, fed us some Lenten cabbage soup, and then poured us tea.

"I have something to treat you with too. One minute, one minute."

She dug through a chest, lifted something out, and placed in front of us . . . some halvah—exactly the kind that they had in the writers' supply.

"Halvah!" my companion cried out in wonder.

"*Matushka,* where did you get it?"

"Last night a pilgrim came by and asked to be put up for the night. He gave me this halvah and then rushed off to the service, as it had already started. After he left, he never came back. He apparently found a better place in the monastery to spend the night. Why are you so surprised?"

"Only because the Lord granted me such a small but persistent wish," said my travel companion. "It seemed that He wanted me to wait until I got back to Moscow. But I kept at Him—halvah, halvah! And so He finally gave in: take the halvah, you stupid woman! For everyone who asks receives, and he who seeks finds, and to him who knocks it will be opened" (Mt 7:8).

"Well, you know what you must do?" *Matushka* softly said to her. "Eat it to the glory of God, and just like that, you'll turn your halvah into a hallelujah."[1]

❧ *The Deceitful Onion Bulb* ❧

I noticed that sometimes we try to soften the truth at confession: we downplay the sins of which we are the most ashamed and grossly over-exaggerate the more insignificant ones, trying to direct the priest's attention specifically to those. As a result, all sorts of misunderstandings can arise between the priest and the person confessing, because of which the priest can misconstrue the situation and even give an incorrect blessing. Of course, the specific secrets of other people's confessions are unknown to me for obvious reasons. I can only speak with complete certainty about myself, but I have some circumstantial evidence that suggests that this happens constantly. In addition, I asked some priests of my acquaintance about this and they confirmed it.

For example, one of my good friends, who had carried on an affair with a married man for several years, went to confession to an old priest, who was, by the way, very strict, and still she received a blessing to go to communion and she went. The fact of the matter was that she, among the rest of her sins, added subordinately that she had a "boyfriend." The priest apparently understood this as something innocent, like a bull terrier, and sympathetically nodded his head.

The same thing sometimes happens with priest's blessings. Here much depends on how adequately, in what form, and with what words one describes the situation for which one wants to receive a priest's blessing and subsequently often receives it.

Here is an example. I was sitting by myself at my *dacha* one autumn—my husband was on a business trip, the children were in Moscow, the neighbors were all gone. It was quiet and still. I fired up my computer and spread out my work—I could work with no one bothering me, dusk was falling, nature was all around, and it was beautiful! Suddenly someone's heavy steps rustled at my window—were some homeless dogs running around? Then I saw a man's head passing by my window; he was heading straight toward my front door. Knowing that I sometimes forget to lock it, I went straight there. But it was too late: the strapping figure of a man with an enormous backpack stood on my front porch.

"Who are you looking for?" I said, not recognizing the sound of my own voice, and cowardly hoping that he had simply mistaken the address.

"Me? You, Olesia Aleksandrovna!"

"Oh? And who are you?"

"I attended your seminar at the Literature institute yesterday, and I showed you my poems afterwards."

I remembered. He really had approached me at the institute and had given me his poems. They were very bad. He had asked me if it was possible to rent a *dacha* where I lived. I answered that I didn't know. Nobody was renting anything out at the moment.

"And what do you want?"

"I just decided to stay with you until I find a place to rent here," he answered, already lowering his backpack onto the porch and getting ready to drag it inside.

"Wait a minute," I blocked his way to the house and showed him the chair on the porch. "I already told you that nobody is renting anything out right now. I also don't remember agreeing to you staying here."

"But the priest gave me his blessing!" he tried to put me in my place. "Oh, my phone is dead. Give me a charger to use, will you? And why are you keeping me out here on the porch?"

I thought a little. Maybe it was my husband who invited him to stay with us and just forgot to tell me, and he really couldn't call my husband to confirm because his phone was dead.

"Which priest?" I asked him, just in case.

"The one at the church."

"What church?"

"The one right here, close by. I passed by it and thought, let me just go inside. The priest was there. I asked him, could I crash with Olesia Aleksandrova and her husband, the priest, until things resolved themselves? I'm learning how to write poetry from her. So he gave me his blessing."

"And did you tell him that we don't know each other and that we never invited you? That my husband isn't home, and that it would look all wrong if you stayed here with me in his absence?"

"Well, he was in a hurry. The service was about to start. He didn't have the time for me to go into such detail. He gave me his blessing, so I have his blessing. So will you give me a charger or are you going to just make me sit here like this? Don't you plan to do what the priest blessed you to do?" His voice started to take on a commanding tone.

I was taken aback, but immediately collected myself.

Oh, if he hadn't been so rude, maybe I would have considered it. Maybe I would have arranged something with my neighbors, who were in Moscow that evening but kept the keys to their *dacha* with me, but my fear and amazement instantly turned into determination, and I asked:

"What is your name and where are you from?"

"My name is Grisha. I'm from Kaluga."

"Here's the deal, Grisha. You can take your backpack and go straight to the train station. There you can buy yourself a ticket to Kaluga and go with God! You'll be home in two hours or so."

"What about the blessing?" he frowned. "Where is your Christian obedience? Where is your humility? It could be that Christ Himself came to you in my image and that you are driving Him away (Heb 13:2)!"

Truth be told, something inside tugged at me. I almost gave in; but then, taking advantage of the pause, he made a fatal error. He dug into a pocket and took out a pile of papers:

"Here, you haven't even read all of my poems yet!"

And he thrust his talentless compositions into my hands.

Then I realized who was standing before me. I understood everything. It was, of course, the devil himself. A dark angel. A tempter. A total lack of talent. The seducer had tried to take on the image of an angel of light: "I was a stranger and you took me in" (Mt 25:35)! The Lord simply cannot appear in the image of an impertinent graphomaniac!

I thrust his papers back into the backpack and said:

"I only read other people's poems during my office hours at the Literature Institute. It's time for you to go."

"Should I really go? Shall I leave my backpack with you?"

"Why would I need your backpack?"

"So that I don't have to drag it around right now! I'll come by sometime later to pick it up."

"No," I cut him off. "You don't need to come by later. You don't need to throw your blessings at me. You don't need to come here without an invitation."

And I locked the gate after him with relief.

But there were times when I myself was guilty of cowardly deceit . . . I would rapidly mumble the shameful sin and stretch out and exaggerate the small sin. Of course, this happens almost without your knowledge, and the realization of this tendency comes only in hindsight.

And so, it was Great Lent. I had a blessing from my spiritual father to commune at every Liturgy, but I had to prepare. In other words, I had to attend the evening services on Tuesdays, Thursdays, Fridays, and Saturdays, read the communion rule each time, confess, and receive absolution from the priest. I was forbidden to partake of communion without having observed these rules.

My spiritual father decided that such an experience during one Great Lent would be extremely beneficial for me. And he took responsibility for this blessing—at that time it wasn't the custom to commune more than once every three weeks or every month.

That is why I had to confess to a different priest each time. But since I was confessing practically every day, and spending my time either in church or at prayer, the range of my repeated sins was relatively narrow. That's where I caught myself. Self-justification! The deceitful belittling of my heavy sins!

Here, for example: at home, I would take a few potatoes, a carrot, or an onion from my sister-in-law, my brother's wife—we lived together at the time—in secret. And not only would I not ask her permission, I wouldn't say anything to her about it later. It's a good thing that I admit this to the priest, repenting of taking something without permission. Why didn't I confess it by its proper name? "I stole!"

So with a heavy heart, I went to the church. I met a priest in the church courtyard, and told him:

"Dear Father, forgive me! I stole something!"

He staggered back.

"And what did you steal?" he asked me strictly.

"I stole an onion," I cowardly told him half the truth. Then, casting off any self-justification, half dead from shame, I sighed: "Produce!"

"Come to me after the service," was all he said.

I stood through the vigil and awaited the priest with a sinking heart—he's going to give me a penance, I thought, and rightly so! That's what you get for stealing, thief!

After a while, the priest came out of the altar and walked straight toward me. I shrank back instinctively . . .

In the meantime, his eyes had lost their former strictness and were now radiating only goodwill.

I stretched my hands forward for a blessing.

"You don't by any chance work at the produce market, do you?" he asked, compassionately looking me in the eyes.

"No," I answered.

Poor Father! These were such difficult times of half-starvation, when you couldn't buy anything in the stores—you could only be given it. So he thought: why couldn't this repentant sinner who stole produce now help a priest by getting from her retail network at least some rare buckwheat groats, some long-grain rice, maybe some Dutch cheese with which to break the fast. It wasn't Lent for the Orthodox year round!

Oh, if only I wept like that over my real sins! The deceit in my onion, the hypocrisy in my carrot, the self-righteousness in my potatoes, all beginning to sprout!

❦ *How I Lost My Voice* ❦

In general, my voice is rather mediocre and not very well suited to singing. But in kindergarten, I sang my heart out, danced, and performed at concerts, then studied piano during my school years and as a young adult. All this continued until our apartment, located on the upper floor, was inundated by a tropical-like torrent of rain from the burst attic pipes, which all but drowned us and ruined my favorite piano. It was restored several times afterwards by piano tuners: the felt on the hammers was replaced, new strings were attached, the pegs were fixed and retuned, but it would fall out of tune once again almost as soon as they left. All this interrupted my musical activities.

But I was still obligated to sing sometimes. Once in 1983, for example, my husband, our little children, and I spent the summer at a country parish in Vladimir Diocese, where a young hieromonk who was a former resident of the Lavra served. The church was a sad sight: services could only be held in one of its side altars, since the rest was in deplorable condition, and no one bothered to restore it—the Soviet authorities weren't interested, the countryside residents were too poor, and attendance in general wasn't very high: Saturday night vigil and Sunday Liturgy barely attracted twenty old ladies.

The priest served alone, and there was no one to sing and read on the kliros, so he assigned me there as reader and singer.

Then, after moving to Peredelkino, I started to attend the local Church of the Transfiguration. Since my husband and I were on good terms with the rector, I asked for his blessing to read and sing on weekdays with the old ladies. Soon, I became a full-fledged member of the discordant old women's choir. I even gained some recognition among the parishioners there. In any case, several pious old ladies would come up to me and say:

"You read so well! So clearly, so articulately, we can hear every word. May the Lord save you!"

At other times, my acquaintances at the church commented:

"It turns out you can sing so well! What a voice you have!"

I began to be entrusted with reading the commemorations, and someone even asked me to read the Psalter for his departed loved ones and slipped in a donation with his list of names.

In short, I was very happy in my newly discovered career. For it was very pleasant that "in the midway of this [my] mortal life, I found me in a gloomy wood,"[1] but still I was able to take on an entirely new activity. I had similarly attempted drawing, and even bought some paints, brushes, and a canvas stretcher when my husband was on a business trip. I devoted myself to drawing day and night without any boundaries, simply as God moved me, for I knew no rules and had not the least experience or even the slightest talent: nothing but pure inspiration.

But on his return, my husband didn't even want to look at my drawings.

"When a woman in her forties abandons all her work and begins to draw, not knowing how to even draw a rabbit or a house with a chimney, that is the first sign of schizophrenia."

Just like that.

For this reason, I was extremely happy with my success as a singer and reader, even if it was in such an intimate, modest, and limited circle.

Moreover, my voice seemed to grow stronger, louder, and more confident from the time that it began to resound within the church walls, and when I read my poetry aloud at that time, many told me that my voice sounded melodious and resonant.

Even Veronica Losskaia, expert on the work of Marina Tsvetaeva and the wife of Fr Nikolai Losskii, admitted to me:

"The way you read poetry is remarkable! It's like you're making music . . ."

But where is this all leading? In the early nineties, the monasteries began to be reopened in Moscow. My friend, an abbot from the Lavra whom I had known for a long time and whom I often visited there, was assigned to one of the reopened monasteries not far from my house. What's more, another old acquaintance of mine from the Literature Institute, a married priest, was also assigned there. Finally, the Father Superior of that monastery held such prayerful, poignant, and moving services there, with such angelic singing, thorough confessions, and deep sermons full of wisdom, that I began to attend services there exclusively.

In the meantime, Pascha approached, and my friend, the abbot, together with his friend, the married priest, meeting me after a Paschal service, suggested that we come together the following evening to celebrate this wonderful feast. Our house was being remodeled at the time, so my husband, the priest; my son, who had been just been ordained a deacon; and I came to the monastery and settled into a cell to partake of food and drink that "maketh a man's heart glad" (Ps 103:15).

Word after word, parable after parable, homily after homily, story after story, we sat together until late; finally my friend, the married priest, sat down at an old organ that stood in the abbot's cell. Then we came to the most important part of the evening.

We began to sing the song about the Samaritan woman:

"I am a Sa-ma-ri-tan!"

Then followed a Cossack song with many verses, with a florid embellishment, a repetition of "this is not for me, this is not for me."

"They offered hi-i-im, they offered hi-i-im, they offered hi-i-im
A sword so sha-a-a-arp!"

In short, our voices grew stronger, louder, richer, with wider vibrato; we sang joyfully and with abandon, splitting into thirds, holding a countermelody, and every fiber of our souls felt the words come to life: "What is so good, or what is so fine, but for brethren to dwell in unity" (Ps 132:1)!

Finally, our repertoire of spiritual and folk songs ran out—well, there are some Soviet songs that aren't so bad. My friend from the Literature Institute, now a priest, played his heart out without even looking down at the keys, his fingers flying with a life of their own. On he played, spirited and lively, tapping the beat with his left foot, while my friend the abbot soundly clapped in time.

Our souls burst open at that continued sung "a-a-a-a!" or better yet, the stressed vowels "eh-a! eh-a!"; out of our souls sprang the bird of joy, which began to flutter about the monastic cell:

"I came out into the garden
A gypsy maiden was there
Geh-athering grapes!"

Suddenly, the door of the cell quietly cracked open, and the head of the Father Superior appeared.

We didn't even notice him at first:

"I blush, I pale . . ."

And then everything grew still.

"Now, now," he said, "do you at least know what time it is? It's after one in the morning! The walls in our monastery are this thin—they are shaking from your singing. The brothers can't sleep. The folks from the neighboring houses are leaning out of their windows wondering what sort of a nightclub the monastery's turned into!"

In short, our celebration came to an end. Leaving in disgrace, we said to the abbot:

"Forgive us! Forgive us!"

And hanging our heads in shame, we went home.

A few days later, I stood before the cross and Gospel, confessing to the Father Superior, whom I loved and respected very much.

"You didn't forget anything?" he asked after I had listed all my sins.

"I don't think so."

He covered my head with the *epitrachelion*, read the prayer of absolution over me, and I reached both my hands to him for a blessing . . .

"You also love coming to a men's monastery at night, drinking wine, and belting out songs as loud as you can, isn't that right?" he couldn't resist adding.

"Forgive me," I stammered.

And that was it. Since then, I've lost my voice—it's gone. I can't sing a thing. At Liturgy, I can't even finish singing the Creed to the end . . . something inside me closes up and only a shaking, rasping sound comes out . . .

And rightly so! That's what I get for going to the men's monastery at night, for drinking wine with the monks, and for singing delightful and wonderful songs there!

❧ *Money for Sabaoth* ❧

When my husband became a priest in the mid-nineties, the people were still religiously unenlightened—in a way, many were simply savage. People began asking Fr Vladimir, and consequently me, as representatives of "the whole Orthodox Church" for the entire period of its existence: why did the Church persecute Protopope[1] Avvakum, why did it participate in Sergianism, why didn't it distribute one ruble per homeless person out of the Christ the Saviour Cathedral building fund, etc. As if that wasn't enough, our area of responsibility grew to include our brother Catholics: Why don't they have processions with the cross? Why did they burn down Galilee? What about Joan of Arc!?

The average awareness of the former Soviet person did not distinguish between Orthodox and Catholic, like two Chinese people who seem alike at first glance.

Once, my husband and I went to someone's house, where one very intelligent lady, an art historian, said, word for word:

"No, I won't set foot into an Orthodox church now! Once, my friend and I were walking by a church. We thought, let's go inside. As soon as we entered, a priest began to walk straight toward us, swinging a smoking censor right at us, as if to say, get out of here! Let me at you! What a racket! So we shrank back and ran out of there! Why did he kick us out like that?"

"He was simply censing at the image of God that is within you," my husband explained.

"Not quite at the image of God! He was swinging right at us! He wanted to hit us! He was kicking us out!"

My husband had many such trials, misunderstandings, and simply amusing cases, especially in the beginning.

Once, a young man with a ponytail came to talk to my husband—he was obviously a monk "mimic"—not a professional, but an amateur, one could say—a self-proclaimed novice.

"Father, how is it that the Masons no longer work in stealth but leave their marks everywhere now? Even the icon of the Transfiguration in the Cathedral of the Annunciation in the Moscow Kremlin has an inverted pentagram on it. And the cathedral in Suzdal has five-pointed stars on it

. . . and the Cathedral in Arkhangelsk has one on its central dome . . . they're everywhere, everywhere!"

"Oh," sighed my husband. "You shouldn't interpret things that way. Cut an apple open and you'll see the same kind of star . . ."

"There you go," the young man livened up, "that's what I'm trying to say—they're everywhere, they've even made their way into apples! Interesting, how did they manage that one?"

Another time, an interesting character came to him and announced:

"I don't have any sins."

"What do you mean?"

"Just that! No sins. I'm a teacher."

My husband was at a loss as to what to say. He had often been dismayed by the fact that certain women came to him for confession, already in the prime of life, having spent many years in Soviet atheist conditions of life, well acquainted with, let's say, the ups and downs of emotion, who only repented that they lacked "purity of prayer." Such admissions seemed to him to be the height of pride and vanity: in other words, the penitent considered herself perfect in every way and in no way lacking: she had meekness, humility, patience, love for others, self-sacrifice, charity, and everything else, except purity of prayer.

But this was the first time that he had seen anything like the case of the teacher.

"Even the saints had sins," he began. "Even they had things to repent of and lament over! The only sinless one is the Lord God!"

"Maybe the saints had sins, but I don't," announced the teacher.

"Really? Well, maybe you really are a saint." My husband hoped that such an absurd conclusion would bring the "penitent" to his senses.

But he simply nodded, unfazed:

"Maybe. I already thought of that myself."

My husband coughed and almost choked, then thought that this teacher must be joking, or must be in spiritual delusion—perhaps he was testing him; so he went farther down the same dangerous path, guided by the logic of the absurd:

"Well, if you are a saint, maybe we are going to pray to you someday? Bring me your photograph, we'll place it on the iconostasis. We'll serve a moleben to you! Light candles! Bow to you!"

The complete idiocy of such a statement, he thought, should put everything back in its place. The teacher must have guessed by this time that the priest was on to him, and that the priest had hoped to finally bring him to an adequately repentant state of mind for confession . . .

But he only stood in front of him and unflappably nodded his head, mumbling something under his breath.

"Since you have nothing to repent of, we have no need of confession or absolution," said the priest. "You must be some sort of unique model of a human being. No one like you has ever been born on this earth!"

But—oh the horror! Even this absurd statement the teacher took literally!

And so? My husband had managed to forget about this strange penitent, when after a while the latter unexpectedly appeared with a large folder in his hands.

"Here," he said, presenting the folder.

"What is this?" my husband said in surprise.

"My photographs, enlarged, just like you asked, for the iconostasis. To pray to . . ."

He was met with silence.

My husband spent some of his workdays at the Media Office of the Moscow Patriarchate on Chistii Pereulok. He was on his way there one day, when he saw that the entire area in front of the Patriarchate gates was filled with people: it looked like a protest or vigil.

They saw him, dressed in his cassock and cross, and began to beg him:

"Father, take us to the Patriarch, the police won't let us through."

"What's going on?"

"We have signed petitions and appeals."

"But what do you want? What are you appealing about?"

"We're fighting for the immediate canonization of Grigorii Grobovoi by the Patriarchate. He resurrected the dead, and now he's under criminal prosecution, but he's a saint! So we came to demand his immediate canonization."

My husband remembered that this Grobovoi was either a sort of cult leader or simply a con man, or both: he had promised the grief-stricken mothers that he would resurrect their children murdered by the Beslan terrorists[2] and had taken enormous sums of money from them ahead of time. But looking at these die-hard followers of Grobovoi, who were ready to raze the Patriarchate to the ground, my husband understood that any arguments against their guru would fall on deaf ears and only serve to inflame their passions the more. So he said:

"What, did Grobovoi die?"

"Of course not!" They answered, dismayed. "He's alive!"

"Then he can't be canonized!" My husband replied, happy that he so readily escaped any further conversations. "Canonizations only take place after death."

"They never take place during life?"

"It's impossible! It's not done that way," he said strictly. "Come back as soon as he dies."

"Well maybe he will never die! Maybe he's immortal!" one of the women proclaimed in awe-stricken reverence.

"We-e-ll! Then he can never be canonized," concluded my husband.

And strangely enough, as loud and up-in-arms as they had been a minute ago, so suddenly did they quiet down and scatter in confusion—they had to weigh the matter hurriedly and digest this information in order to come up with the most proper conclusion for their guru, in order to answer the question: what would be better for him—canonization or immortality?

Soon afterwards, a bald old man came to see my husband in that same place on Chistii Pereulok and placed his business card on his desk. On it was written: "The Lord Sabaoth."

"Well, hello," said my husband. "How can I help you?"

"We need to save the world," the visitor sighed heavily. "The world is perishing!"

"Then you must take the proper measures," advised my husband. "Who better than you?"

"Well, that's what we have to figure out," the newcomer confided. "I'm planning to go to Jerusalem, otherwise the world will perish!"

My husband shook his head sympathetically.

"But there are issues!" his guest threw up his hands.

"What issues? Your issues?"

"Well, yes. I need to get to Jerusalem somehow!"

"I don't think this poses a problem for you . . ."

"If there is enough money for the ticket," his guest said confidingly. "But what if there isn't? And the world is perishing! So what—just let it perish?"

My husband stayed silent.

"I feel sorry for the world! I created it with such love! I just want to say to them: what have you done, oh, you scoundrels, you scoundrels!" And he even held up his dried-up little fist in the air and shook it at the scoundrels.

My husband felt a little sick to his stomach.

"So I've come to the Patriarchate," the guest got down to business. "Surely you don't want the world to perish, do you?"

"Well, no," agreed my husband.

"So stop beating around the bush, give me money for my ticket to Jerusalem! Where is your accounting office?"

My husband showed him the way with relief.

A little while ago, when I was cleaning up his office and putting business cards away into a box, I read the words "The Lord Sabaoth" on one of them. "Creator" was written in cursive underneath. The address was written in the lower left corner, briefly and to the point: "Jerusalem, Mt Zion."

❧ *Kalliping* ❧

All these stories would seem improbable to me, had I not heard them from the horse's mouth. But if you look around and observe, even the grotesque has become accepted and claims to be the norm.

Take, for example, the driver who, seeking revenge on a highway patrolman for giving him a ticket, bit off his thumb—bit it off and spat it out. Or the cannibal who posted online an invitation to anyone who would like to be eaten by him. A man who responded to the invitation and visited the cannibal was really eaten—fried, cooked, and made into a meat jelly.

"One cannibal invites another cannibal to lunch."[1] Or the young girl who gave birth to two children from her own grandfather ... These truly hellish pictures have become part of everyday life. You know, a touch of the exotic.

My spiritual father, who studied the problem of evil, explained to me why the evil one needs man, so much so that he never—until the very day he dies—leaves him alone.

"Man," he said, "originally had something that the father of lies does not—an essence and the ability to create. Therefore, the adversary needs man to feed on his essence parasitically and to use his creative gift to invent ever new kinds of evils."

When he was telling me this, I remembered a friend from my youth, Lenia, who came up with a new genre of painting and even took it to the Paris galleries. He called it "Kalliping" (a play on the words "calligraphy" and "painting")—a kind of counterpart to painting. In other words, this new form of art was intended to sound like "beautiful writing in painting." So there! After all, "kallos" in Greek means everything beautiful, wonderful, elaborate, honorable, noble, glorious, brave, attempted with honor, successful, joyful, fair, complete, good, excellent, superlative! But that's in the Greek.

With Lenia, it was in Russian, from the word "kal" (that is, fecal matter).

He painted on toilet paper with brown paint of different hues, then crumpled up the paper and either pasted it onto a panel or made special exhibits where he would just toss it into wastebaskets. This was then displayed in rooms with dark lighting, where even the walls were covered in handprints of reddish-brown sludge ...

They say that the exhibit was well received and had good press, gathering him some admirers and even followers and students. And if not for a convoluted family situation that uprooted Lenia and sent him spinning like a top—who knows?—maybe he would be famous now the world over. But at least a certain writer appeared in his stead who gleefully advertised fecal matter on television as healthy foodstuff ...

Is it really possible that the evil one couldn't even come up with this on his own, without the help of man?

❧ *Good Material for a Television Series* ❧

A parishioner of my husband's church once overhead the following conversation. Some women who had come to the church to pray said amongst each other:

"Fr Vladimir—which one is he?"

"He's the really tall monk whose wife is a poet."

"What, she writes poetry?"

"Yes, she does."

So this same parishioner recently and most logically noted to me:

"When you write about Fr Vladimir, do you always call him "my husband" in the text? That seems a little disconcerting and . . . indelicate."

I agreed with her. So from now on, I will call him "Fr Vladimir," as is proper.

When he began to serve in church in the mid-nineties, there was an enormous number of con men who played the role of Orthodox people who were in some sort of trouble and needed the priest's help. Others imitated monks and walked the streets with church mugs, claiming to collect money for the church building fund, but they were soon found out. Before putting in their contribution, people would ask them to recite, at the very least, "Our Father."

So I was approached by one such man, disheveled, red-faced, reeking of alcohol, but dressed in a cassock. I was stuck in traffic on Tsvetnoi Boulevard, and he was walking among the cars.

Seeing my prayer rope hanging from my rearview mirror and my icon of St Nicholas the Wonderworker on my dashboard, he rolled back his eyes:

"Money to restore a church!"

"Do you know 'Our Father?' Go on, recite it!"

He straightened up like a student who had been called up to his desk by his teacher, looked up with effort, and pronounced:

"Our Father, who art in heaven, hell oh be . . ."

He faltered.

"Don't worry," I encouraged him, "that's OK, try again."

"Our Father," he announced fairly clearly.

I nodded.

"Hell oh be . . . thy . . ." he mumbled, and quickly ran off.

These swindlers constantly crossed paths with Fr Vladimir. They would come during his assigned time in the church and tell him such stories that it was simply impossible not to give them money. I think he was even sorry that he gave them so little and not everything that he had: he did have to leave something for his family. What else could he have done? They would come to him pathetic, frozen to the bone: "Je ne mange pas six jours."[1]

One unfortunate foreigner, who claimed to be a piano tuner, said: "Do you need your piano tuned? I haven't eaten in three days. I have no money to go back to my hometown."

As it happened, our piano was in terrible need of a tuning after a flood.

Fr Vladimir brought him home:

"There you go, get to work."

As it turned out, he was not alone but had with him a six-year-old son. They were both hungry. They spent the entire day at our house, had some food, but had nowhere to spend the night, so they spent it with us.

Then it turned out that this was not his only son. There was another one, a younger one. Their papa worked and the boys hung around nearby, playing. I asked, did they need to eat something? The little one could spend the night together with the six-year-old.

Then it came to light that his wife, the mother of the children, was also nearby—in the room for mothers and children at the train station. She was there with her nursing babe. We threw them in for good measure. So while the dad worked, pulling the felt lining onto the little piano hammers, the mother cooed over the baby and the sons played war. Starving as they were, there were used to eating like all normal people—three times a day, at breakfast, lunch, and dinner. But we had a different rule at home. We had coffee for breakfast, a sandwich for lunch, and a real meal only for dinner.

So the nursing mother made a comment:

"You don't seem to eat so well . . . no calorie intake. We eat your food and then just get hungry again."

Fine. They lived with us like this for several days. The hammers lay all over the house, and the look of the dissected piano gave rise to a suspicion in our hearts: what if this talented master had decided to create a surprise and turn the piano into a harp? So I said to him:

"Will you finish soon?"

He said to me:

"If I were to do it the real way, it would take me half a year, but I'll manage in a few months."

Meanwhile, the baby was screaming, the boys were playing tag, the young mother decided to have a laundry day, and all of us with our own children and other members of the household felt completely out of place, like we were in their way.

So I told the piano tuner:

"Thank you very much. Let me pay you for all the work you've done, and we can part ways. Whatever you have left, just leave it. We didn't have any plans to play the piano right now anyway."

And he answered:

"Oh no. I'm not going to leave until I finish the job! The conscience of a master doesn't allow such a thing."

The whole affair ended dramatically. We paid the money, moved the family to the church, where they were allowed to spend the night in the church house. The next morning nothing prevented them from buying tickets to their hometown and going home. But I still ended up the guilty party who had done them wrong: I had kicked out parents with children! There was a baby who was still nursing! I hadn't fed them well enough! Oh and by the way, their sleeping quarters had been too cramped for their taste. So in the end, they didn't get anything good out of their time with us.

And even then they didn't leave. They invaded another family in the same manner, took apart the piano, broke the lid . . . then vanished without a trace.

In general, though, the stories told by those who came to the church for help were all typical stories, and it was impossible to distinguish truth from pure falsehood. Everyone was poor, wandering, hungry, unable to buy medicine, and without a place to lay their head.

One day a woman came to see Fr Vladimir—completely miserable, overweight to the point of obesity. She sat down and broke into tears. She just sat there and the tears poured down her face. Finally, she managed to quell her sobs enough to say:

"I came to Moscow with my little boy. We were robbed on the road, and my son got sick—fever, chills—and I have no money to buy his medicine. And our relatives whom we came to see say that maybe he's contagious, and they won't take us in. I've already sold the clothes off my back to buy him medicine and go home, and in the meantime, we're living at the station. We haven't eaten in three days."

All my husband had was a 500-ruble bill, which he gave to her and requested:

"Please, take this and break it in our bookstore, take half for yourself and give me back the other half."

She took it, left his cell, and was out the door and on the street in a flash. They barely saw her leave. Even her weight, it turned out, was not a hindrance. And so what—was she lying or did she really run off to treat her ill child?

But there were other stories that were more elaborate, custom-made for the situation. A man came to Fr Vladimir with the face of a criminal. He said:

"Father, I'm a mafia boss called Viper. I served time in a concentration camp and was recently released. There, in the camp, we were visited by a priest. He directed me toward Christ. But the other convicts—the really bad ones—didn't take to him. They said that 'pop' is just going to hear our confessions then give us up to the cops. So they condemned him to be stabbed to death. I found out about this and spoke out against it, but I could see that they would still do him in. So I warned him to get away and not come back. He never showed his face again.

"In the meantime, I was set free. The first thing I did was go to Fr John Krestiankin in Pechory, and told him everything. 'I believe and I confess.' I've been monk material from my mother's womb, as I am physically incapacitated. Bless me to go to the monastery, if only because my former partners from the penal colony have already sent out a letter saying that Viper's not longer a mafia boss but has turned into a stool pigeon. Now they're summoning me to a meeting of mafia bosses. What do I do?

"So, Fr John Krestiankin says to me—I don't bless you to go to the meeting. Go to the convent in Ussuriisk Region. You're not a threat to the nuns since you're a eunuch, and you definitely won't be found there. He gave me some money, but only enough to get as far as Moscow. Also, Fr John told me go to the Church of the Holy Martyr Tatiana in Moscow and that the priest there would give me the rest of the money to reach Ussuriisk Region."

What was to be done? My husband, of course, didn't have enough money to take him all the way to Ussuriisk, but what he had, he gave to Viper. Then he sent him to Fr Tikhon Shevkunov, the abbot of Sretensky Monastery, because Fr Tikhon really respected Elder John Krestiankin, and his monastery was not poor—in any case, not in comparison to our family.

But Fr Tikhon, as an experienced spiritual father, immediately saw through this Viper. In the end, it all came down to the fact that my husband had simply paid him for good material for my book, which he immediately delivered to me.

Here is another one, also with a certain creative flair and imagination.

One time, in the evening, when Fr Vladimir's hours at the church were coming to an end, a middle-aged man flew into his cell, all out of breath, by all appearances someone respectable who had recently let himself go a little. In other words, he was dressed in a good suit, but it was wrinkled and dirty; a good shirt, but the cuffs and collar were soiled; and finally, he reeked of alcohol and urine.

"Father, here on this check is my bank account number—it's made out to the bearer, and the bank is right here on Romanov Pereulok. All the money in the account I give to your church, the Church of the Holy Martyr Tatiana. My white Volvo is parked in the courtyard of the Central Telegraph Office—all my documents are inside and the key is under the carpet. Take it and use it for the church. I don't want it to go to waste! All I ask of you is your prayers! . . . I am going to a meeting right now that might not end well for me. But I place my hope in your holy prayers."

"But what has happened?" asked Fr Vladimir.

"I have a wife, Tatiana. I funded the construction of a church in Iceland for her and sent her there because my former partners are after me here. They claim that I owe them money, they want to take my business and have already set the clock ticking on my head. I wanted to come to an agreement with them, but they kidnapped me and tortured me for a whole week in a cellar in the forest, chaining me to the radiator. In the end I agreed to get them everything they asked. But I said that giving away a business is a complicated matter: I needed to draw up the paperwork, and this would take several days.

"They let me go, but I have to meet them at an appointed place this evening, otherwise they would kill my family. But I don't want to give them everything, so you take the money from the account for yourself. And the car. Just pray! They have inside contacts in the police, so . . ."

My husband looked at him in amazement, at a complete loss for what to do. Should he allow this man to go to the dangerous meeting? Should he confess him?

But the latter looked at his watch and jumped up—"Oh, I'm late already, well, give me your blessing!"

He was about to run out of the cell and into the hallway. But, taking several steps, he came to a sudden halt, slapped himself on the forehead, and spun round:

"Father! I'm running late, but I have no money—not a cent. And my meeting is in Butovo! Give me some money for the taxi, please, or I might not make it!"

Fr Vladimir said naively:

"But it's rush hour, the traffic is so bad right now! You'll make it so much faster on the metro!"

The man looked and looked at him, and pierced him right through to the bones with his gaze, as if to say, hey you, I gave you my entire bank account, my white Volvo, and you're too greedy to give me enough money for a taxi! So my husband gave him the money.

The paper with the bank information he tossed in the trash. One of our financially aware friends saw it and broke into laughter, it was such nonsense.

Nevertheless, these con men with their stories had to work hard for their money! Oh yes! They sold their material. For cheap. I recently saw an announcement in the newspaper: "I will sell you the story of my life as subject matter for a novel or material for a television show. For cheap. Only a thousand dollars."

We got away with much smaller losses.

❦ *A Blessing to Smuggle* ❧

A priest's blessing carries enormous power. I had many opportunities to be convinced of this. And even in those cases where I may have retained a trace of doubt—through human weakness but with good reason—any lack of faith was eliminated.

In the eighties, the rector of the Church of the Mother of God of the Sign on Ryzhskaia Street was Fr Vladimir Rozhkov. Then he was transferred to the Church of St Nicholas in Kuznetsy, but I often went to visit him there as well, first and foremost in order to pray during his reading of the Canon of St Andrew of Crete. I believed that no one possessed such piercingly repentant intonation, no one could so prayerfully and artistically recite and understand that divinely inspired spiritual work. Having once heard it, it was impossible to forget either the magnificent baritone of Fr Vladimir or his naturally clear diction, or his carefully placed accents, or the musical ending of every prayerful phrase.

But I went to Fr Vladimir in Kuznetsy much less frequently than when he was the rector on Ryzhskaia Street. Back then, I listened to his sermons with a rapidly beating heart, and especially loved when he served the Liturgy: speaking in laymen's terms, it left a very deep impression on me, moved me to tears, and grabbed hold of my heart. One of his altar servers, who subsequently became a priest himself, confessed that he felt the same way and added that Fr Vladimir himself always prayed with tears of repentance.

In short, I loved him very much. And he must have sensed the heartfelt attachment of this sheep in his flock, because he also began to treat me with trust and sincerity. Honestly, if there had not been such a gap between us in status and age, I would have considered us friends! In any case, I would sometimes drive him home in my car, visit him at his *dacha*, or come to his house with my husband. He would call me at times, and we would talk on the phone for a long time; he would give me books to read, tell me about his research and writing plans, and even tried to convince me to be his assistant.

I continued to attend his church for the Great Canon every Great Lent; then, in the year 1990, he called me up to him after the service:

"Will you drive me home?"

"Of course, Father! And you, will you give me your blessing? I'm going to France tomorrow with my children."

"To France? Listen, I have an enormous request for you. My favorite old noblewoman lives in Paris. She is the cofounder and patron of the Russian House at Sainte-Geneviève-des-Bois.[1] I'll just give you a few things to give to her, OK?"

We went to his house, and he handed me over an enormous icon and a platter wrapped in a soft rag.

"This is all part of the historical legacy of the Meschersky family. I looked for these items in antique shops; she will be so happy. The platter even has the Meschersky family coat of arms on it! Give this to her and tell her that I love her very, very much!"

Fine. He wrote down the telephone number, I took the parcel with the gifts, and came home. I packed it away properly, when my husband, seeing that I was planning to transport all that over the border, cried out in a great voice: what are you, an antiques dealer? They're going to confiscate it at the border for good, and detain you too!"

He had a good point! I hadn't thought about that—I'd never taken anything like this before over the border! I called Fr Vladimir in the middle of the night, woke him up, and shared my misgivings with him.

"I'll just pray about it," he replied in a sleepy voice. "Nobody will check through any of your things!"

He simply said this and hung up the phone. But I, to be honest, didn't fall asleep until the very early morning. Since my baptism, I had become painstakingly law-abiding. Before, I had considered it beneath my dignity to: arrive somewhere on time (I was always late), cross the street where I was supposed to, or buy a ticket for public transportation. I had often ridden the train in St Petersburg illegally without a ticket. I had even been kicked off one time in disgrace in Bologoe, but I just waited for the next train and made it to my destination without a ticket anyway.

But then—I quit cold turkey. I can't cross the street on a yellow light. I began to show up at events early—at first ten minutes early, then twenty, then, I'm ashamed to say, forty minutes! An hour!

Basically, I called him early in the morning:

"Fr Vladimir! They'll take everything away! What a pity it would be! And they'll arrest me!"

"Everything will be fine, don't think twice about it! I told you, I'll pray. No one will even take a second look at you. Well, go with God! May the Lord bless you. You're doing all this out of love! Love conquers all."

So I set off with the children to Sheremetevo[2] with a heavy heart and our precious cargo. I filled out the customs declaration. Looking around me and wiping the cold sweat from my brow, I wrote a dash through the space for "antiquities" with a trembling hand. The children and I walked toward the first checkpoint, the conveyor belt. I saw customs officers checking people in front of me, opening suitcases, feeling their way through belongings, digging through everything thoroughly, taking things out, while the people stood looking on in tears. How terrible!

Then it was our turn. They checked my tickets and passport, where my children were written in, they glanced over my customs declaration . . .

And at that moment someone called them over to registration.

They thrust the passport, tickets, and declaration into my hands, closed the gate behind us, and the two or three of them rushed off to where they had been called. So we just took our things and went to check in our suitcases. In order words, just as Fr Vladimir had promised, no one searched any of our things or even paid any attention to us.

In Paris, I called Princess Antonina Lvovna and told her that I had brought her some gifts from Fr Vladimir Rozhkov. She reacted very strongly:

"Oh, dear Fr Vladimir! What a dear he is! He is such a dear, such a dear! I love him so much! And you—do you love Fr Vladimir too? Do you understand what an incredible person he is?"

I answered her sincerely—yes!

We agreed that we would meet at Alésia Church, next to the church itself. She drove up in a Mercedes and gestured to me to get in quickly.

"I'm not supposed to pull over there," said the princess when I had sat down next to her, holding the precious package on my lap. "Let's go out somewhere—to a restaurant! Do you like restaurants, my dear?" she asked, pressing on the gas pedal.

I examined her out of the corner of my eye with interest. She was an elegant, elderly lady, thin, with her hair done, and wearing a rather short black velvet pencil skirt and a matching jacket. I later discovered with surprise that she was just under eighty years old then, which meant that back home she would be considered ancient. In the meantime, she deftly turned into a narrow street and came to a sudden stop in front of a fabulous restaurant with a carpet strewn out the front door and a freshly shaven, liveried doorman standing at the entrance.

Since we would have many such get-togethers with the princess and since they would all begin under the same circumstances, i.e., the meeting time at Alésia Church at eleven o'clock, the Mercedes, the restaurant, etc., and then later, closer to evening, some adventure would arise, I won't describe these first restaurant outings, but the subsequent ones, when I came with my husband.

The only important thing that I would like to stress is that we brought and handed over her family heirlooms—the icon and platter with the coat-of-arms—unimpeded, safe and sound.

"You see, and you were afraid, O you weak of faith," happily exclaimed Fr Vladimir Rozhkov. As they say: "Do not be unbelieving, but believing" (Jn 20:27).

Approximately half a year after that, my husband (who, by the way, was not yet a priest) and I were getting ready to travel. At first, we would go to Geneva, where I had been invited to give a lecture at a university and to conduct a literary evening at the Russian Club. Then we would go to France, all the way to Paris, where the publishing house Éditions Gallimard had released a book of my prose.

Then we received a call from Fr Vladimir—how are you, what are you doing?

"Are you planning to go to Paris?"

"Yes, but not right away, not directly—through Switzerland."

"Switzerland is a beautiful country, but Paris is better—and you'll see the princess there!"

I stayed silent, sensing a trap.

"I'll give you some gifts for her," he continued. "No, this is not like last time. It's just some silly little things. Will you give them to her?"

"Well, only if it's not like last time . . . of course I will!"

"Wonderful! My daughter will come by and give it all to you."

To be honest, I had already agreed to take some things into Switzerland—an acquaintance of my Swiss friend from the Russian Club had begged me to give her some souvenirs, and I was expecting her at any moment.

She rang the doorbell and right then and there, in the half-darkness of the entryway, thrust some sort of package into my hands, hurriedly thanked me, bowed, and vanished.

A little while later, Fr Vladimir's daughter also arrived, bringing a one-liter bottle of vodka and a small, but considerably heavy, package.

My husband and I began to pack for the road. We looked inside the package for the princess and saw ten 200-gram tins of black caviar: that was what Fr Vladimir had humbly called "some gifts."

I don't know how it is now, but back then the law allowed for no more than one or two hundred grams. And we had two kilos!

Despite the lateness of the hour, I started calling Fr Vladimir:

"Fr Vladimir! It's in metal tins! They clink! The other time at least nothing clinked so loudly. This time they'll discover everything and take it all away. It would be such a pity!"

"So I'll pray about it!" Fr Vladimir answered, unfazed. "They won't take anything away! May the Lord bless you! And the princess will be so happy! She loves caviar very much. How else could I make her so happy? I love her so much!"

"By the way, we're going to pass through more than one border patrol. There's Switzerland and then the entry into France!"

"Nonsense!" Fr Vladimir noted. "I'll pray about Switzerland, too, and France! No one will so much as glance in your direction. They don't need anything from you! Oh, what a beauty the princess was in her youth, and so intelligent! She will be so happy."

My husband was quite skeptical about the whole thing—some princess, some old noblewoman dressed to the nines, caviar in metal tins, which would, of course, make a loud clinking noise. Then we had to take out the "souvenirs" for our Swiss friend in order to distribute the contents throughout the suitcase. These turned out to be little bits and pieces of semiprecious stones. Commercial quantities of them! If I hadn't known that Swiss lady well, I would have suspected that she was planning to put them on the market . . . well, this was the end! The tins would clink. The customs agents would force us to open our suitcases and find inside—all that garnet-agate-carnelian-amber sparkle! Smugglers!

Approaching Sheremetevo, we felt ill. They were going to gut our suitcase at any moment, and I, blushing, would feign cluelessness—oh, really? Caviar is not allowed? What semiprecious stones? That's costume jewelry . . . Oh ho, they would really believe me then . . .

We submitted our passports and declaration forms:

"Why are we traveling without money? Or did you just not declare it?"

"Because we're poor," I said.

"Yes, we know that type. They're the ones that will bring back ten tape recorders and fur coats!"

He waved his hand at us.

"You're free to go!"

He didn't even notice that we hadn't yet placed our suitcase on the conveyor belt!

We arrived in Geneva, delivered the jewelry to my friend, and happily discovered that the vodka hadn't exploded and the caviar tins hadn't opened, I gave my lectures, conducted my literary evening, and received payment for both lecture and travel expenses. We were already planning to buy our train tickets to Paris when we discovered that a note had been placed in our passports: entry to France only allowed via Charles de Gaulle Airport. We were trapped—this time the tins would definitely clink! What if Fr Vladimir's prayers wouldn't work on the Swiss Calvinists and agnostics? And last but not least—airplane tickets were very expensive here; all our money would go to cover them.

"Why fly?" said my Swiss friend, parading around in her amber. "We'll get in my car, cross the border, I'll drive you until Bellegarde, which has the nearest train station from Geneva on the way to Paris. You'll buy your tickets there and calmly proceed from there."

"What about the border? We told you—we only have permission to enter France by air."

"Nonsense," she waved her hand. "We'll risk it!"

We took our vodka and our caviar and went to storm the border. I, of course, appealed to the Lord in my thoughts to save us "by the prayers of Archpriest Vladimir Rozhkov," and everything went off without a hitch. At that early hour, the Swiss customs agents and border guards were apparently drinking their morning coffee and eating their petit déjeuner, and the French, by all appearances, were recovering from their soirées of the night before, since we didn't meet a single person on the entire trip to Bellegarde. And there, as we had intended, we bought our tickets for the high-speed train and reached Paris a few hours later.

There I called the princess and told her that I had come with my husband and that we had brought some gifts from Fr Vladimir. She was ecstatic and exclaimed: "My dear, how I long to see you!" She set our meeting time at eleven o'clock at the Alésia Church and drove up in her Mercedes. My husband and I climbed in, and she drove us to the glamorous By the Angels restaurant, which was still empty at that early hour. We were immediately surrounded by all the waiters with the chef d'hôtel at their head:

"Princess, how happy we are to see you! You look fabulous!"

They obviously knew her well there, she was a regular patron . . .

"Princess, would you like your usual? The port?"

"We'll start with an aperitif," she suggested. "Yes, we'll start with the port. Well, here's to our meeting!"

I took a small sip, as, to be honest, I was not used to drinking port on an empty stomach at eleven o'clock in the morning.

"Olesia," the princess reacted strongly, "what are you, a nun?"

"N-no," I said slowly and uncertainly. "Why do you say that?"

"Well, you're not drinking anything!"

And the princess showed me her empty glass.

Then they brought out some sort of unusual food—many different dishes. We ate, drank wine, and engaged in lively conversation, joked, and laughed to no end . . .

We had Veuve Cliquot, an expensive champagne, for dessert.

So it was not surprising in the least that we left for the car "with joyful steps."[3]

We had not taken the vodka and caviar with us into the restaurant—the princess had ordered us to put it all in the trunk. So we still hadn't given her those things. So now I asked her to open the trunk; I took out the package with the vodka and caviar, opened it, and offered the princess to have a look inside.

"Fr Vladimir asked us to give you ten tins of caviar," I said, not without pride. "Here it is! And a bottle of vodka."

"What a dear he is! I don't think he's appreciated enough where he is. I love him so much," said the princess, taking out one of the tins and turning it around. "Well, all right, now you must come with me to the Russian House! I've taken a fancy to you."

She placed the tin back into the bag, put the bag onto the back seat, where she also threw her light coat; I also sat down, and my husband took a seat in the front, next to the princess.

We roared off. To be honest, I hadn't even thought about it: if we, in our thirties, had walked to the car considerably tipsy, then the eighty-year-old, albeit young-looking and charming, princess had exited the restaurant leaning, or rather hanging on to, the strong arm of the maître d'hôtel. So how could we even think about driving to Sainte-Geneviève-des-Bois with such a driver?

"My son always scolds me," said the princess, as if she was reading my thoughts, turning around and looking at me in the back seat. "I love to drink a little and have a good time, and then take a drive! But, as ill luck would have it, I once mixed up the roads and drove into a tunnel, and what a nuisance, drove right into the opposite lane! My son took away my car after that! He said: 'You're going to get into a car accident someday and be killed!' But I can't live as correctly as he does. I get depressed! So he finally gave me back my car."

We were flying down the highway, and from time to time she would glance at my husband, then at me. The other cars swerved away from us and were instantly left far behind. At that moment, I understood her son very well and sympathized with him.

"I would like to meet Lidia Aleksandrovna Uspenskaia very much," said my husband. "Doesn't she live in the Russian House?"

"Oh," the princess rolled her eyes and stepped on the gas. "She is so proper, so strict! She is virtue itself. I'm afraid of her. I think she must judge me for my frivolity. So you can go see her if you want while I rest a little in my room."

We were already approaching the Russian House.

The princess left the things in the car, escorted us to Lidia Aleksandrovna's door, and then disappeared. We knocked.

Lidia Aleksandrovna, the widow of Uspensky, the author of books about the theology of iconography, turned out to be a very miniature, thin, neat old lady. She was like a little bird, but a strict bird, exact in its bearing, and clean, because there are different kinds of birds. You have the predatory, omnivorous seagulls; the impudent, disheveled crows; the chatterbox magpies; and the wagtails. Then you have the miniature chickadees and the elegant swallows—messengers from another world—and Lidia Aleksandrovna was one of these. It felt as if our conversation was resumed rather than starting from nothing, like we had already had this discussion at some other time, and we had been interrupted at the most interesting part, and were now taking it up again from where we had left off. We spoke about Metropolitan Nikodim, for whom she had worked as a secretary in Paris, and his relationship with the Catholics. We didn't even notice that two hours had flown by . . .

Suddenly, the door opened with a bang and our princess appeared on the threshold: she had thrust the door open with her foot.

"How long can you hold these wonderful young people up," the princess exclaimed. "I miss them already! I want to take them to the Russian cemetery!"

Lidia Aleksandrovna took her in with a strict glance.

But the princess would not be subdued. "Aren't you bored? You're probably discussing something academic, covered over with the dust of time . . ."

"It's terribly interesting!"

"What is it—some sort of intellectual theology? Something acutely specific? Thrilling indeed! Will you come with us to the cemetery?" she asked Lidia Aleksandrovna.

"You go ahead. Go in peace. We'll finish our talk some other time," Lidia Aleksandrovna released us.

We got into the princess's car, though the cemetery was within walking distance.

Some North African kids were running around with a ball near the cemetery. The last remaining sunlight was warming them. We entered the church, put up some candles, prayed, then walked from one grave to another: from Bunin to Berdyaev, from Fr Sergii Bulgakov to Felix Yusupov.

"I don't like cemeteries," shivered the princess when we moved back toward the car. "I love life!"

She took out her key, it beeped . . . Alas! The car was unlocked.

"I didn't lock the car!" the princess exclaimed, rushing to the back seat where all our things had lain and from where she still hadn't taken the bag with the caviar and vodka.

"They stole it!" was all she said.

Sure enough, my husband's fine, orange buffalo leather suitcase that he had brought back from America was gone. It could be folded until it was the size of a man's purse. It could also be unfolded like a suitcase and fit everything. There had been an enormous amount of ten-frank coins in the side pocket—about forty, which I had placed there in order to buy gifts. But most importantly—the bag with the vodka and caviar was gone. That caviar, all ten 200-gram tins of it, for whose sake and by the prayers of the rector and archpriest Fr Vladimir Rozhkov the Lord had dimmed the eyes of the Moscow customs agents, so that they looked but did not see, and had also taken the Swiss and French border patrol out of the game. All that was left on the back seat was the mink coat of the princess!

What, the mink coat? You will probably ask. That should have been the first thing they took . . .

Oh, no! The thing is that the thin mink lining was unnoticeable from the outside. The exterior was a simple black raincoat, a trench. The integrity of aristocrats is such that they don't flaunt their wealth in order not to stink of money. They are modest glamour and veiled chic. The plebeians have it all backwards: a golden chain lies on that oak.[4]

We looked around. The North African youths were no longer playing ball. All was quiet and dark.

"Princess, are you very upset?"

"Yes," her face fell. "But I myself am to blame. What was I thinking, forgetting to lock the car? I'm so upset about Fr Vladimir's presents! Ten tins of caviar! My son is going to scold me so much, so much! Just don't you tell him. Well, what now—back to Paris?"

We sped back in silence.

"You really do value Fr Vladimir?" the princess asked once again. "You understand what a dear he is, what an incredible person?"

"Yes, we understand."

"Thank God that we had managed to give the princess that ill-fated caviar and vodka, had shown her all ten tins," I said after we parted ways with her. How would it have looked if all that had happened before she had seen it with her own eyes! How we would have defended ourselves! She would have been sorely tempted to think that we had eaten it all on our own! How terrible . . ."

Happily, the princess called Fr Vladimir and told him herself how she hadn't taken the precaution of taking his gifts out of the car, and how she had been robbed . . .

He was very upset. He couldn't let it go for a while. He even tried getting upset with me, but as soon as I noticed that, I said to him rather curtly:

"Fr Vladimir, that's enough! Your prayers have a limited area of influence. You asked for us to be allowed over the border and they let us through. You asked for us not to even be noticed—we weren't noticed. You blessed us to hand over the gifts to the princess? We did that. But did you ask for us and the princess not to be robbed after that? No, you didn't. Did you bless her to lock her car? No, you didn't. What do you say to that?"

He had nothing to say.

❧ *Payback* ❧

Our conversation turned to the subject of payback. It all began when the priest Fr Valentin, who served just outside of Moscow, started talking about theft.

"Priests are the most professional experts on their communities. After hearing the confessions of commercial employees in our little town, I've come to understand that we have an epidemic of thievery."

"What, do they steal their own products?" said the surprised Irina Lvovna, my neighbor at the *dacha*, who had come over to "sit out the dark": in our neighborhood, the electricity was often turned off, but only individual power lines, not altogether. So this time it was the power line of Irina Lvovna's *dacha*. Now she sat with us in the light of a large lamp, drinking tea and listening to the priest with great interest.

"Well yes, they even steal their own products, sometimes, then they cheat by falsely weighing them and miscounting items. It's even considered the normal thing to do," sighed Fr Valentin.

"And what do you do? Do you chastise them for this?" Irina Lvovna asked with interest.

"It would be useless. They just answer me: how am I supposed to feed my children, or pay rent? So I just . . . scare them."

"What do you mean, scare them?"

"With the threat of payback. I tell them—you will pay for every stolen ruble tenfold. That scares them."

"How do you mean?" Irina Lvovna wouldn't let up. "Who will they answer tenfold to? The police?"

"He means that God will put them in such a position that they will be taken advantage of and will lose more than they stole themselves," I said. "Even my children can do that math almost from their very cradle."

"What, did they steal too?" said Irina Lvovna, horrified.

"No, they didn't steal, but sometimes the cashier at the metro or the store would miscalculate their change to their advantage, and they, noticing this, would take the extra money as if nothing was the matter, thinking that well, God sent it their way. Then, in literally two or three days, they would have to pay it back: they would be shortchanged somewhere else at the first opportunity, or they would lose their wallets completely. And this always happened when I gave them a lot of money—either to pay their school for their traveling expenses somewhere, or pay their share for a trip to another city. In short, since they experienced it themselves, they will never take anyone else's money."

"Whatever you want men to do to you, do also to them" (Mt 7:12), cited Fr Valentin.

"Well yes, in the area of discipline, this is good, of course. But in life it's not like that at all," Irina Lvovna waved her hand. "Some people steal and steal and it's nothing to them . . ."

"That means that things are very bad for them," sighed Fr Valentin. "The first sign that God cares for a person is when their hidden misdeeds overtake them from without. They become their own reality."

"How do you mean?" asked Irina Lvovna.

"You judged someone—and you immediately found yourself in the same position as that person. Or you lied and it became true."

"It's true," I recalled. "I have a friend who would evade military service by pretending that he had asthma. And as soon as he received the white ticket for exemption from service, he got sick—with asthma. Or sometimes I'll lie that I'm sick with a cold because I don't want to leave the house, even though I'm completely well, and I'll immediately get chills and a stuffy nose."

"Or if you laugh at someone, just wait, you'll find yourself in a similar unfortunate situation," concluded Fr Valentin. "As our parishioner, who's a bit of a holy fool, says, whatever you make fun of will become your own misfortune."

"No," Irina Lvovna firmly shook her head. "That never happens to me. You're all living in a fairy tale . . ."

And she went home, as the electricity should have been turned back on by now.

Now I must say a few words about Irina Lvovna. She was a fifty-year-old widow, but not an unhappy old widow, broken and aged by the loss of her husband. No, she didn't allow herself to be weakened by grief; on the contrary, she took herself in hand—even took courage from it—and began a new life. What's more, her words took on a certain finality and her gestures a certain authority. Her clothes fit her curvy figure quite neatly, she dyed her hair in the color "Golden Beach," and, I assume, wasn't against meeting a suitable man of her age in order to spend the rest of her life with him. Perhaps she would have done so already, because she did have certain admirers, but her overly inflated sense of self-worth (which she just considered to be a high standard) always got in her way.

We lived across the street from each other, and had grown closer over the last year or two. In any case, she had begun to drop by, but not without a certain formality: only after a phone call and my invitation, which was always given formally. She would come to consult with me, however guardedly, and sometimes even to speak candidly, but in subtle hints, dropped almost by chance. In short, I began to discern that a real candidate had appeared on the horizon, judging by her inspired manner in describing a certain Spanish translator who had already invited her to a presentation of his book of translations, and was now inviting her to a Christmas reception hosted right at the residency of an ambassador of some Latin American country.

It seemed to me that she found it pleasant just to say those words aloud—"reception," "ambassador," "residency"—but even without that, her ego soared to unprecedented heights.

Two or three days passed, and suddenly she uncharacteristically appeared on my threshold—without a preliminary call, in an agitated state, and even a little disheveled.

"Well, Irina Lvovna, did you go to the reception?"

"Oh, you can't imagine what it was like! I don't even know if I should laugh or cry . . ."

And she giggled, but a little nervously.

"At first that Spaniard of mine very subtly proposed to me."

"Please accept my congratulations!"

"Then my fiancé took me to the ambassador's, where we had a fabulous Christmas dinner. The Christmas tree was all lit up . . . candles . . . ladies in cleavage-baring dresses. Our Russian celebrities. Waiters in white tuxedo jackets walked around everywhere serving food and cocktails . . . the most interesting conversations. Then suddenly, in the very heat of the evening, my intended," here she again giggled nervously, unable to hold back, "vanished. He was gone for ten minutes, twenty minutes, half an hour, an hour! Suddenly someone from the ambassador's staff—I don't know if he was a porter or a footman—came up to me and said: 'Your friend is asking for you.' I said: 'What? How? Where is he?' And he told me: 'Come with me.'

"They led me out of the hall and took me along the corridor. From a distance I heard someone's shrieks, cries, pounding, a terrible commotion . . . They told me:

"'There. Your friend has been trying to get out for two hours already without success. Talk to him, calm him down while the reception is still going on.'

"I looked—sure enough, it was the door to the men's room, and my Spaniard was beating on the door from the inside and yelling:

"'Get me out of here!'

"I said to the footman accompanying me:

"'Yes, let him go at once! Why are you keeping him there?'

"But he only answered me in broken Russian:

"'We would love to, but he locked himself in, and now he can't open the door. We're not going to break the door down!'

"'Break it down!' I said. 'He can't sit there forever. At least break the lock.'

"'It's impossible from the outside,' he said. 'We already gave him screwdrivers and knives under the door so that he could try and break it from the inside.'

"My Spaniard heard me and started to howl:

"'Irina, I beg you, don't leave me! Tell them to let me out!'

"I said to the footman again:

"'Break the door down, what are you waiting for?'

"'We're afraid to, His Excellency the Ambassador would be very unhappy if we broke the door down in his residency. How would the Honorable Ambassador use the bathroom?'

"And he left.

"'Well, how are you doing in there?' I asked my fiancé.

"'Well, not bad, in theory,' he answered. 'It could be a lot worse. As it is—it's clean, there's somewhere to sit if you put down the lid on the toilet, and there's a nice soft rug on the floor. If worse comes to worst, I could spend the night on it.'

"'I like that! What are you thinking, spending the night on a carpet in the bathroom? How did you get into such a decadent mood? Take courage!' I tried to lift his spirits. 'I'll go and ask the Honorable Ambassador to take personal measures . . .'

"Suddenly the same footman reappeared:

"'No-no-no, I beg of you. His Excellency the Ambassador doesn't like to be disturbed during a reception.'

"So what could I do? I went back to the hall, and there they were already serving the main course—twirling some sort of bird on a spit over an open fire. Everyone was applauding, happy, drunk. Only my quote-unquote 'fiancé' sat locked up in the toilet, beating against the wall like a butterfly against glass.

"I came back to the door, and sure enough, there he was causing an uproar—loudly pounding against the door, trying to beat it down with some sort of battering ram.

"I asked him:

"'What are beating the door with?'

"'My shoulder, my own shoulder. These new locks with the flimsy hardware are no good, you know.'

"His voice, though it came through, sounded somehow distant. The door was evidently thick, and strong.

"'Why don't you at least take a bath while you're in there,' I told him. 'Why just sit there?'

"He answered:

"'I would gladly take a bath, but there's no tub. Just a shower.'

"Soon, the guests began to part ways—completely drunk, happy. The same footman appeared.

"'Come on, now, do something,' I said to him. 'Use a chisel or something, at least, or just break the door down.'

"But he only answered me again—the Honorable Ambassador, he won't be happy . . .

"But I was getting sick of it all—I started to threaten him:

"'Look, you be careful, or you'll have an international incident on your hands. Our citizen was held captive in your bathroom, how would that look? I could say it was an act of provocation!'

"He finally brought a tool, like a drill bit or a chisel, inserted it where the round handle was, and tried with all his might to unwedge the lock. But it was no use! It was a good, solid door, a strong lock.

"While we busied ourselves in this way, the ambassador had escorted his guests and headed for his bathroom, to which we were trying to gain entrance with that chisel. We had started to work on the hinges, but all in vain.

"'What's going on here?' the ambassador asked, frowning.

"The footman told him:

"'Here's what happened. The guest locked himself in, and the lock caught. We tried to saw out the lock—that didn't work; break the door down—it won't budge. And the guest has been in there for three hours already in the most terrible state.'

"The guest was already screaming at the top of his voice:

"'Call EMERCOM!'[1]

"They were already ready to call EMERCOM, those Latin Americans, and they did call them . . . but they were told that no, this was on the territory of a foreign sovereign country, and they couldn't just come to us like that on a whim, they had to meet and vote on it!

"The Honorable Ambassador, meanwhile, was barely still standing—truly, this was hardly the time for him, after a Christmas dinner, with a Christmas tree and a roaring fire, after the meat on the spit and hot drinks, to sort out international affairs! But what if they would really be stormed by all kinds of people right now, who knows, what if they would poke and prod their way through the entire residency with their microphones and cameras?

"'We are extraterritorial here,' he explained to me for some reason.

"In the end, I calmed our prisoner down by telling him that professionals were on their way to free him, so it would be better for him to rest before their arrival on that little rug, while I myself returned to the ravaged hall, settled into a large armchair, and dozed off.

"In the morning, our people from EMERCOM arrived. The Honorable Ambassador emerged right on cue—rubbing his bloodshot eyes, he came out to meet them.

"In one stroke, they sawed out a little window around the lock, released the captive to freedom, dug around in the lock, and said to the ambassador:

"'What kind of a bootleg lock is this? Where did you get it, on the black market?'

"'It's a good lock! A Spanish one!' He defended himself. Then he said. 'My colleague in the economic section probably bought it on Mozhaiskii Market! I've suspected him of fraud for a long time!'

"My fiancé was finally free. He embraced the ambassador:

"'Well, now you can pour me a glass of whisky, friend!'

"So off we went to some distant room, into which yesterday's guests hadn't been allowed; we sat down on the couches there, and he and the ambassador drank themselves silly, so silly that I had to call a taxi and almost carry my fiancé home myself. There."

"Great story," I said. "And I'm so happy that you have a fiancé, Irina Lvovna."

"What are you talking about!" she quickly jumped up. "Don't you get it? I was just calling him that out of a sense of irony! Do you think that I can marry a person who has disgraced me the way he did? He spent the entire night in someone else's bathroom! It's a joke! No, such things don't happen without a reason. These things only happen to a certain type of person."

"You exaggerate! I'm telling you—it could happen to anyone . . ."

"No, excuse me, not nearly anyone! This could only happen to a clown! Ha-ha-ha! It's just funny! He slept, you see, curled up on that toilet rug in the bathroom! He even yelled to the EMERCOM people that he was extra-territorial! Then he went and got drunk! What a sad, sad man! And how did he make me look in the ambassador's eyes? My late husband, by the way, was a Party member, a journalist! My new suitors have some competition. I have, after all, high standards, a high sense of self-worth!"

"But what difference does it make to you, Irina Lvovna, what that ambassador thinks of you?"

"What did I look like to him, I'd like to know? A fool! But I have a very high standard of living!" She couldn't seem to let it go. "If something like that happens to a person, it's a sign of their poor internal state of affairs. It's an alarm bell for me."

Apparently, that night at the ambassador's residency left quite a mark on her, because every time she and I met afterwards, she recalled it in one form or another. Most of all she blamed her at-the-time fiancé. She not only wished never to see "that Spaniard" again, but refused to speak to him on the phone altogether.

And so, one evening, having bathed and locked all the windows and doors to keep the cold January drafts out after her hot shower, she went to bed, read a little, and before turning off the light, decided to use the bathroom, and the door slammed shut behind her! How did that happen? She wasn't planning on locking it! But it happened—she tried to open it, but the door wouldn't budge. Something had jammed inside. She pushed against the door with her shoulder, her hip, but it hurt too much, and it wasn't budging! It was a strong door. So poor Irina Lvovna stood in just her nightgown in her tiny "facilities," with no one to help her.

I repeat, she lived in the house by herself after her husband died. Her upstairs neighbors were in Moscow, and the others were out of earshot. She was completely helpless. She didn't even have any tools on hand—they were all on the other side of the door. There wasn't even a soft little carpet on which to lie down . . . just cold tile underfoot. Scream or not scream, no one would come anyway, no one would set her free—not tomorrow, not the day after tomorrow, not in a week. Irina Lvovna became despondent. On the one hand, the situation was most comical and idiotic, but on the other hand, it was even tragic. No one would come there in one week, let alone two! A month! Though she blew the very Horn of Jericho![2] The upstairs neighbors would perhaps come in the spring, with the first greenery. The phone, of course, remained in the bedroom.

She began to think how she could get out. The problem was that she and her husband had at one time added on to the *dacha*: it was a small house, and they had widened it. That presented an absurd problem: there was a window in the bathroom, but it opened onto the boiler room. And it wasn't that simple to just crawl out into the boiler room, because there, under the very window, were the stairs leading to the cellar. A person jumping through the window, if anyone could even be found willing to do that, would risk falling three meters down, and not onto an even surface, but onto one of the steps. Some thrill-seeker could perhaps crawl out and try to creep along the narrow ledge lining the walls of the boiler room, but that's what would make him a thrill-seeker!

Irina Lvovna, on the other hand, was the esteemed widow of a Party member and a journalist, a lady, what's more, with a curvy figure. She sat and sat in her place of captivity, but there was nothing else to do—so she opened the window and crawled out. She flattened herself against the wall, and oh so carefully, step by step, with a prayer on her lips, began to inch along over the black abyss, until she reached the entrance to the boiler room, where there was an even surface and from where the descent of the stairs started.

All good. She made it that far. But the boiler room was locked from the outside! And the key was in its spot on the key holder next to the hanger, so this was also just the appearance of freedom, but actually a trap. On top of it all, it was January—bitter cold, the time of the famed Epiphany frost! The boiler was being heated under the house, but here, in the boiler room, it was freezing cold. What's more, Irina Lvovna was in her nightgown, and barefoot—she had tossed her slippers off when she was crawling along the ledge. Then she saw some sort of bundle in the corner and remembered: she had stashed some things of her late husband's away at one time, and kept some old things here—curtains, towels. She had always intended to give it away to the homeless, but had never gotten around to it. So she searched through all those things and found some clothes for herself: her husband's worn out, striped terry robe and slippers. She wrapped a towel around her head. She threw a curtain around her shoulders like a shawl for extra warmth. She tried to open the door to the boiler room, but immediately understood that it was useless. Next to the door was a thick, unshuttered window. She hit it with a brick and it shattered.

Irina Lvovna took out the glass, nearly cutting herself, crawled out into the snow, began to walk toward the door to the house, and realized that it was all locked. She had closed the security latch herself, had shut the windows with her own hands. Now what?

She wandered off wretchedly in her size forty slippers, in her robe and curtain, through the whole neighborhood, and came directly to me. She began to knock on the door, then saw a light in the window, and started to throw snowballs at it.

I was home alone. I couldn't see anything that was going on underneath my window from my lit room. Then I turned off the light and peered out. A strange human figure was standing on the snowbank, wrapped in rags. I got scared and started to look for the stun gun that someone had given me the year before and that lay somewhere, uncharged. But suddenly I heard a heart-wrenching shriek—the figure knew me by name, and the voice sounded familiar.

I carefully opened the door, and Irina Lvovna, bare legged, looking highly fantastical, even exotic, all covered in snow, tumbled inside.

"Irina Lvovna!" I burst out in surprise. "What a great disguise! What are you, celebrating Yuletide? I never expected it from you . . . you're all covered in filthy rags!"

And I broke out laughing.

"Don't you laugh at me!" she said curtly, before launching into the explanation for such a ridiculous appearance and her late visit. "I used to laugh at people, too, and look what came of it!"

She was all shivering, and now, in the warmth and in the light, she looked very pitiable—not a trace was left of her high sense of self-worth . . .

I seated her on the couch and listened to her incoherent rambling while she drank tea with raspberry jam. Finally, having warmed up a little, she announced:

"I didn't believe a word of what you were saying here, that what goes around comes around. But it's all true! God is looking out for me after all! He really taught me a lesson!"

"Of course," I replied diplomatically, "He cares about everyone!"

"Not everyone!" she quickly and peevishly retorted. "You simply don't know that! For many years I closed and even locked that door to the bathroom, and it always opened, without fail! And now—this was all done on purpose! Do you understand? Especially for me! Tit for tat! Payback! To teach me a lesson!"

And she lay down on a pillow, covered herself with a throw blanket, and fell asleep.

"And how is your Spaniard doing?" I asked her a few days later.

"He called me yesterday. He said: did you hear the news? I asked, what news? He answered: that Latin American ambassador was promptly reassigned. His replacement will be sent soon. So we're expecting a huge party in the residency in the near future—to welcome the 'new guy.'"

ᔇ The Delusional One ᔈ

There is a term in Orthodox asceticism—spiritual "delusion." This is when a person begins to have a high opinion of himself and imagines that he has followed God's bidding and has "overcome the order of nature."[1] In our time of ignorance, of abundance of spiritual paths to follow, excess, and self-importance, victims of such "delusion" have greatly multiplied. This is understandable, for after the fall, man became proud and ever searches for ways to satisfy his pride, but "if you gaze long into an abyss, the abyss will also gaze into you."[2]

For example, I had a friend who would "warm up her drinking water." She would sprinkle some powder from her hands into a glass of water and drink the water, which had indeed become warm, claiming that it was healing water. In the end, she was diagnosed with some sort of illness, from which she literally dried up and began to look like the iconic Baba Yaga.

Another acquaintance of mine dabbled in spiritualism and went in so deep that spirits began to appear to her in waking and talk to her without the use of a ouija board. They instilled in her the idea that she was the Earth Mother, and that she was able not only to prophesy, but to shoot flames from her eyes. I heard that she would walk around her *dacha* neighborhood and submerge it into total darkness, extinguishing one light after the next. Then she caused a fire in her own *dacha* and the whole thing burned down . . .

Also, I knew a boy who had paranormal abilities—he could read whatever he was sitting on. They would place a newspaper on a chair; he would sit on it and read the front-page articles. But—thank God—he was baptized, and this dubious talent left him.

Yes, it sometimes happens that the evil spirits will immediately leave their victim as soon as the person is baptized and "renounces Satan."[3]

But it also happens that they prevent or even stop a person from being baptized. Once, my friend was driving his delusional brother to a priest with the request to baptize him. They agreed that this would take place the following day. But that same night, this brother sat down in his room in a lotus position and saw Jesus Christ come down from the icon and say to him: "You don't have to be baptized, you've already achieved great heights." So the baptism never took place because the delusional brother said, why should I?

But sometimes the demons delude the baptized as well—churchgoing people who partake of the communion of the Body and Blood of Christ. It is impossible to bring these types of people to their senses without God's direct interference.

I had an acquaintance named Boris, whom I had at one time, having just been baptized myself, considered practically a saint. First of all, he regularly fasted and was an ascetic. Second of all, if he said anything at all, it was simply "yes, yes; no, no," as it is instructed in the Gospel.[4] Third of all, he never looked you in the eye, considering this to be impertinent, but instead always looked slightly lower down and to the side, constantly lowering his eyes. He held his gentle hands before him, on one of which was wound a long prayer rope: there was no bustle in them, no loud gestures. He would hint—and very subtly, humbly—that he'd reached 500. In other words, he was making 500 prostrations per day! It was discovered, also through certain implications and utterances of his, that he slept on the bare floor. And what was most impressive—in a tent. This tent wasn't put up just anywhere, but in his own apartment, since he was forced to share a room with his grandmother. So he was an ascetic and an anchorite at the same time. A stylite of sorts: his tent measured one and a half square meters! So he sat in it for days and nights at a time, only emerging from time to time on especially important spiritual matters.

He never laughed excessively, for as it is said, "Hell is ever-mocking." His only friend was a spiritual brother who was also practically a saint: this friend lived in Moscow, but traveled over the hills and far away every Friday to visit an Orthodox elder and serve as an altar boy for him, reading in church, helping to answer letters, and participating in the Holy Mysteries with him.

So, the good man who helped me to be baptized would bring them both to see me, so that they could feed me spiritual bread, so that I would finally see the spark of eternal life in the faces of mortals and would myself be inspired to follow in their footsteps ... I would meet them with much reverence and awe and ask them questions about the Faith and the Church. But apparently my questions seemed to them so basic, my spiritual ascent so low, that they, coughing somewhat strenuously and even exchanging coughs with one another—cough, cough!—and visibly lowering themselves to my level of relative simplicity, would answer with a few carefully and unhurriedly chosen words, and then again grow silent, lowering their gaze and noiselessly moving their lips—probably in prayer.

Basically, our theological get-togethers were not successful—in addition, something or other was said about women—those vessels of weakness and sin—to the extent of, can anything of worth be poured into such a vessel? So we all parted ways for a while.

However, several years later, Boris and I ran into each other at a service in a monastery and returned to Moscow together. We traveled together all night in the same car, and I was amazed by the obvious changes in him. Now he was open to the world—talkative, inspired, and smiling. By the third hour of our conversation, he informed me that he had ascended to the highest step of the Ladder of St John Climacus and had achieved complete passionlessness, so now he had no reason to hide from the world because the world wouldn't ensnare him anyway. By the fifth hour, he told me that he held the Jesus Prayer in his heart constantly, and by morning I learned that the Lord Himself had appeared to him, had taken him to the seventh heaven, where everyone, including the Mother of God, St John the Baptist, and the Apostle Paul, were dwelling.

At that point, the train arrived in Moscow and we parted ways.

Then, in another two or three years, we met on the street and he blessed me with a large sign of the cross.

"Are you a priest?" I said in surprise.

"I am more than a priest—I am an apostolic descendant by grace. Symeon the New Theologian wrote: let him who has not had a personal experience of Christ dare to participate in the priesthood! What, do you think that our priests and bishops have been made worthy of such a meeting? I assure you—no, they only know of it by word of mouth, from others. But I—I know it from God Himself!"

"Oh, really?" I said, at a loss of what to do. "Have you spoken of this to any priests or bishops?"

"What's the point?!" he waved his hand. "They're all brainwashed. They're afraid! I asked them: 'Did you ever see the divine light in the chalice while preparing the mystery of the Eucharist?' And I could tell from the looks on their faces that none of them had. But now I manage without them—I just concentrate on internal introspection and Logos-meditation, and through that, I partake of spiritual communion. After that, the path to awareness of the energetic aura of the spirit was opened to me. I can enter into the realm of the airy tollhouses after death, I can ascend to the divine spheres of the spirit . . . and anyway, I was appointed the chief commander there in the presence of the elder and the Mother of God."

I began to feel uneasy, and hurriedly bowed to him and said goodbye, walking away with a heavy and agitated feeling inside.

Soon I saw him on a television talk show, where he kept trying to either make some sort of passes with his hands, or to catch some sort of invisible beings flickering before his eyes . . . But I was most shocked when he said that God had revealed his new name to him, which was something like "Bomkinchondro Gottopaddakhai."

I didn't even know how I should pray for him . . . I kept seeing him the way I had known him in times past: young, full of desire to go into the desert and forget himself and the world there for the sake of Christ.

Two more years passed.

One day a hieromonk of my acquaintance was planning to chrismate and commune the paralyzed grandson of his parishioner, a very old woman. But he had to travel far and was uncomfortable taking public transportation with the Holy Gifts. In short, I drove him there in my car and we went up to the apartment together. The sick man lay on the couch in the room there, thin, with long, grey hair. The priest asked everyone to leave the room so that he could speak to him in private, and the old lady and I sat down in the kitchen.

"Boren'ka had a stroke! But he's still young!" sighed the old lady. "He can't speak, he can't move! The Lord definitely tied him up! Shut up his mouth! Clothed him in a shirt of humility!"

"What are you saying?" I exclaimed. "As if God was a paramedic or a priest warden!"

"I only say what I know. Boria brought a whole revolution onto his own head! He kept saying—I'll ascend to the seventh heaven, I'll overturn everything there and bring it all to order! Yes, he said that. And the Lord, you see, said to him in reply: just you get up off your couch, you fool! Or just turn over . . . and he can't! And before that he kept boasting: I'm the chief commander! Called himself Bobkinchondro or something . . ."

A strange suspicion arose within me . . . I glanced inside the room . . . the priest was bending over him, anointing him with chrism. When he moved a little to the side and began to read the prayers, my suspicions were confirmed . . .

"But he rejected the Church herself," I said, dismayed. "How can be given communion? What if it's against his will? It could turn out that it was done by force . . . or did he manage to repent before all this?" I asked the old lady carefully.

"Maybe, maybe not . . . the Lord had already closed his mouth and taken away his hands. So we don't know if he's for it or against it—but it doesn't even matter," she grumbled. "As for 'by force,' I'll say this to you, my dear: maybe the dead don't want us to pray for them either. But we don't ask them: we just pray and that's all! Maybe our enemies don't want our prayers either. As for atheists—it's a fact that they don't. The same applies to babies. Are you going to ask their permission? The psychologically ill belong in the same category. It turns out we pray for them without their permission, perhaps even against their will. We carry them along by force . . ."

The old lady made a gesture with her dry little hands as if she was truly dragging someone along with all her strength by a rope, and that person was resisting.

"The only thing is, the soul is a Christian by nature!" she continued. "The soul desires this in any case! So there is no 'by force' in the end!"

When we bade farewell to the old lady, I went to see Boris in spite of everything. He lay, victorious and still, his gaze affixed unmovingly on the ceiling. His facial features had sharpened, and he looked more like a sculpted image of his own self. It was as if the artistic idea of the Creator had shone through in his image: a faster, ascetic, chain-wearer, and passionbearer. A hesychast and stylite.

A thought wandered into my mind, that perhaps the Lord had indeed fulfilled "his heart's desire"? And as bold as his ancient grandmother had seemed to me, something inside me urged me to agree with her, especially as she herself was already gazing into that place where earthly logic falls apart and the laws of our fallen world cease to exist.

❧ *How the Vatican Shod Our Bishops* ❧

My husband was going to the Council of Bishops, which he was required to attend as part of his priestly duties. Around the same time, the journalist Dorenko had made a thrilling announcement on the radio, just in time for the start of the Council: he claimed that there was a special boot shop in the Vatican that made shoes for the Pope himself, and conjointly for the entire Roman Curia. And now, apparently, hearing about this wonderful shop, our archbishops had also sent their orders there and were now sporting their Catholic custom-made shoes.

My husband, who had a constant problem with footwear—all his shoes rubbed his feet raw, were too tight, fit wrong—became very interested in this unexpected piece of information, and meeting his old friend, an archbishop, at the Council, immediately relayed everything to him.

"Really?" the bishop said in surprise. "Strange, I haven't heard a word . . ."

And as if they had planned it, they both lowered their gaze and began to examine the papal footwear on our bishops.

The first one to catch their attention was an elderly bishop from central Russia. He slowly walked along, shuffling his feet, shod in plaid felt slippers.

"Maybe he has bad feet," guessed my husband's friend, the bishop.

The next to come along was a younger bishop from the south of Russia. He had simple imitation leather boots

"Well, he's still young, he's just a vicar bishop," noted my husband's friend, the bishop.

The third to appear was a seasoned archbishop from Siberia.

He wore visibly used shoes with worn-down heels, beige ones that were relatively dirty.

"His cell attendant let that slip," our bishop reproachfully shook his head.

But the other bishops, on closer inspection, had shoes that were not any better, if only cleaner and in better condition.

"We-e-ell," my husband sighed, disappointed, "the Vatican didn't expend much of an effort."

"What, were you really hoping that the Catholics had shod us?" the bishop smiled.

Then my husband remembered that his bishop-friend's diocese was in Belarus and that he had suffered much at the hands of Roman Catholic priests and bishops there, who were luring members of his parishes to the Byzantine Catholic Church. And he thought—maybe it was better that our bishops were shod in the old-fashioned way. If worse came to worst, they could stop by a shoe store in Thessaloniki on their way to Mt Athos, and, unsuccessfully trying to remain incognito, hastily try on one or two pairs, until they were discovered red-handed and called out to by a zealous Russian pilgrim or pious tourist:

"Your Grace! Your blessing!"

What of it? That actually happened . . .

❧ The Little Cloud ❧

Once, when my husband, Fr Vladimir, was on duty at his Church of the Holy Martyr Tatiana, a middle-aged woman and her adult daughter came to talk to him. They both had tortured, unhappy faces.

"Father," they said, "we have a poltergeist in our home. Grandfather, who's deceased, comes to us at night. We can't bear it anymore. We don't feel comfortable at home. Someone advised us to come to you. Please come and bless our apartment."

"But what's happening at your house? Why have you decided that it's a poltergeist and that it is specifically your grandfather?"

"Who else could it be? When he passed on to the next world, that's when it all started happening. A little grey cloud began to appear in our kitchen in the evenings. It just hangs there over the table, and at night it becomes more dense and begins to stink."

"Begins to stink?"

"Well, yes. It smells, and we can't say that it's a faint smell. It reeks. A terrible odor. A stench. And it grumbles."

"What do you mean, it grumbles?"

"It curses and swears. It's not above an obscenity sometimes. And all that in the voice of Grandfather. It's all we can do to not run away."

"Was your grandfather properly buried? Was he given a Christian burial?"

"No, and we don't go to church ourselves. And he was such a blasphemer! He could hardly walk, and spoke with difficulty, but still spoke such blasphemy! He would find his voice very quickly. Where did he get his strength? But now he is just driving us insane. Believe it or not, I am a doctor myself, a senior physician," said the mother, "and as soon as the little cloud began to appear, I thought, that's it, I'm going crazy, I'm having hallucinations. I went to see my colleague—the senior physician in neurology—and started to tell her about all this. I thought maybe she could prescribe me some pills, administer some treatment. She said to me: I'll come over and we'll see what this little cloud is all about. She came and I sent my daughter to spend the night with a friend. Closer to midnight, that senior physician and I sat in the kitchen, and there was that little cloud: stinking, cursing; we were uncomfortable listening to it! And suddenly the head of neurology admits: this little cloud is not in my area of expertise because it is not a product of your psyche, since I saw it as well. So we would need some other specialists to help. My daughter heard about this the next day and admitted that she was also seeing the little cloud every night, but was scared to talk about it, thinking that she would be sent to the psych ward."

"Fine," said Fr Vladimir, "I'll come bless your apartment, and take a look at your little cloud at the same time."

I drove my husband to the given address. As soon as we entered the clean, spacious apartment, a little dog, a lap dog, suddenly jumped out at him from a corner and broke out into an angry, yelping bark, trying to bite his foot and pulling his cassock to the floor this way and that.

"Come here, dear, come here, you ball of fur!" I bent down to it. "We smell like our cat, that's why she's barking at us."

"R-ruff!" It violently snapped its jaws, barely missing the fingers that I had just managed to pull back, and began to choke on its frenzied barks.

"Chakra,[1] what's wrong with you?" the mistress of the apartment gently addressed her. "We can't understand it: she's been barking like that since morning. She always used to be such a peaceful, affectionate little dog."

"Let her think about her behavior," the daughter picked up the dog and shut it up in the bathroom.

In the meantime, my husband went through into the kitchen; the mistress led the way, desiring to show him where exactly Grandfather was appearing in the form of the foul-smelling and acerbic cloud.

"Don't worry," he assured the two disconcerted women. "I once blessed the department of journalism nearby and came to sprinkle holy water on a closet full of cassette tapes, metal film reels, and other cinematic equipment; when I sprinkled the holy water and said three times—'Let every evil demonic activity be put to flight'—the shelves collapsed and the film reels scattered all over the floor. The professors themselves, who were present at the time, said: 'Apparently, there was a lot of evil encased in them.' We'll put to flight your little cloud, too."

And at that very moment, the crazed lap dog tore into the room, having somehow managed to escape the closed bathroom. Hatred and fury burned in its little black button eyes that could otherwise have been cute. It threw itself at my husband, but the women rushed to intercept it, and got there in time to grab it and take it back behind the closed door. But this time they also locked the door.

Fr Vladimir laid out his Book of Needs and Gospel on the table, placed his holy oil, holy water, candles, and little box with charcoal there, and began to light up his censer.

The dog was in a rage, snorting and howling in a low growl. One would think that it had changed from a lap dog into a Rottweiler.

We were forced to bless the apartment under the accompaniment of that crazed barking.

But Fr Vladimir read the prayers and the Gospel, marked crosses in holy oil on all four sides of the apartment, and moved through the entire space of the apartment with his holy water, brush, and the powerful words: "Let every evil demonic activity be put to flight!" He generously sprinkled the cursed place over the kitchen table, the windows, doors, objects, walls, curtains, closets, couches, chairs . . . then it was the bathroom's turn.

The daughter opened the door and tried to pick up their prized trophy dog, but it snapped at her finger, ran out, frantically ran about the apartment, rushed into the kitchen in a panic, and, while the priest sprinkled the place of its recent confinement, jumped onto the stool, from the stool to the kitchen table, and there, continuing to bark in the same harsh and severe manner, relieved itself and soiled the table.

"A-a-ah!!" the frightened women cried out in horror, seeing the obscene traces next to the holy oil. "Chakra's possessed! She's never been like this since the day she was born, she was always so tidy, please forgive us, forgive us! Grandfather's spirit must have lodged itself in her—that blasphemer!" they said, trying to come to her defense. They were all disheveled and red in the face.

But the dog wasn't finished. It jumped up, grabbed the brush out of Fr Vladimir's hands, and began to tear it to pieces, wallowing on the floor and growling.

They managed to take the brush away with great difficulty, caught the dog again—this time using a robe instead of their bare hands—and again locked it up in the bathroom.

We left, having comforted the poor women and assured them that worse things have happened during house blessings. We told them that sometimes the holy water prepared for the blessing suddenly begins to boil and splash the people present, scalding them; that their grandfather had obviously summoned the evil spirits when he was still alive; that such things happen . . .

Two weeks later both of them—mother and daughter—appeared in Fr Vladimir's church.

"Well?" He asked them. "How's your little cloud doing?"

"It dissipated," they notified him, "it's gone. We'd almost gotten used to it. We almost feel as if we've kicked Grandfather out. As for Chakra . . ."

"What happened?"

"She threw herself under a car, on her own. We took her on a walk back then, as soon as you had left, and let her run around the garden. Suddenly, she ran away and took off at breakneck speed, and so we lost her. She was like our child. It was probably Grandfather paying us back."

At this Fr Vladimir couldn't help himself and said:

"Your Grandfather's been in the grave for a long time now. But you keep blaming him for all your problems. Admit it, what were you yourself doing in that apartment? Why did you name an innocent dog Chakra?"

They exchanged glances and looked down:

"It was nothing. We just invited some psychic mediums to our home when that cloud appeared. For a long time they walked around the apartment with some sort of sticks and spinning frames, burning incense, making strange movements, but they couldn't get rid of it. And before that, we had simply summoned Grandfather's spirit—just to find out how he was doing over there. We got a brochure at the flea market: a guide to spiritualism. So we decided to try it out, just once. He himself wasn't happy about it. He just said: "You shabby tramps, I'll get you for this!"

And? Well, it turns out he kept his promise.

❧ Sokratis ❧

That summer, the monks of Holy Trinity Monastery honored me with their trust: by doing so, in a way they accepted me into their male monastic brotherhood. I mean, of course, my three monk-friends—two iconographers and a poet.

It was a hot summer, and under cover of night they would go out through a secret gate, to which only they had the key, get in my car, and we would drive to Lesnaia Lake. There we would build a fire, drink instant coffee out of a thermos, make instant noodle soup, and—why hide it?—sip Sokratis Greek cognac, which in the confusion of *perestroika* had been imported in large quantities to the small city of Troitsk and was being sold in the only shop on Market Square.

At times, the monks would come to my white Troitsk house on a hill, and then we would sit under the apple trees in the garden, look up at the stars, have deep conversations about things great and small, and drink this all down with that same vitalizing, philosophy-inspiring, Hellenic tonic. Those were happy times.

And at other times, either one or another monastic brother would approach me in the monastery with a typical black wallet made of thick rayon, put money in my hand, and ask:

"Listen, my uncle is supposed to visit me here shortly—I would love to sit and have a good heart-to-heart with him, treat him to something, talk for a bit; we haven't seen each other in a long time. Buy us a few bottles of Sokratis, please, will you?"

Of course, I bought it. Then other monks found out about this, and also began to approach me with their black wallets. I couldn't turn them down, either. But as it turned out, I would have to make three separate runs to the shop on Rynochnaia in one day—three runs for two or three bottles at a time!

So is it any surprise that the sales clerk knew me very well and would reach for the case of Sokratis at my very appearance?

And so, one time, I ran out of toothpaste. Since this little shop of mine sold everything that the Troitsk supply offered—Korean soups, vodka, cognac, potato chips, Snickers, safety pins, soap, eye shadow, etc., I set off there at my usual pace.

"Hello," I leaned in through the little window.

"Hello," the salesclerk cheerfully replied. "Your usual?"

And, without waiting for a response, she placed several bottles of Sokratis in front of me. "You want two or three today?"

After that, I stopped buying cognac for the monks.

"That's it, brothers," I said. "As it is, I'm already known around here as the local drunk. What if my husband comes and we go to that store to buy soap or something, and they greet me with: 'Hello! Your usual?' And plop! Put a pile of bottles in front of me. What would he think?"

But the summer was already coming to an end anyway; a new abbot had been assigned to the monastery, who "tightened all the screws" and ordered the secret gate to be boarded up, while one of my iconographer-friends went to an elder and told him everything about the Sokratis.

"Make it so, Father, that I and my monastic friends, the iconographers and poet, would stop drinking completely," he asked the elder in a fit of repentance.

So what happened? The elder sealed him with such a sign of the cross that he returned to the monastery a complete teetotaler. What's more, he began to feel such revulsion for any wine that "maketh a man's heart glad" (Ps 103:15) that he couldn't even put it in his mouth. Even if he would, at times, have liked to—you know, in theory—take some comfort with his brothers, in his own circle of friends, the thought would turn his stomach.

As for his friend, the other iconographer, for whose sake he had also implored the elder—that is another story. His stomach wouldn't turn at all; on the contrary, his soul was very inclined to drink. But only after a few sips, he would break out into a terrible allergic reaction. It was so bad that he had to be taken to emergency to pump the alcohol out, which would bring him back to life.

So my friends, the monk-iconographers, no longer drink. Fifteen years have passed, that elder has already passed away, and they keep sipping away at nothing but their green tea or herbal infusions.

"Well, fine," I once asked them, "but why didn't it work on our third monastic friend? He pays it no heed, it's like a drop in the bucket to him. Or is it like the Gospel says: 'One will be taken and the other left' (Mt 24:40)?"

"You know what?" they said to me. "Let's not do that! The judgment of God is a mystery. All we have to do here is be still, stand on tiptoe with bated breath, and put a finger on our lips. 'Whatsoever the Lord pleased, that hath He done!'(Ps 134:6). Also, in the life of St Anthony, it was said to him from the very heavens in answer to his curiosity: 'Anthony! Keep your attention on yourself!'"

∾ The Late Husband of Mother Seraphima ∾

Monasticism is a deeply voluntary matter. It is not in vain that a moment exists in the monastic tonsure when the tonsuring abbot (elder) asks the one being tonsured:

"Why do you come brother/sister falling down before the Holy Table?"
"Do you come to the Lord voluntarily and of your own mind?"

And he or she replies:

"Yes, Reverend Father."

But I know of cases that took place in our time, after the Babylonian captivity,[1] when inexperienced neophytes were either lured into the monastery or tonsured almost by force. This can be explained first of all by the fact that neophytes are sometimes characteristically ignorant, imbalanced, and prone to spiritual misalignment. Either they fast until they are half dead, or they begin to arrogantly insist that fasting is an outdated and obsolete institution. They either take the priest's word as truth to the farthest extreme, or they don't follow any spiritual instruction under any circumstances. Second of all, when new monasteries began to open, monks were in immediate demand. That is why such immature types were taken and tonsured, those who weren't ready to be novices or who had neophyte complexes.

I heard one such story myself from a monk from a distant northern monastery. He once came to an elder in order to ask his blessing to successfully defend his thesis at his university. The elder, thinking for a long time, said to him:

"Actually, you need to become a monk."

He was led away by the spiritual children of the elder and taken to the monastery. Before he had a chance to come to his senses, he was tonsured at lightning speed. So began his trials and wanderings from one monastery to another.

"But why didn't you just tell the elder that you didn't want to follow the monastic path or at least that you weren't ready?" I asked him.

"I didn't even know that I could say that," he admitted. "I thought—the elder has spoken, so now I must follow his instruction, though the earth should crumble beneath my feet. I was afraid that the Lord would punish me for disobedience. And the elder's spiritual children also insisted: the elder said so, now you don't have anywhere to hide! It's decided."

But there were also more subtle methods of persuading someone to enter the monastery. Even I was almost caught once—in any case, my heart began to go pitter-patter and turn in that direction against all odds, and I began to struggle with it. This is how it happened.

In 1995, my husband was ordained to the diaconate of the Russian Orthodox Church, and at the time he served at Sretensky Monastery. For some reason, I fell under the temptation of thinking that since he was now a clergyman, he could also be tonsured into monasticism. What about it? They could say: "Fr Vladimir, go ahead and do it 'for obedience's sake.'" But what would I do? I didn't want to part with him under any circumstances! This fear was completely unfounded and was simply suggested to me by an evil spirit, ever striving to dismay the Christian heart.

And so, Mother Seraphima, who had just recently become the abbess of Novodevichy Convent, having heard from someone that a certain deacon's wife had for a long time driven a car, took a great interest in me: Metropolitan Iuvenalii was ready to donate his black Volga to her convent, but would wait until the abbess could find a driver. So she turned to me with the request to become her driver; that way the convent would have its own car, and later one of her novices could learn to drive, and she would release me with gratitude.

The abbess was very much to my liking: she came from an old noble family that had served the Church, the Tsar, and the Fatherland for a long time. The New Martyr Seraphim Chichagov was her grandfather; he had in his time fought for the canonization of St Seraphim of Sarov, whom we considered our family patron saint, since he had saved my father from certain death during World War II. Her great-grandfather had served as Minister of the Imperial Navy during the reign of Nicholas I, and her great-great-grandfather, Admiral Chichagov, had been celebrated for defeating the Swedish fleet near Revel.

As for Mother Seraphima herself (Varvara Vasilievna), in addition to never being a Party member—about which she loved to repeat: "The Lord was merciful to me and allowed me to escape membership in the godless Party"—she was a professor, a doctor of chemical sciences, a respected member of many academies around the world, a USSR State Prize laureate, a recipient of two orders—the Order of the Red Banner of Labor and the Order of the October Revolution. She was responsible for some important discoveries in the rubber industry—among other things, she invented the suit in which Yuri Gagarin flew into space. All in all, she presented what they call a "one-of-a-kind" human being.

After discussing with the abbess the possibility of releasing me from my duties for the Art of Literature seminars that I was leading at the Maxim Gorky Literature Institute, I agreed.

Metropolitan Iuvenalii's people immediately made the papers for his Volga car out to the convent. I was designated as the authorized driver, and my life began to course through the streets of the newly opened Novodevichy Convent. I must say that at the time the monastery only owned the church with its candle shop and three rooms located within the church itself:

in the farthest room was the reception area of the abbess, where mostly unfortunate women broken by grief came to see her. (One of them had been kicked out of her one-room apartment by her son, who had brought in his young wife; another by her drunk and abusive husband; a third—a very young person—was sent by some monk-spiritual father of hers who had forbidden her to marry her beloved: "If you marry him, you may stop coming to see me!" So she had chosen her spiritual father over her groom.) In the middle room was the kitchen with the dining area, and in the third, a separate room, some needed things were stored by the convent. In theory, the monastery had also inherited some half-decayed buildings that would in time become the sisters' cells, but this would only take place in the unknown future, as there were no funds for their restoration. For now, the potential nuns had nowhere to lay their heads.

They lived each in their own place and came to the monastery from the world "for their obediences." Even the abbess continued to live in her Moscow apartment on Vosstaniya Square, where I would pick her up every morning at eight thirty in my car, drive her to the monastery, deftly turn in through the gates, which were invariably flung open with hurried willingness by an elderly guard, and only then would I exchange my car for the black Volga.

It would be parked next to the church itself. The Pobeda make car of Metropolitan Iuvenalii's young hierodeacon, which he kept in immaculate shape, was also parked there, and in the mornings, inspired by the example of the untiring owner of the Pobeda working nearby, I would polish the Volga and shake out the rugs, which I almost never did with my own car, thinking—possibly without reason—that "it would be safer that way" (a year before that, my perfectly clean and brilliantly polished Semerka had been stolen under my very nose).

Later on, when the car would be ready for the abbess's departure, she and I would visit "the sponsors," i.e., various authorities and charities that could possibly fund the monastery's restoration. But not only did no one hurry to provide the money, it seemed to me that they were not planning to give any at all, in spite of the fact that the abbess's visits would be preceded by inspiring letters and convincing arguments in defense of such a use of their resources. We were completely unable to direct the current of finances in the direction of the decaying convent. They just looked at us with a considerably suspicious and wily smirk (as if to say, we can't be deceived, we're no fools!), almost as if we were asking them at the very least to change the course of the northern rivers . . .

I even tried to take advantage of my membership in the Russian PEN Center[2] for this purpose. After getting the phone number of the press secretary Khakamada, who was at the time a deputy of the State Duma, I introduced myself as a writer (probably in order to raise the status of my request in her eyes) and recited to her on the phone a rather "charismatic" speech on the countless spiritual, aesthetic, as well as practical benefits that Irina Mutsuovna could receive in exchange for her sponsorship . . .

The press secretary strictly asked what I meant exactly by "aesthetic benefits?" I answered that the restoration of such a magnificent convent would bring aesthetic pleasure and recall the beautiful image of the Grand Duchess Elizabeth Fyodorovna[3] founding her convent . . . that I meant it in the sense that this would be a "beautiful gesture." In addition, its abbess was an aristocrat, the granddaughter of a martyr, who was herself an academic and had never been a member of the Communist Party of the Soviet Union.

I even hinted, not without poetical expression, that Irina Mutsuovna could, by doing this, boost her own—stammering a little, I still managed to say it—image, as well as that of her forthcoming pre-election campaign, and what's more, even enter history in the most worthy way.

It seemed to me that I pontificated so convincingly that I almost saw before my very own eyes the image of Irina Mutsuovna entering the course of history: in white clothing, with an elegant wreath of lilies—that was how Irina Mutsuovna appeared to me in my mind, and thus for a moment, history seemed to me not unlike the heavenly kingdom . . . such a wondrous moment did I have . . . such a fleeting apparition . . . [4]

But it ended, as it should have, with the troubles of life's vanity, throes of hopeless grief, and raging, gusty storms.[5]

My fellow conversationalist, having consulted with her supervisor, harshly responded that Irina Mutsuovna doesn't see why she should really help namely the Orthodox people, and not Jews or Muslims or someone else. It was clear (as was to be expected) that neither the image of the Grand Duchess, nor that of the abbess-academic, had in any way inspired (at least aesthetically) the former Communist activist and teacher of Marxist-Leninist political economics. And now I sadly glanced over the featureless, imported, low-quality product in which Irina Mutsuovna loomed on the television screen . . .

But the abbess also had difficulty with her novices. She had under her direction only one real nun who was already experienced in the monastic life. She had been promoted by the abbess and now sold candles. But there were problems with her, too—it was her previous monastic experience that got in her way: she would constantly announce to the abbess:

"We didn't do it that way in our convent . . . our abbess always said . . ."

The abbess would grumble at her:

"Let her go back and sit there in her old convent, why did she want to come to us so much?"

This nun also started a quarrel with me. She believed that I was taking the monastery car and driving away to do "my own errands" and that I filled my own car with monastery-intended gasoline, which I would receive at the gas station with state-issued tokens. She even shared her suspicions with the abbess, who simply asked me: "How do you buy gas for your car—with tokens or with money?" I answered, "With money," and she believed me. But surprisingly enough, the nun didn't stop at that, and learning who my spiritual father was by roundabout ways, contacted him to complain about me.

He asked me at confession:

"Have you ever filled up your car with the monastery's gasoline?"

Then I understood how the enemy of mankind rages against and torments the brides of Christ![6] I felt sorry for the nun, and the thought that I had abandoned my husband and children, my writing, having rushed to help the abbess and await "godly adventures" just for the sake of stealing the monastery's gasoline seemed so silly to me.

It was not much simpler with the rest of the novices. I think that many of them hadn't gotten the chance to even become regular churchgoing people: when we all read the communion rule aloud together, they did it as if they were seeing the prayers for the first time and with strained amazement attacked the words syllable by syllable: O-the-good-ness-of-God . . .

Moreover, it turned out that the abbess had no ability whatsoever to lead, i.e., to give orders, insist, or make reprimands. This seemed especially strange in view of the fact that when she worked in the world, she directed entire laboratories and divisions. But she had such highly developed, even excessive, respect for human freedom, that the abbess treated her novices almost as if she was giving them total freedom of choice—and perhaps this was her way of expressing a sort of opposition to the Soviet authorities, which ever strove to repress the individual.

This created definite disadvantages in her relations with the willful and still spiritually imbalanced novices, who continued to think that even in the monastery they were "in their own right." Her low-toned, endearing voice always sounded intelligent, respectful, and gentle. Conversations with the novices went approximately like this:

"Valentina, wouldn't you like to wash the floor in the church today?"

"Oh, Mother, I'm not really in the mood, there's something wrong with my back."

"Tatiana, how are you feeling, would you be against it?"

"No, Mother, I'm not really feeling up to it today."

"And you, Natalia, how do you feel about it—wouldn't you like to work a little for the glory of God?"

"I have heartburn today for some reason. No, let Larisa over there wash it."

"Larisa, what do you say to my proposition—will you wash the floor?"

"Mother, I get all sweaty, I'd rather read the *Lives of the Saints* aloud at lunch . . ."

I felt sorry for the abbess, looking with confusion at her newly appointed and capricious novices, and said:

"Mother, if we don't need to go anywhere, let me wash the floor."

"To the glory of God!" the abbess happily replied.

This usually had a great educational effect: in ten minutes, all present novices were crawling on the floor and scraping off the wax and dirt.

"As my late husband would say," said the abbess when we got into the car afterwards, "the Soviet regime has spoiled people: everyone has begun to think that he must do as he wishes." The most surprising thing is that she didn't have any solutions for this: no solutions, and her conviction still lives on.

Generally, and especially in times of serious difficulties and trials, the abbess would very often refer to the authority of her late husband: "As my late husband would say . . ." Coming from the lips of the abbess, this would sound peculiar but touching. It was obvious that they had spent many years together and had lived in complete harmony.

In truth, they didn't read the *Lives of the Saints* at mealtimes, but the book *Olkhovksy Convent*, about an ideal and peaceful women's monastery. It was a completely fictional place that never existed. For monasteries are places of blood, pain, suffering, and sweat. But there, everything seemed to be peaceful, smooth, and full of God's grace, which really just made it saccharine and sugary sweet. Our novices would sigh languidly: "If only our convent was like that . . ." Finally, I couldn't take it any more and said to them: "So go ahead and create one like that yourselves." They just shrugged their shoulders: "But how, how?" I said: "You can start by obeying your abbess!" But the next day, everything would start all over again:

"Elena, would you be so kind as to peel some potatoes for the sisters?"

"Oh, Mother, how can you say that, I've had ringing in my ear since morning! And then my hands always look so terrible after I peel potatoes! Such dirt underneath my fingernails!"

In spite of the abbess's initial assurances that I wouldn't have a lot of work ("You would just have to pick me up from my apartment and take me to the monastery, then home from the monastery in the evening, and take me here or there in the city, nowhere far, steps away!"), I ended up driving from morning till night. But the abbess herself, I think, couldn't imagine what a whirlpool the Lord would place her in.

I dropped the abbess off at the monastery at eight thirty, and drove her back at nine o'clock at night, or even ten sometimes, or even eleven. And in the interim, I had to go about on monastery affairs practically the whole day.

So, we drove with the abbess to some textile factories and chose the material from which the novices' monastic habits and summer dresses would be sewn: the monastery was being given a little *metochion*[7] with a church, a yard, vegetable gardens, and fields, so that it could be self-sustaining. It was assumed that the novices would take on the spring sowing as soon as the snow melted from the fields, and that they would spend all summer until the beginning of fall in the countryside. So they needed light, but monastically modest, dresses for their work in the fields.

However, the abbess categorically disliked the fabrics being offered to her at the factory. At first, they were all too faded and acutely unattractive, as if a genuine ill-wisher had laid his hand on them: they had either cucumbers on a dirty-blue background, or purple flowers on a yellowish-green background, or orange houses on a purple background . . .

"Who is responsible for this, who could draw and think all this up?" she said in disbelief. "No, how am I supposed to dress my sisters in such ragged, old-ladyish, slovenly uncouthness? I think that even the clothes that nuns wear should be tidy and, if possible, in good taste. The appearance of the monastic is also a homily. It would be wrong if someone should turn away from a nun in disgust at seeing her dreadful appearance. We have a long way to go until we can become holy fools! We shouldn't try to imitate them—they have achieved spiritual heights that are beyond us—we would only make the demons laugh at us! No, what is a nun? She is the bride of Christ! What, is it proper to offer to Christ the worst, the mostly slovenly and dowdy things? Well, no! Of course, we should never take pride in anything—especially in our clothing or external appearance—but a proud person, no matter how you clothe them, be it in rags, be it in shabby, torn trousers, will still find an object to be proud of—they will take pride in their torn socks, in their dirty collar . . . so humility—that is an entirely different matter."

At last, we got lucky—we found a plain blue cotton print with small white polka dots, and the abbess summoned the seamstress to choose designs.

"The thinner girls should have one style, the plump ones something a little different . . ."

She sat there, kind, elderly, nervously looking through the patterns as if she was planning to clothe her own daughters. I had in the same manner gone shopping when I traveled abroad, worriedly buying clothes for my daughters: for the elder, Aleksandrina—slender, brown eyed, with chestnut hair—one style; and for the younger, Anastasia—strong, blue eyed, blond—exactly that, something a little different.

This choosing of fabric and designs by the abbess for the monastery sisters' dresses touched me so much that when we got into the car, I exclaimed from an overflow of emotion:

"How happy, Mother, must your nuns be under your wing!"

And then she suddenly told me something, ever so quietly and carefully, in her so pleasantly low voice:

"Well, what about you? Maybe you can join me too, eh? We would serve to the glory of God together! Monasticism—it is, after all, an angelic rank!"

And she looked and looked me as at "one of her own" . . .

There was always a running theme in the abbess's reflections:

"Well, the Lord placed me at eighty years old as the abbess of a once enormous monastery. But who am I? What will I tell him at the Final Judgment—'Lord, I'm old, I'm sick, I'm infirm; the novices that I was given are incapable, disobedient, the monastery is in ruins, there is no money, and so I didn't do anything!' Is that what I'm supposed to say to Him? No, since He determined that I should be here, I must, though I should die here, restore the monastery."

She would repeat this constantly—both when some hope would begin to glimmer from the side and when the matter seemed hopeless: and then, on top of everything, Great Lent began—the time of profound temptations and sorrows.

Finally, the time came for the transfer to the monastery *metochion*. The *metochion* was located close to Domodedovo: you had to drive on Kashirskii Highway, and then, before reaching the airport, turn right toward the city of Zukovskii, and after that go left, and drive another ten kilometers, then turn right again and drive on a concrete road for approximately three kilometers.

We arrived there with the abbess and three novices—that's all that we could fit in the car. The priest who had served in that church, but was now being transferred to another parish, gave us the keys and a blueprint of the property; with that, he left.

So the abbess, having explored her new holdings, stood for a long time in the middle of the field that was soon to be cultivated by the inexperienced city novices. The icy Lenten March wind blew at her blueprint and was seemingly ready to carry off into the distance her small, dry, completely aged figure—there, to the darkened forest—but the abbess continued to stand her ground, tearfully looking over the place where she, an eighty-year-old abbess, chosen by God, was supposed to facilitate the manifestation of the glory of God.

From that moment on, I would drive to the *metochion* almost every day—sometimes even twice a day, when I had to drive all the novices there for a church service. I also drove all kinds of household goods there, as well as provisions, and even a sheep and goose that had been donated to the monastery: I placed them in my backseat in a basket, where they bleated and gabbled. I also drove a hieromonk who was supposed to serve there and become the monastery's spiritual father. He was an intelligent and charming man, and we didn't become friends so much as conversed and understood each other. And so, once we were driving from the convent after the Liturgy; it was March, the snow was beginning to melt, the rooks had arrived, the birds had begun to sing, criss-crossing sunbeams pierced through the car—it was like we were sitting in a shining jewelry box. He said:

"It's difficult to decide to enter into monasticism, isn't it? But it would be so good, so good!"

I thought that he was speaking in general terms.

"Yes, yes," I said, "yes—yes!"

We drove a little bit more, and he began to counsel me confidingly:

"You just have to do it, that's all! But we don't have any humility, any patience, any obedience, so we must fight! Why do we hold on so hard to this earthly life?"

He began to frown, all golden in the rays of the spring sun.

I nodded, but stayed silent.

When we were already approaching Novodevichy, he couldn't help it and exclaimed:

"Monasticism would suit you so much! It's all joy, it's such beauty, freedom from the world! Just think, the Lord Himself would be your Groom!"

Here I looked at him with growing suspicion. Something stirred and scraped in my soul; I began to feel like a *kolobok*.[8] When this hieromonk was hearing confessions at the *metochion* the next time, I didn't go to him.

And so, one time, since I was also required to drive monastery guests, I was supposed to drive home a veteran bell-ringer. Long ago, he had rung the bells at the monastery for Paschal matins; this was still during the time of Emperor Nicholas Aleksandrovich. Now he was an ancient and dried-up little man. His friends had driven him to the monastery, and it fell to me to drive him back. I asked him:

"Where should I go? What's the address?"

He replied:

"I don't remember the address, but I do remember everything by sight. You drive, and I will show you the way."

He sat in the front and began to direct me: straight, to the right, to the left. We passed Liusinovskaia, and somewhere near Tulskaia metro station he suddenly exclaimed:

"Quickly, turn left, over here, under the bridge, right after the tram."

"Is there a road here?" I asked him with doubt, as I had never seen cars turning into here.

"Of course, don't worry, I always take the tram here. I recognize the place."

What else could I do—I turned where he told me to and drove along the tram rails. But something was wrong—there were no cars, the concrete ended, though two clear lines of the track shone in the sun. Finally, we began to encounter more and more trams. They were placed in a strange order, like seals on icebergs—here and there people crowded around them, whose faces grew long with amazement as soon as they looked in our direction. I began to get a very real sense that we had driven into some sort of tram yard, but I shook it off as a pointless thought—in other words, at this point, it didn't matter: we still had to find our way out somehow. I continued to slowly and stubbornly move along the tracks in the direction indicated to me by the ancient bell-ringer. We turned once more, and here the old man joyfully announced:

"It's here, here, I recognize this place, now drive out into the street!"

And just as he said, there was a street ahead, an extremely wide and bustling one. What was the street? I had lost all sense of direction, which, to put it nicely, even in familiar conditions is not very good; you could say that, on the contrary, I suffer from a certain "topographical idiocy." Now it was doubled by our adventure through the tram yard. In short, we drove onto an unfamiliar street, and here I saw on the opposite side a very long, almost a kilometer-long, concrete house. This house began approximately where we had driven under that tramway archway (or "bridge," as the bell-ringer had called it), and here, after all our trials, we emerged again near this endless house, but in the wrong direction of traffic.

"Oh, I think that we're driving in the right direction, but on the wrong side of the street," said the old man.

This experience with the veteran bell-ringer helped me to understand that I must slowly bring to an end my service as the abbess's professional driver: I myself was also moving forward, although under obedience, the right way in theory, but practically speaking in the wrong direction! As Abbess Seraphima's late husband would say, according to her, everyone sees signs tailor-made for them in the developments of their life. So it was time for me to recognize my worth, to bow out, say "thank you," and quietly take my leave.

But it was Great Lent, the busy season at the convent, and half the sisters were lying ill at home; they needed medicine, documents needed to be delivered to the Patriarchate, and humanitarian aid for the sisters picked up from the Danilov Monastery. I was to drive straight through the front gate: "Abbess Seraphima's car!" "Abbess Seraphima? Drive on."

The abbess herself had to be taken to the hospital clinic. And so she and I got stuck in such a hopeless traffic jam that our trip was beginning to lose purpose—not only would we not make it on time, but standing in one spot, pressed in by cars on all sides, we were already thirty minutes late.

At first, the abbess was nervous and kept rushing me, though we drove directly up against the car standing in front of us, but then she resigned herself and began to look around the street.

"What's that little restaurant there?" she asked me, pointing in the direction of an enormous window. That wasn't there before. My late husband would often take me out to dine, so I know."

"It's a Chinese restaurant," I replied. "It's good, but very expensive. An American Slavicist once invited us out to eat there."

"Expensive?" the abbess said in surprise. "Strange. I went to a Chinese restaurant in Italy with my late husband, and it was very cheap. Chinese restaurants are usually cheap."

"They are very cheap in Paris and America, there's a lot of them there, and a lot of competition." I said. "But that hasn't reached us yet: that restaurant is for now the only one of its kind in Moscow."

"Yes," the abbess agreed. "In Italy, of course, they wouldn't survive if they ripped off their customers. They have their own wonderful ethnic restaurants, as well as French ones and whatever else. My late husband and I ate out quite often both when I traveled abroad for conferences and here at home in Moscow . . . sometimes it was only in those places that the 'Soviet' flavor would disappear."

I tried to imagine how someone standing aside and listening to this conversation between the abbess and her driver would react, and smiled.

"Why are you smiling?" she asked me strictly.

"I'm smiling because I am beginning to understand that you are a very fortunate person!"

"What made you come to that conclusion?"

"You are the granddaughter of a martyr," I began, "you had a wonderful, loving husband, the Lord blessed you in your work, you made extremely important scientific discoveries that are very useful to people, and even in your venerable old age the Lord has bestowed upon you His trust and has chosen you to be the abbess of a beautiful monastery in the very center of Russia!"

"You're talking as if you're saying the eulogy at my funeral," she laughed, dismayed. "Can it be that you're thinking of leaving me?"

"Yes, Mother, I am," I admitted.

"Why? Something doesn't suit you?" she said with concern.

"Everything suits me very well. But I have a husband, children, work that I love . . . The monastery has a car now, and I will find you a driver. As for me—you can see for yourself, I'm no driver! If we get a flat tire somewhere on the highway at night in the rain, what would we do? Stand there, cry for help, get wet, look for some men, rely on solidarity among drivers on the road . . ."

"Well, all right," she said dryly. "I understand that it's not working out with you and monasticism. Then please at least find me a driver, a church-going one. As my late husband would say, there is no greater madness than to trust a deceitful man. A driver should have your trust. He's the person with whom you share your initial reactions when you sit down in his car."

I found her one. This was my handyman, Sasha, a chemist by education who fixed my car. At the time, he had just begun to come to the Church, and he liked the idea of driving Abbess Seraphima.

The hieromonk who had become the spiritual father of her convent was soon transferred to another place, where he at first became rector and then bishop. I met him recently in the courtyard of the Patriarchate on Chistii Pereulok. He recognized me and was very happy to see me:

"Well, how are you? Listen, I have a little convent starting in my diocese. It's hard to find words to describe the place: it's paradise! Imagine: the cleanest little river, with water like a holy spring, reflecting the sky, clouds, stars, and moon. Pure poetry! And over the river there is a sloping hill onto which several birch trees ran up and froze, admiring the view. And that's where the convent is, right by the birch trees. What do you think?"

"It sounds wonderful, *Vladyka*, I also have no words!"

"Well, your children have already grown up, right? What's stopping you now from coming and joining me as the abbess? I would give you your own car! You could drive just like you used to."

I was so shocked that I lost the gift of speech for several minutes. But I somehow managed to say:

"But I have a husband! What about him?"

"What about your husband? What about him? We'll take him, too. We'll find a place for him, too. It's a large diocese. We'll tonsure him, too. You'll be in one monastery, he in another. Just like Peter and Fevronia!"[9]

He stood there, radiating from inside, happy that he had thought of everything so well. I didn't want to disappoint him. I just said to him, sighing:

"As the late husband of Abbess Seraphima used to say, stand where you are, do what is appropriate, and what will be, will be!"

❧ *The Angel* ❧

That winter, my life was very difficult—first of all, I was very tired: it was almost ten years since my husband had become a priest and we had moved to Peredelkino. I had worked as his driver practically from morning till night and would drive him before the crack of dawn to Moscow and back at an hour when all normal people had already dined, soaked in the bathtub, and were now sitting and peacefully watching television. Second of all, for some reason, I was chronically frozen: it was so cold outside that the rooms in our decrepit Peredelkino house didn't heat to higher than fifty-three degrees and the pipes constantly froze. For this reason, we always had to be on the watch—place plastic water bottles full of hot water around the pipes, keep the heated oven open, keep a thin stream of water running, watch the switched-on lights and make sure that they were on only one at a time, not all at once. In the worst case, what would happen is the electrical fuses wouldn't be able to handle it and our house would be cast into total darkness. And as we know, there is already more than enough darkness in December.

Then there was the Christmas Fast on top of everything . . .

In short, I was completely worn out and awaited Christmas with impatience: after that, there would be more daylight, then there would be Christmastide, then it wouldn't be long before Cheesefare Week, and then Pascha would come with the sun, warm breezes, and birds.

So, lamenting and struggling, I suddenly understood what it was that I wanted and what would be a true comfort to me: to see my guardian angel. After all, I mused, he had been given to me at baptism and has been with me all this time; he stays near me in my room, is secretly present in my car, but I don't feel him, or see him, or hear him.

This wish of mine became quite a temptation! Even people who have the least understanding of spiritual life know that if a sinner begins to see bodiless spirits, it only speaks of his completely darkened state. And if my wish were suddenly granted and I saw my angel, it would mean one thing—goodness gracious, it was time for me to seek treatment. But still, I wanted it so much, so much, as if he was my very favorite being, as if I was languishing in estrangement from him and awaited an impending reunion with him.

It was terrible—I couldn't pray for the Lord to reveal him to me, neither could I free myself from this insane wish. In short, it became an obsession.

Soon Christmas Eve would come. I thought, "I'll go to communion on Christmas Eve morning during the Liturgy of St Basil the Great, and then I will ask the priest's blessing to commune on Christmas Day as well." I felt depressed and was falling apart.

So that's what I did. I went to communion on Christmas Eve and also received permission for holy communion on Christmas Day. I immediately felt better. Music began to play in my soul, my internal candle was relit—I felt its warmth.

It was just too bad that on Christmas my husband was scheduled to serve not in his own Church of the Holy Martyr Tatiana, which my children and grandchildren attended on great holidays, but in the Church of Christ the Saviour. The little children would definitely not last through the night service there: there was nowhere for them to sit or curl up. Fine. Let my husband serve with the Patriarch; I would go where my children would be, both young and old. Then after the service, I would pick my husband up and take him home to Peredelkino.

I drove him to the Church of Christ the Saviour and returned to Peredelkino to take my daughter and granddaughter to the Church of the Holy Martyr Tatiana. I turned onto the highway, drove along the deserted road; the trees were all covered in frost, the drifting snow blew along the ground, I was in no rush and looked around in admiration. And here was the place where I had to slow down, turn on my left-hand turn signal, and press on the brakes, because I had to turn left and enter through the gates. As soon as I made the ninety-degree turn, I suddenly saw a solid black car that had just crossed the solid line and was aiming straight for me at a frightening speed; it was making directly for my driver-side door, and in those precious seconds, I understood that this was the end. This was it! But on the other hand, I had such peace in my soul, and I heard a voice—also very calm and articulate—distinctly say to me:

"Don't be afraid! Don't be afraid! Don't be afraid!"

Then, at the very last moment, the driver of the car flying straight at me swerved to the left, hit me slightly in the left side panel, after which he flew along the towering snowdrifts another five meters until he crashed into a metal fence: the fence sprang back and stopped the suicidal flight of the car, which still managed to make a hole in it. A man of northern ethnicity jumped out of this BMW and rushed to the back door. He threw it open and lifted out a child of about seven years old in his arms. He held him and held him up high, then the boy began to stir and stood on his feet.

We were all whole and unharmed.

But I continued to sit in my car, which after the impact had turned to the right and had buried itself nose first into a pile of frozen snow. A true miracle had just taken place, and my soul was celebrating while still unable to admit and recognize this. I was especially taken aback by the voice I had clearly heard: "Don't be afraid! Don't be afraid! Don't be afraid!" I felt that the speaker must have been near me at that very moment, right there with me.

Well, after that, there was a lot of hustle and bustle—I had to take my daughter and granddaughter to church in a taxi, wait for the police, ask someone to pick up my husband after the midnight service in Peredelkino, and so on and so forth. That's beside the point.

I understood that the Lord had heard my secret complaints and had comforted me with the assurance that my angel, even if he remained unseen by me, was ever by my side. I walked and he followed. I slept and he stayed over me. I wrote and he looked over my shoulder. I languished in loneliness, but I was with him. But also, I became angry and he heard my rebukes, my unfair and venomous words . . . and that meant that everything that happened to me was not in vain: someone took it seriously, and it was all counted and recorded in a book that would be read at the Final Judgment.

And so, it would seem that my problem was resolved in full. My requests were granted. Rejoice, sing, live! "See then that you walk circumspectly, not as fools, but as wise" (Eph 5:15). But in fact, it was not so!

Because in a considerably short time—it was already Great Lent, in March, the month of oxymorons, when seemingly disparate beginnings and ends meet, when scenes of childhood, youth, and our continuing years of maturity mysteriously come together in time; when the frailty and transience of life are especially distinctly felt, and with them, its boundlessness and transcendence; when both the inescapable approach of the Fateful Day and its ephemeral nature are keenly felt, the image of this unseen angel once again appeared as a desired and longed-for object. I walked among the black, shriveled, wicked snowbanks and tried to imagine where he was, but was still unable to find him. I searched for him as for my beloved, and couldn't find him! I called him, but heard no response!

It was all happening again: "A dark and foul flood of evil thoughts rises up within me, separating my mind from God. Do thou dry it up, O my intercessor!" My angel, my angel!

But soon Pascha arrived at last. Everything became exactly how I had dreamed it would in the beginning of winter. The sun shone out, the birds began to sing, the jasmine bush on my porch began to perk up.

Several days later, my husband's parishioner came to visit him at the Church of the Holy Martyr Tatiana, having just returned from the Holy Land, and brought him a Paschal gift.

It was a photograph of Isidor, Patriarch of Jerusalem, taken on Pascha, when he himself communed believers in his church. In the photo, he stood on the ambo with the chalice in his hands, carefully administering the Gifts with the communion spoon. Next to him, on the same side at the chalice, just slightly askew, was the silhouette of a snow-white angel with a burning candle in his hand.

∾ Heavenly Fire ∾

On August 18, I was in a tour bus headed for Mt Tabor. This was the high point of our pilgrimage: to ascend at midnight to the summit and there, on Tabor itself, in a Greek monastery on the Feast of the Transfiguration, to pray at the Divine Liturgy and receive communion. We pilgrims had already visited the Tomb of the Lord and the manger in Bethlehem, crossed the Judean desert, and visited the monasteries of St George the Hozebite and St Gerasimos of the Jordan, whom the lion had served. We even stopped at Cana of Galilee, where Christ had performed His first miracle. Now the other pilgrims were boisterously discussing our tour guide's program for the day.

"See, at eleven we meet at the foot of the mountain, then climb up. At twelve, vigil and Liturgy. At three in the morning, the descent of the grace-filled cloud."

"What? Does the grace-filled cloud descend on the dot?"

"Well, yes, since it's part of the program."

"Do you believe it?"

"I doubt it . . . I think it's some kind of trick. The Greeks are always up to something. How can you plan something that you have no control over in advance?"

It was quite a motley group of pilgrims, diverse in social status, age, and level of "churchliness." There were the pious, quiet ones, the "constantly prayerful," the "advanced in spirit"—they were always reading akathists on the bus out loud, and over a meal, all you ever heard was "but my priest told me this . . . ," "but my elder told me that . . . ," "but *my* spiritual father . . ."

But there were also the completely uninitiated. One of them was an old dried-out village crone with the angriest eyes, a pile of money, and a crutch, with which she beat her fellow travelers' legs at the slightest provocation. So, she didn't like that I took the front seat in the bus, which had a great view, and she drove me away. She didn't say a word, just scraped me off my seat and sat there herself. In Cana of Galilee, the tour leader took us to the gift shop, where the old crone couldn't make herself understood to the cashier, who spoke only Yiddish and English, so she asked me to translate. When the time came to pay for the gifts and she pulled out wads and wads of dollars from her purse, at which I couldn't help but stare in astonishment, she barked at me: "What are you goggling at?" and elbowed me in the side, covering her money with her hand. Finally, she let slip that her very rich son had sent her on this pilgrimage. And all who had the opportunity to feel her crutch became convinced that her son was not just a real businessman, but simply a jerk.

Another equally offbeat person on this pilgrimage was a man, around forty five, brawny and conspicuous, but a bit simple, and his unhealthy lifestyle had left traces on his already wrinkled face. He admitted that his wife had sent him on this pilgrimage in the hopes that maybe the trip would change him for the better. He was planning to go to the Tomb of the Lord in only a white undershirt, but our tour guide, a young hieromonk, asked him to come in more appropriate clothing, so he changed into a black T-shirt with a white skull on it.

"This is how I am. I like to make jokes," he explained good-naturedly, drawing his hand over the picture on his chest.

After we visited the Tomb of the Lord, at lunch, when our conversation began to encompass more exalted themes, he joined in.

"I believe in God, too!" he admitted. "And I know that He helps me."

The hieromonk joyfully nodded.

"It's very good that you feel that way."

"What's there to feel? I see it like I see you. One time I woke up—head pounding, throat dry—I'll die, I think, if I don't drink something. But there's nothing in the house, and my wife's at work and took all our money with her. Well, damn, I thought. So I left the house, started walking down the street, looking down at the ground the whole time—that's how rotten I felt!—and suddenly, right in front of me on the pavement—you won't believe it!—five hundred rubles! Well, Lord, I said, you didn't let me down. You understood! Glory to You! I walk into our store and I'm on my way to the usual section, and here my neighbor comes up to me—'Hey, Vovchik, I borrowed two hundred from you before. Here it is.' At that, I couldn't contain myself, and I said, 'Lord, what is this? Enough already! At this rate I'll get really drunk!' But I took the money. So, there you go! How can you not believe after that?"

Our hieromonk bashfully chuckled and lowered his eyes.

"I had another situation like that . . . I once met this floozy . . ."

At this, everyone stopped listening to him, and the meal was ending anyway.

Now he was sitting, sprawled over two seats at once, in the bus that was taking us to the mountain where the Lord had transfigured.

"Come on!" he said. "It's those Greeks, they make those clouds with chemicals! Maybe they shoot some kind of capsule with the fog in advance, and it explodes on a timer and descends in the form of a cloud. And they rake in the dough with the pilgrims . . . Well, I'm not going to buy anything in that monastery on purpose. I even heard how in one monastery the monks wiped the icons with sunflower oil, then told the old *babas*, 'Look! It's streaming myrrh!' Oh boy, how they started howling, and in came the cash!"

"That's all nonsense," the hieromonk said, upset. "That is impossible! Of course, that's just what they need—to slather icons with oil! Monks don't swindle people!"

"Quiet, quiet!" the akathist-singers shushed them.

So we arrived at the hotel. We dropped off our things there, rested for a bit, read the rule for holy communion, and it was already time to go to the foot of Mt Tabor. From there, we had the option either to walk up or take a taxi because buses didn't travel up the mountain.

While we rode, all the conversations were about the cloud. Everyone was worried—will it appear or won't it? Only I, for some reason, remained indifferent. It seemed to me much more important that we were celebrating the Feast of the Transfiguration at the actual spot where it happened "at that time," and continues to happen at the Liturgy, "now and ever and unto ages of ages." While I climbed the mountain, I understood that I didn't need anything else to bolster my faith: no streaming myrrh, no clouds.

The Greek monastery was already full of people. Other than the Greeks themselves, there were Orthodox Arabs, Jews, Serbs, Romanians, Georgians, and—of course—our Russians and Ukrainians:

"Khalia! Khalia! I saved a spot for you!"

Such a crowd could never fit inside the church, so the Greeks set up a portable altar, something like a veranda adjacent to the church's altar, so that people could stand in the courtyard of the monastery under the starry sky. I squirmed my way forward and stood right at the rails separating the improvised altar from the rest of the monastery. Here I stood the entire service, until the very end of the Eucharistic canon.

The moment that the priests began to commune in the altar, only a few meters from me, a whisper began to spread through the crowd.

"There it is! There it is! The cloud! Look up!"

I looked up and truly did see how, down on top of the cupola of the church, onto the very cross, a slate-grey, tight, tidy little cloud descended lower and lower down, until it covered the cross, then the cupola.

And the moment when the priest came out with the chalice to the makeshift ambo and exclaimed, "I believe, O Lord, and I confess!"[1] while all the people streamed toward him, the cloud seemed to pop, spreading itself all over the monastery and swaddling the people with its soft, moist, foggy breath. And immediately—here, there—flashes, flashes, lightning flashes! At first, I thought this was the effect of flashing cameras trying to capture this miraculous scene. But having received holy communion, I moved away, and looking more closely, I saw that the entire area, both in the skies and on the ground, was filled with these joyful, festal fiery birds, snakes, and lightning-bursts, dancing in zigzag patterns in the air and illuminating joyful faces and upraised hands that tried to touch or even grab that heavenly fire come down to earth. "I came to send fire on the earth, and how I wish it were already kindled!" (Lk 12:49).

And—joy, rejoicing, reverence, life, life!

The angry old crone saw me in the rejoicing crowd, and something kind, childlike, and simple-hearted glanced from within her. She grabbed my hand with her entire paw, and—filled with emotion—shook it. It must be that this fire has the same essence as that grace-filled fire that comes down to the Tomb of the Saviour on Pascha. It didn't burn, though it didn't light any candles, either . . .

All this continued until the very end of the Liturgy. Then the heavenly light began to weaken, and the fog began to dissipate. It was time to leave.

Together with my little old lady, we left through the gates and tried to hail a taxi to take us back to the foot of the mountain. Suddenly, we saw our man coming through the gates—the same one who had suspected the Greeks to be avaricious fakes.

"It's like I'm drunk!" he exclaimed. "Drunk, but I drank nothing! Take me with you."

And we took him into our taxi.

"That's it," he said. "I give up. They beat me!"

"Who beat you?"

"Who? Those Greeks, that's who! Everything seemed so natural, so accurate. God must arrange it all for them! And I almost caught one of the lightning flashes! I even left them twenty euros. 'I acknowledge it,' I told them. I believe, so to speak. Oh, mommy, mommy!" And he suddenly lifted a fist to his head and struck himself, hard, three times on the forehead.

"Well?" I asked myself—the same self who had been so smart before and had said things like, "Well, my faith doesn't really need these miracles!"

But that version of myself was no longer there. She wasn't answering. I didn't even try to find her.

❧ *Corfu* ❧

St Spyridon of Trimythous is considered to be the patron saint of Corfu, though he never lived there, being from Cyprus. In Cyprus, he carried out his Christian service, performing miracles and great feats of prayer and charity, but his relics were transferred to Corfu in 1456 from Muslim-occupied Constantinople, and since then he has physically remained there, defending and assisting anyone who turns to him in faith and prayer.

I love St Spyridon very much and have felt his love, protection, and help so many times that I actively feel his presence in my life: if you call out to him in prayer, he will respond. And now, here in Kerkyra, nearing his relics and standing before them waiting for them to be opened, I feel the joy of MEETING. For truly: "God is not the God of the dead, but of the living" (Mt 22:32). This is one of the most astonishing revelations of Christianity.

It is said that, in his time, he never allowed his island to be occupied by the Turks who seized increasingly more lands all around: in 1537, the Janissaries, preparing to take Corfu, laid a long-lasting siege on it. The downfall of Kerkyra, its main city, seemed inevitable, but its occupants turned in prayer to St Spyridon, and the Turks were annihilated, in spite of the fact that they far outnumbered the Christian defenders.

During 1386–1797, the Venetians became masters here, then the French came for a while, but in 1799, the Russian fleet, commanded by the great Admiral Ushakov (since then added to the ranks of the saints and especially revered here in Corfu), defeated them and liberated the island. Then in 1815, it fell under British control, and as a result, the English language remained behind: the locals have traditionally been fluent in it ever since.

The feeling remains that it was the Venetians, not the Turks, who set the tone here: the capitol of Corfu, Kerkyra, is reminiscent of Venice, Genoa, Padua, and Malta, while in the main Orthodox churches—that of St Spyridon and the cathedral in which the relics of St Theodora are kept—the church singing during the Greek service is accompanied by very careful, delicate organ playing that seems to mimic the human voice. All the Corfu folk melodies also speak of its distinctive character, its freedom from Muslim persecution and influence. And it seems like the ancient Phaeacians[1] have been living here since time immemorial, with their lack of bloodshed or catastrophic mingling of nationalities; they are a Christ-loving and peaceful people. It was they, the Phaeacians, led by their king, Alcinous, who welcomed the almost despairing and cunning Odysseus and brought him at last to his native Ithaca.

There are always Russian pilgrims in the Church of St Spyridon. They are instantly recognizable, even if they are quiet—not only by the women's headscarves, but by a certain triumph in their faces. After the services, when everyone has approached the cross and the priests have had their breakfast, the attendant opens the reliquary and a moleben is served before the relics. Approaching the reliquary, adorned all over with expressions of gratitude to the wonderworker for his blessings, you can see the entire body of the saint. There it is, in the flesh, filled with the Holy Spirit, immune to corruption for the past seventeen centuries.

The Greeks have a custom: if you want to thank the saint, order an image to be cast for you out of silver, or buy a symbolic representation, of the miracle committed by him. On their reliquaries and miracle-working icons hang silver carvings of legs, arms, eyes, heads, if not entire bodies; in other words, these are given in gratitude for a miraculous healing of that body part. There are also images of babies who were born by the prayers of the saint or the Mother of God. There are images of ships—these must be offerings for deliverance from storms at sea. St Spyridon's reliquary is similarly covered in such gifts.

I understand these expressions of gratitude very well, even if it looks strange from the outside: why, let's say, would the saint want these silver trinkets, or the Mother of God flowers? But the grateful heart so wants to share its gratitude, to touch the relic once again with all its soul—not with cries and prayerful groanings this time, but with an affected and gladdened heart: "Glory to You, O Lord! Thank you, St Spyridon, for hearing me and responding, for delivering me from impending misfortune!"

* * *

I also once felt an overpowering desire to give the Mother of God a golden cross on a chain in a burst of gratitude. To this day, it hangs on the Kazan Mother of God in the Moscow *metochion* of the Lavra. Here is the reason I donated my little cross to the icon of the Kazan Mother of God: My son Nika was going to be ordained a deacon and in preparation was collecting all the necessary documents. This proved to be a fairly labor-intensive matter. He had to present a document from the institute from which he graduated, from the military recruiting center, from the church where he served as an altar boy, from the Housing and Utility Management, from the psychological health center verifying that he is not a registered sex offender, from the narcotics unit stating that he is not a drug addict, and on top of all that, many other medical documents, down to blood and urine analyses.

It took him almost half a year to assemble all this—in part because he had lost his military service card and was forced to get it reissued in a torturous and dangerous manner: the military commissar, who had a shortage of recruits, went out of his way to seize my dear son, shave off his already deacon-length hair, and send him somewhere far away to march to songs on some training ground.

But finally he gathered all the necessary documents: he had stood in line for the analyses, he had spoken to the psychiatrist, he had even walked away from the military commissar in victory. My husband had already given him money both for his deacon's apparel, which cost a pretty penny, and for his life expenses in general—around three hundred dollars (a fair sum in those days). He packed all this away into his briefcase and set off for the Patriarchate. There he found that the bishop to whom he had to give all the documents was absent. It was his day off—a church feast day. So he took his little briefcase and went off with it on his own affairs—to church for the service, and then to sing at an event. He was at the time the conductor of a church choir, and his singers would often earn a little money by singing at events hosted by rich people. There he was paid one hundred dollars, fed, and released into the night. He put the money with the rest   into that briefcase—and stepped out onto the dark street, into a blizzard and blinding snowstorm. In his joy, he decided to take a taxi home. At that moment, a taxi drove up. Nika sat in the front and put the briefcase between himself and the driver. They drove off. Then the taxi driver said:

"Money first."

What was going on? He'd never heard that before.

Then the tax driver slammed on the breaks, bent over him, opened the door, and shoved Nika out right into the snowbank. The briefcase he held onto and kept in the car. He slammed the door and roared off.

So Nika remained without his documents, with no money, no certificates, no military card, not even his passport. A day passed, then another. The bishop asked my husband:

"Why isn't your son bringing me his documents? Did he change his mind?"

Nika, meanwhile, was at a total loss: his passport, fine, he could renew it, but his military card . . . that military commissar would lose his mind: he had just issued a new card for him a few days ago, and he just went off and lost it again. No, the bird wouldn't escape that cage a second time, the fish wouldn't evade those nets, the commissar wouldn't let him go again . . . and what about the medical tests! The psychiatrist! The Housing and Utility Office!

To be honest, all this just killed me: I knew that Nika wouldn't be able to get back what was stolen from him for a while. He would put it off, procrastinate, give in to all-too-typical temptation instead of overcoming it and showing his resolve; perhaps this was the Lord's way of testing his will to become a deacon? He might irritate the bishop with his delay—and they might refuse to ordain him at the Patriarchate. It sometimes happens that God offers a person something only once. Their life will lead them ELSEWHERE.

I walked around all gloomy and depressed, visiting all the Moscow churches, praying, asking on behalf of my son. In the meantime, two weeks had passed and the third had begun. It was already a hopeless matter. I came to the church of the *metochion* of the Lavra to the Kazan Icon of the Mother of God—a small icon hangs there to the side, a little lower than eye level, you must kneel before it and raise your head to look at it. I began to beseech Her and suddenly felt such consolation coming from Her, such love: She was alive, and heard me, and was responding.

I didn't even have a chance to unlock the door when I heard the telephone ringing long and insistently.

"Was it you who lost your documents? Are you interested?" asked the creaky voice of an old woman. "My son found them. He will call you."

And she hung up the phone.

Her son began to call me from pay phones to set up a meeting. He promised to return the briefcase for a hundred dollars. But each time that I was ready to rush off to our appointed place of meeting, he would call and change the address, as if he was afraid of someone. Finally, we agreed to meet at the Manege.[2] I jumped out of the car without gloves and began to run across the snow. Fifteen minutes later, a huge meathead appeared and knocked me on my shoulder:

"Come with me, don't turn around. If I notice someone tailing us, you can look for your briefcase in the dumpster."

"But where's the briefcase?" I asked.

His hands were empty.

"Like I said, walk."

I scampered off after him. He led me in silence—now and again slyly turning around and casting his gaze all around him with evil little eyes— along Bolshaya Nikitskaya Street, and then we turned the corner onto Nezhdanovaya Street (there is a church there with an icon of St Spyridon with a little piece of his relics), walked across a garden, and turned back. At Gazetny Pereulok, he stopped:

"It doesn't look like we have a tail. Money first. A hundred bucks."

"Only in exchange for the briefcase," I insisted. My naked hands had frozen in the cold air, my lips wouldn't move.

"I make the conditions here. I always did it that way and everyone was willing. If you don't give me the money—I'll leave and you can find your briefcase yourself."

I handed him the bill with shaking, disobedient hands. He put it in his pocket.

"Go to Aleksandrovsky Garden.[3] There a person will approach you and give you the briefcase."

"What person? Where is my guarantee that he'll give it to me?"

"I told you: everyone was always happy with my way. Well, as you like, I'm going," and he began to walk in the direction of Tverskaya.

I rushed off to Aleksandrovsky Garden, greedily looking into people's faces. In twenty minutes, a woman with the pleasant face of a schoolteacher came up to me and handed me a bag in which lay the briefcase.

"I have to make sure that everything is there," I muttered. "It could be empty."

She shrugged her shoulders and headed for the metro.

"Wait," I said.

But she ran away, and I didn't chase her.

Inside the briefcase, I found all the documents—the passport, the military card, the urine analysis. The only thing missing was the money for the deacon's equipment, for living expenses, and what my singer-son had earned that terrible night.

A month and a half later, he stood on the solea with an orarion, waving his hand lightly in the air and singing the Creed along with the choir.

That was when I offered the Mother of God that little golden cross.

* * *

Some wonderful, intelligent Russian people, having earned their living not through scheming, but through skill and righteous labor, had built a wonderful house on a mountaintop here in Corfu, twenty-five kilometers from Kerkyra, in a place called Agios Stefanos; they invited my husband and me to stay there.

Whenever I leave my house and set out on some travels to distant shores, I always feel a certain discomfort, as if I were leaving my loved ones to fight alone on the front lines under fire and shrapnel, while I, leaving behind the battle lines, run away and lie low in a deep bunker—so chaotic, anxious, and difficult is ordinary Moscow life. At first, having escaped from its stronghold, I feel lost and look back with considerable guilt: I didn't finish doing this, I promised to do that, but didn't do it—I have so many personal and professional (literary) debts. Like Gulliver, I feel ensnared by thousands of invisible Lilliputian threads tied to stakes beaten into the ground: any movement is difficult. And yet, the idleness of the traveler almost seems criminal to me.

Then I begin to convince myself, as if I was defending myself in front of someone, that a person should, after all, extract themselves from the turbulent current of everyday existence, to estrange themselves from it, shifting his perspective; for the eye, seeing the "usual," glazes over, and stops distinguishing the primary from the secondary, the vital from the unnecessary. And in general, in order to understand your own, you need to discover the foreign. On some turns of their earthly path, a person must absolutely stop and catch their breath. Maybe they must even finish taking in everything that they have experienced in their haste, think through everything that they have accomplished thoughtlessly and meaninglessly—on impulse and instinct—and thoroughly examine the whirlwind of events that had burst upon them and had as yet remained unrecognized and unnamed, stuck in the depth of their subconscious. Maybe they must even reach their internal and true self, swimming their way through that flurry of indistinct images, that sea teeming with creatures, and emerge at the last, having reached their firm shore. So traveling is also a labor, I try to assure myself, as if I was defending myself from someone's rebukes. Moreover, I have an editing commission from the *Journal*—to write twelve short stories about love. So I am, after all, not idle but working. Isn't it work to draw out short stories from the dull current of the days? It's not simple to expostulate about love, is it?

Then, examining the surroundings from my high mountaintop, I suddenly stop hearing that scolding internal assailant as well as his co-interrogator, both of whom are capable of poisoning your life with such reflections. I simply say, "Hallelujah! Rejoice, my soul, enjoy, thank the Creator!" And I slowly begin to feel my interior becoming like my exterior—like Corfu, with its shining sky and glistening sea—I feel my exterior, that irresistible beauty of God's world, taking over and defeating the fragmented and damaged landscape inside.

It seems obvious to me that many issues within our national character can be explained by the terrain and climate. For seven months of the year, it's a low, leaden sky, which is never even visible in big cities, depressingly bitter cold, unpredictable torrents of rain, poor weather, nightfall, darkness, gloom. And then, we have those endless expanses: fields, meadows, woodlands, steppes. Nothing to rest your eyes on. You shrink internally and curl up, trying to preserve any warmth, exerting yourself until the point of exhaustion, like the children in the painting of the *Peredvizhnik* painter Perov (one of The Wanderers), dragging their terrible load behind them in the snow. Everything is achieved through heroic effort, labor, and struggle. There comes a point when the Russian soul becomes torn; it aches and is metaphysically fatigued. You just want to sit in a corner, focus on one immovable thought and drink something hot in order to warm up and soften your soul, hardened by trials.

* * *

The island is in itself a symbol: a certain reserved expanse, cut off from the rest of the world and open to the sky, a microcosm, like a human soul fitting the entire world within itself.

Here, on Corfu, you have everything: mountains grown over with olive trees and ravines, heights and abysses, rivers and little lakes, sand and rock, exotic birds and hedgehogs, poisonous snakes, greedy wasps, magnificent bougainvillea blooming everywhere, and rhododendrons. It's just like the soul, with its chasms and heights, dark underground rivers and daybreaks, its creeping creatures and its glorious blooms.

How amazing: I read somewhere that all this olive grandeur is manmade. Supposedly, this was all naked cliffs, but the Greeks put up terracing and planted forests of olive trees.

But that is difficult to believe: first of all, there is no visible terracing, though there are trees. Second of all, they are everywhere—in almost every corner of the island, even the unpopulated ones, and even on the inaccessible cliffs. Third of all, there are four million trees here, and only a hundred thousand residents.

Corfu is not large in size: sixty kilometers in length and twenty-five in width, and even that is at the widest point in the north. To the south it narrows, eventually jutting sharply into the sea. But its roads all weave in and out of the mountains, forming a multifaceted serpentine pattern; sometimes they clamber upward, sometimes they descend to the very sea, so you can drive on them slowly and for a very long time—sometimes it's difficult to pass an oncoming bus or impossible to pass a car ahead of you crawling at a snail's pace, so you're forced to plod along behind it at the speed of a horse pulling a cart, but it is exactly that slow pace that allows even me, sitting at the wheel, to examine the scenes swimming past me to my heart's content.

Look on, soul, look on, dear, be curious, get your fill of joy, respond with love, become a pure "hallelujah!"

* * *

Not only did St Spyridon save Corfu from non-Christian adversaries, but he also twice stopped an epidemic of the plague, saved the residents from earthquakes, droughts, and hunger, cured mortal diseases, and even— this, too, happened—resurrected people from the dead. Perhaps the miracle of the four million olive trees also occurred not without his participation? Over in that direction, the Albanians under Enver Hoxha tried to build terraces on their cliffs and plant vineyards;[4] they even invited the Chinese as advisers. But nothing came of it: the vineyards dried up, and nothing was left but the hideously dug-up cliffs.

Or perhaps that happened in Albania because it was there, when it was still called Illyria,[5] that the wicked Arius was sent into exile after the condemnation of his heresy at the Council? Arius was there, and here we have Spyridon.

The day after visiting St Spyridon in Kerkyra, we went to examine the coast. It's all carved into coves, each one different from the last. At the foot of the hill on which we were staying, it's rocky, but if you drive farther south of the island and then turn to the east, there are sandy beaches. The Ionian Sea is there, completely calm. But if you drive a little farther and curve around the jutting end of the island, you will reach the tempestuous Adriatic Sea. The waves are such that you can't get into the water—they curve round, knocking you off your feet, and drag you out to sea. But if you continue your travels and cross over the northern part from east to west, and then turn to the south, you will again find the Ionian Sea, without any waves. I don't understand how this can be. My husband laid the map out onto his lap and guided me along every fork in the road, and I drove, trying to remember the magical names of the towns and villages—Kassiopi, Kalamaki, Perithia, Acharavi, Agios Spyridonos, Roda, Sidari, Peroulades. There—we've just covered the entire north.

Everything was as it should be—my husband showed me the way, and I obediently drove the car. A nice woman who had married relatively late, but very happily, recently told me:

"We are so happy in our family because you told me a secret and I took your advice."

"What secret?" I said, interested. "I don't even remember what I told you."

"When I was getting married, you told me that the most important secret to marital happiness is preserving the cult of the husband. I've been following your advice religiously, and see how good everything is between us!"

* * *

Some bird was constantly rapping the reflective window of the villa where we were staying: knock-knock-knock. We would open the door and look out: who's that knocking? We would even ask, who's there? And that bird would just keep tapping—knock-knock-knock—from the morning on. One time, having difficulty distinguishing between truth and reflective reality, it crashed into the glass and bounced back, then it sat immobile for a long time on the ground, not understanding anything, not realizing . . . and only when my husband touched it in order to pick it up and put it onto the grass did it awkwardly flap its wings and crookedly fly off several steps away.

There are so many possibilities for symbolic interpretation and edification here! Aren't we the same with our neurotic psychological projections? We fly at our own reflections in others and crash, bouncing back . . .

When the bird was trying to get into our house, pecking with its beak, I always thought: why does folk tradition state that a bird flying into the house is a sign of death? And I would carefully close the glass door to stop it from finding its way in after all.

* * *

To this day, there are legends about St Spyridon as if he were actually present in his church, turning his head in the direction of the holy altar during the Liturgy, and that he walks at night: during the frequent changing of his vestments, the soles of his slippers are discovered to be worn through. In addition, there are many personal testimonies of how he healed the incurably ill, notifying them of the impending miracle with his appearance.

And so, the villa where we were allowed to live for a while is located on the crest of a forested mountain, from which you can see the unbelievably and seemingly unnaturally blue sea, and in the distance—Albania with its bald cliffs. We observed its shores through a telescope and saw nothing but deserted, naked shores by day and total darkness by night. It was as if external darkness reigned there, while here, on Corfu, dwelt God's world: clear, powerful stars of enormous size, a blinding moon, a silvery sea, and the living greenery of the olive groves.

* * *

Time and again on Russian estates you come across the German manager, the English housemaid, and the Greek gardener, and I like that. Why not? The German here is named Werner. He is seventy years old. He arrived in Corfu as a student, rented a house from a Greek family, where a little girl was growing up, and he waited for her to become an adult. Finally he reached that day, married her, spent his entire life there, and now checks the plumbing, pool water, and air conditioning for the Russians; his free time he spends walking around Kassiopi with his wife, now an older woman, standing on the pier, squinting at the sun, sitting on a bench at the shore near the Three Brothers tavern, and watching the fishermen carry nets from ship to shore filled with various fish and sea monsters. Werner's face is stamped with total bliss and goodwill toward life.

The housemaid is called Caitlin; she is a tall, beautiful woman with a reddish tan and light blue eyes. She assiduously scrubs the white floor with her mop, and sometimes after her departure, you're scared to step on it. I also saw her in Kassiopi: she was sitting on the backseat of a motorcycle, gently embracing the elderly Greek sitting in front of her, and had even laid her cheek against his back.

As for the gardener, I don't even know his name: he turns the sprinklers on in the garden, mows the grass, trims the roses, and leaving suddenly, throws a sloppy, chewed up cigarette butt onto the road paved with smart-looking, neat stones. My husband thinks that his relationship with the owners isn't the best: his cigarette butt is an image of terrible dissonance in this place, like a challenge to the world order.

We count the days on our fingers and realize that today must be, thirteen days before ours, the Greek Church's celebration of the Birth of the Mother of God: a helicopter with a banner flies overhead: "Alithos Anesti! Truly Christ is Risen!"

* * *

A person with a cold is cold everywhere, but a healthy person loves the wind gusts, the storms, the pouring rain. It is so sweet to stand on the terrace during a thunderstorm—to watch the lightning and listen to the thunder. The olive tree rustles its leaves in the bustling wind, almost murmuring, then oh, how it begins to rhapsodize, a veritable Pythia . . .

In my early childhood, when my parents would send me to the children's camp in Maleevka for the summer, I loved to hear the sounds of the night thunder. I would climb out of bed, come up to the window, and peer into the darkness. I stood in celebratory, mystical terror of the animation of the dark forces of nature. I was a little pagan, looking through the crack at the imbibing of the feasting gods.

Interesting: how did Werner recognize his future wife in the little Greek girl?

He watched how she grew—centimeter by centimeter—how she matured, contemplating her blossoming, and then observed her in the medley of people walking on the shore, cared for her on the mountain paths, walked with her among the olive groves.

Anyway, before our departure for Corfu, I was asked to write twelve short stories about love for the *Journal* illustrating the words of the Apostle Paul: "Love suffers long and is kind; love does not envy; love does not parade itself, is not puffed up; does not behave rudely, does not seek its own, is not provoked, thinks no evil; does not rejoice in iniquity, but rejoices in the truth; bears all things, believes all things, hopes all things, endures all things." (1 Cor 13:4–13:7). Thinking about these stories, I observe Werner circling the house, checking the pipes, and standing over the blue pool for a long time— the swallows fly above him, trying to dip into the water with their wings and not fearing Werner at all.

If marriages are made in heaven, then the Lord, naturally, gives us hints: there he is, your intended! There she is—your fated bride, your wife.

I had a premonition like that. My parents also had that knowledge, or rather that foreknowledge.

* * *

The English housemaid, Caitlin, coughs as she mops the floor. Yesterday, like me, she stood on the terrace for a long time during the thunderstorm and watched the lightning split the sky and the waves dash onto the coastal cliffs. The thunder promised something, portended something. In childhood it was clear what: love. In adolescence also, it was love and creative work. In youth, it was creative work and love. And later, in the twilight years? I don't know, maybe eternal life. The dead stand before you in your thoughts as if they were alive, and there is no proof that they are no longer present. On the contrary, they appear more vividly for some reason, more animated than they were in life . . .

The thunderstorm reveals something similar, having the night before overturned the sea, untied all the boats from the piers, and cast an enormous fish out of the sea.

The Greek gardener arrives in a large red Toyota and immediately turns on the sprinklers distributed throughout the garden by pressing some buttons on the panel with his finger. The sprinklers twist and turn, spouting out water, and it seems as if the entire garden is laughing. The gardener watches, standing right next to the terrace. There the table is already set, and the Russians stand, facing east, reading a prayer before their meal. The Greek understands that they are reading the "Our Father." He nods in time with the words. In a few days, his son will be married, and there will be a big wedding.

I picked up his daily cigarette butt from the ground in his sight in admonition, and he suddenly became dismayed and began to talk, as if defending himself. His son was getting married, but his daughter can't seem to find her match. She's a good girl, with good qualities, smart. I had seen her—they had come here together the day before the thunderstorm. Her face was correctly proportioned, her eyes big and expressive, but in spite of this, she was unattractive. At first it seems that it's because of an unflattering hairstyle, poor posture, the wrong clothes. Her relatives think: we'll just style her hair the right way, put a rose in it, pull back her shoulders, straighten her back, fix her gait, dress her in a red dress that would stand out in the light of day, make her high heels click. We'll raise up the corners of her mouth to make a smile, we'll fill her eyes somehow with fire and light. "Elpida, why don't we make a beauty out of you?" But she just slouches even more and moves her brows together more threateningly . . .

The gardener had probably thrown down that cigarette butt out of pure vexation, automatically, remembering his daughter and shaking his head, and there was nothing in that gesture against the owners of the house.

* * *

When I was still a student in the tenth grade, this is what happened to me. I became ill with pneumonia and was sent to get an X-ray at the Literature Foundation's clinic. It was winter, and I dressed up warmly, wrapped myself up in a scarf, and set out early. In the clinic it was dark and empty. Then, coming out of the X-ray room and walking along the darkened, gloomy corridor to the coatroom, I noticed someone's silhouette at the end of the hallway. And in that very moment I heard an invisible voice right next to my right ear (or rather: the voice sounded off to my right): "This man will be your husband." This shocked me so much that I headed straight for that silhouette in order to better examine it, but because I'm nearsighted, I had to come fairly close to him, and I saw a wonderful-looking young man, tall, very, very thin, even frail-looking, with a face that reminded me of a young Pasternak.[6] I even called him that in my thoughts: the young Pasternak. But what was I supposed to do next? I couldn't just walk up to that surprising and wonderful stranger and tell him that he was going to be my husband, or even offer to get acquainted. So I stood and stood near him, waiting to see if perhaps he would strike up a conversation with me himself; then, putting on my coat, I slowly made my way home with the faint hope: maybe he would catch up with me?

After that, I began to look for him. Since he was being treated at the Literature Foundation, he was either a writer or the son of a writer—that much I realized. So I began to get acquainted with the sons of writers, the adult sons of my father's friends. It's amazing that even if I didn't exactly hit my target, I kept hitting precisely around it; as if while playing Battleship, I would hit all the empty spots on the grid around the ship: these sons, as it later turned out, were acquainted with the mysterious "young Pasternak," and one of them was even his friend.

Meanwhile, a year and a half passed, and I was admitted to the Literature Institute. That year, the first of that September was a Saturday, which was already at that time a day off for all the Literature Institute students except the first-years. It was even called "a day for free writing." So for this reason, the first of September was only attended by first-year students.

At first, I really didn't like it there: it was boring, tedious, hopeless some-how—so much so that I wanted to take my documents right then and there and go home. On the third of September, rain came down hard; autumn had arrived, so I didn't want to go the institute at all. In spite of the rain, all the students, of whom there were now many, crowded into the narrow corridors of Herzen House and looked for the sheets with their schedules; and here, in the crush and squeeze of the crowd, I suddenly saw HIM, that "young Pasternak"; I recognized him from the back. He was standing with a long umbrella, facing the window. I came up to him and looked into his face. He merely threw his glance over me, as if some unnecessary object was standing before him, not worthy of his attention, but I remembered well what had been said to me in the dark corridor that early winter day.

And what then? Nothing. Only at the end of the academic year, on the eve of our exams, did I gather the courage to call him and ask him to share his notes for the exam. Then summer came, and everyone went their sepa-rate ways for vacation. Then the following year began, but it didn't bring me anything either from the man who was promised to me as my husband in the corridor of the dark clinic, except a "Hi" or "Hello" in passing.

At the institute, I studied and worked too hard: first of all, I was part of the translation department; in addition to the other subjects, I was learning French and Hungarian. Second of all, I wrote a lot at night and sometimes, still in the throes of the night's inspiration, I would get up from my desk and go straight to lecture. In the evenings, I would go to all kinds of poets' get-togethers, poetry evenings, etc. My parents were very worried about me and decided to send me to Gagra, to a writer's house that was now vacant due to the winter season. The owners tried to fill it up with coalminers, but even they weren't too keen to be there. To kill the boredom somehow, they would go to dances in the evenings that were organized right in the dining room. What's more, the women danced with other women, and the men with other men.

Once, sitting on my balcony, which looked out onto the sea, and watching the crimson sun slowly bending downwards, I suddenly had a strange feeling—I was completely seized with the decision to immediately, that very moment, call my promised future husband. This expression of will was so irrational that I doubted myself: was it coming from me? What's more, I didn't know the phone number by heart—it was written down somewhere back in Moscow, and I had already called him once about the notes. And if this didn't sound comical enough, I would describe it this way: Some unseen power turned me around and dragged me to the nearest telephone office. But that's the thing, it all happened exactly that way. I went out into the snow-driven twilight, trying not to think any of it through and not to doubt, but simply to obey. I even forced myself not to think about the fact that I would put in the coins for the phone call (I think it was fifteen kopeks), and then what number would I dial? No, I just went to the phone, picked it up, and allowed my hand to dial the buttons on its own, at random.

And he answered the phone.

"Hello," he said happily. "Where did you disappear? I'm sitting here and waiting for you to call. Come see me tomorrow."

"I'll be there," I answered just as happily, standing in a phone booth in the telephone office in Gagra.

In half an hour, all my things were stuffed into my suitcase; in an hour, I was sitting down in the commuter train, the next one leaving for Adler. Two hours later, I was standing in front of the airport supervisor, begging him to give me a seat on the next plane to Moscow.

The next evening, as agreed, I went to his house, and shaking from nervousness, tried to speak only of beautiful and exalted things—all the more because I had seen a book lying open on my companion's desk with the cover facing up. On it was written: *Schelling. System of Transcendental Idealism.* This system was exactly where I was yearning to be.

* * *

There were a few old men and women in church on Sunday in Kassiopi. The young people began to appear with their children toward the end of Liturgy. Two old men and several boys and girls partook of holy communion. By the end of liturgy, the church was full. As it turned out, those people were waiting for a *panikhida*.[7] Then they passed out some food *in memoriam* to everyone in the churchyard: it all resembled a traditional family event. There was a certain natural reverence, not a result of personal experience, perhaps, not achieved through personal struggle, but rather inherited: "this is our tradition," with no trace of crisis or battle. You could feel that the churches had never been closed on Corfu, the icons never destroyed, the church property never taken by force, the priests never shot, belief never forbidden, faith never punished by death . . . and that faith had become interwoven with life, a manner of living, one with the direction of the soul. "God is everywhere."

This aspect of the Greek faith, or shall we say this "national expression of Orthodoxy," is what appeals to the owner of our villa: it's free of fits and seizures. "You will always recognize our people in a Greek church," she says. "They're always frantically crossing themselves and crashing onto their knees before the altar on a Sunday. Even though that's not allowed on a Sunday, it's unnecessary. It's like they want to be more pious than the Church itself, but the Greeks pray naturally, without that neophyte violence of emotion."

I stay silent. I really don't want to fall into judgment here even in the abstract. It's true that the Greeks come to church as if to their own home: they simply walk onto the solea during Liturgy and venerate the iconostasis, then they sit down on the chairs scattered throughout the church in rows, getting up only during the most important parts of the service. It's not tedious that way, and your legs don't hurt . . . and truly, this does speak of a certain natural manner: our grandfathers prayed that way, our fathers, and now we, it's our tradition, it's in our DNA, our religion is hereditary, our faith is national, it's in our subconscious—what's the problem? It's just strange that they don't partake of holy communion on Sundays, as we do—"with fear and trembling"—and the fear arises somewhere in the depths of your soul that this "natural Christianity" may be interwoven on the inside with the strong threads of paganism, especially when every olive tree rhapsodizes like a sibyl.

* * *

When we leave the house, we don't lock the door. "It's absolutely safe here, no one here would steal," our hostess told us before her departure.

On principle, my husband also doesn't want me to lock the car when we leave it somewhere, pointedly leaving the window open: "No one's going to take anything."

* * *

There is an answer to every question in holy Scripture, though there may not be an answer to a concrete question: what should I, someone of no particular importance, do right now, at this time? The human free will is boundless, but simultaneously limited by a desire to always follow God's will, which is often incomprehensible.

An abbot of my acquaintance once said: "If you don't know how to act, just say with all your heart: 'Lord, I love You! Glory to You!'"

* * *

I had a dream about my late father and mother. They were sitting in a room with a glass wall and looking through it into the neighboring room. My husband and I were living there. In other words, they could SEE us.

When I woke up, I took my notebook and started to—no, not write a poem, but simply—scribble. Old Kirsanov, to whom I would bring my poems at seventeen years old, would say to me: scribble more. So I scribbled.

> It's a pity,
> I can't bring my ancestors back to life—
> to dine with me
> under the full moon.
> I can't move them into a little bast[8] house
> over the sea on the mountain
> in a Greek September.
> So do they come to me here in my dreams:
> What isn't a dream—they
> foretell my days.
> What isn't a dream—they assure me that the shores will hold,
> the roads, the paths,
> even the darkness, they say, has its bounds:
> Hereto, but further—stop.
> They affirm: hold fast to the heavenly firmament,

like this somehow.
They show me how.
I say: this heavenly firmament is high,
my hand just slips through.
There is nothing to hold on to—
to what can the hands hold fast
the hands that grow out of me?
When from the plumate expanse—thence—
in spite of
all the earthly laws—
two unseen hands
will reach forth, holding me suspended high, then—
you will see how firm is my step.

I keep thinking about my assignment from the *Journal*: stories about love. Nothing comes into my head except the story of my parents, even though it goes along other lines and is in itself not at all about love, but about the workings of divine providence.

In December 1941, my then-sixteen-year-old father was riding on a train from Moscow with his fellow cadets from the Artillery Institute in Tomsk. In the same car, my grandmother was accompanying her daughters after evacuation[9] —my eleven-year-old mother and my nine-year-old aunt, Lena. They were cold and frightened, but the young cadets, occupying the same compartment, were drinking, joking around, and smoking. They were speaking about poetry and reciting poems. My mother—an intelligent girl—also recited something. Then she got a note from one of the young men. He had scribbled on a newspaper clipping with a pencil: "When I come back in victory, you will be my wife." My mother also took a pencil and wrote in block letters: "Fool." With that, she gave the paper back to the cadet.

In the meantime, it was time for bed. It was cold in the third-class car, which was full of people, no room to swing a cat. In short—my grandmother laid Lena down in her felt boots, with her feet toward the aisle, and when they woke up, they discovered that someone had stolen the girl's boots during the night. Then my grandmother cut off the sleeves of her fur coat, sewed them together, and put them on Lena's feet.

Fourteen years later, my father—now a veteran who had served at the front, a war invalid, a young poet, and a student of the Literature Institute— sat peacefully at home with his wife and mother-in-law. They ate dinner and told each other stories from the war. Papa remembered how he was on his way to the institute, and in his car, a sleeping girl's felt boots had been stolen, and then, in order to shod her bare feet, her mother had cut the sleeves off her coat. My grandmother's face changed, she looked at him with an entirely new expression, and gasped softly. She began to describe those cadets who had joked and read poems; then it was my father who looked at her strangely, got up quietly, began to rummage around, and took out a tiny piece of paper—a newspaper clipping. He unfolded it and handed it to his young wife. On it she read: "When I come back in victory, you will be my wife."

* * *

Not in vain did the Apostle Paul mostly take the apophatic route in his definition of love's expression: according to him, "love does not envy; love does not parade itself, is not puffed up; does not behave rudely, does not seek its own, is not provoked, thinks no evil; does not rejoice in iniquity, but rejoices in the truth" (1 Cor 13:4–6). In other words, it keeps its distance from any spiritual impurity, it flees the endless provocations of self-love, it leans away from temptations as from a thorn prickling and poisoning the soul. It is free from passions that strip the man of his youth, and in this way it remains outside of them, against them, in spite of them, in defiance of them. As for its actions, it is merely written that it "suffers long," and in this action it is sooner directed internally, oriented toward its own depth, as well as in the fact that it "bears all things."

Christ said: "By your patience possess your souls" (Lk 21:19). Love, tried by patience, does indeed gather together the scattered forces of the heart, and centers them in itself, converting the varying energies into a single will of a ruling Eros transformed. This rule is so great that even the powerful and natural instinct of self-preservation gives way before it, and a sacrifice brought to it in love is sweet and desirable to the soul. "Greater love has no one than this, than to lay down one's life for his friends" (Jn 15:13).

This love is commanded to us by the Lord and is called by Him "My commandment": "This is My commandment, that you love one another as I have loved you" (Jn 15:12). "Abide in my love" (Jn 15:9). "By this all will know that you are My disciples, if you have love for one another" (Jn 13:35). Two of the very first commandments begin with "love." Apostle John witnessed that "God is love" (1 Jn 4:8). The Holy Gospel in its entirety is an annunciation of love by Love. In essence, it is all about love; love that is new life in Christ!

Love "does not rejoice in iniquity, but rejoices in the truth; bears all things, believes all things, hopes all things, endures all things" (1 Cor 13:6–7).

* * *

The mistress of the villa where we were staying has two children. Not too long ago, my Georgian friend, Karinka, worked for her as a nanny. Karinka had a university degree in philology, but was forced by circumstances to become a nanny, though she was also happy when I referred her there.

I've known Karinka and her husband, Shalvah, since I was seventeen years old. They had just gotten married when I came to Tbilisi to try my literary hand at translating the Georgian poets. Soon they gave birth to a brilliant little girl, Suliko. She studied music from age three, was taken to a music school at five, and was already playing as a soloist at nine: she played the piano with an adult Georgian symphony orchestra and even went on tour. Shalvah worked for several years as a diplomat in an African country, where they had a house with a pool and a staff: they had a maid, a chauffeur, and a gardener. Then they wanted to go back home, and they returned to Georgia in 1989.

Soon, fleeing the hardships of war, they moved to Moscow. They moved a lot, renting places to live. They tried to sell their Tbilisi condos: two fabulous apartments in the best neighborhoods of Tbilisi. For that money at the time you could only buy a small, one-bedroom apartment in Mariino. Suliko rushed into a marriage—for love, naturally. In a year, having given birth to a little son, she and her husband divorced and she abandoned music completely.

At that point, Shalvah began an intense love affair on the side and soon left Karinka. She remained in a foreign city with no husband, no house, no work, no money, a divorced daughter, and a grandson in her arms. That's when she went to work as a nanny for these well-off people. They grew to love her so much that they almost considered her a part of the family. But after working there for several years, she began to slack off. Some straw broke the camel's back—either she didn't like the tone in her employer's voice; or she remembered that she had graduated from the school of philology at Tbilisi University; that she was the daughter of a writer and had been the wife of a diplomat; that she had at one time had her own luxurious house; that her daughter had been a wunderkind, for whom worldwide fame had been predicted, but who had instead became a single mother with sad eyes and had found a job—and even that with difficulty —in some office selling cotton, and was now flying to Kazakhstan.

Looking at Karinka, I thought: could I, finding myself in a similar situation, in a foreign country, among strange people, have simply forgotten myself and gone to work as a nanny or a cleaner? I don't know; probably, for the sake of feeding my children . . . I was, after all, sent by the ministry of propaganda to perform God knows where; I did read my poetry at both factory residence halls and Red Corners. The female warden would walk in, turn off the running television with authority—interrupting the showing of *The Seventeen Moments of Spring* or an Italian miniseries about Captain Cattani and causing a wave of strong dislike and protests from the poor temporary residence workers huddled together around the television screen—and present me to be picked apart by them, prefacing my performance with an edifying speech about the importance of cultural enlightenment and growth. And then, shrinking inside from bitterness, disappointment, shame, and the general absurdity of the whole situation, I would read my poetry to them. For this mockery of both them and myself, I would be paid seven-and-a-half or, if the performance took place in the region around Moscow, eleven rubles. And what of it: I had two tiny children at the time, my husband had just graduated from the Literature Institute, he couldn't find a job anywhere because he was not a member of the Komsomol, his articles weren't being published—on the contrary, they would be returned, for example, by *Literary Matters*, with a severe rejection or the question, written in red pencil in the margins: "What about your view of Maxist-Leninist ideology?" No, it is sweet to sacrifice yourself in a single moment, to flare up and be burned down, but it is unbearably difficult—slowly and patiently—to carry out your ordeal of love day after day, day after day.

* * *

This Sunday, we set out a little earlier in the morning than usual to Kerkyra to Liturgy at the cathedral with the relics of the holy Empress Theodora. Her relics had also been transferred from Constantinople during its occupation and pillaging. Here also, as at the Church of St Spyridon, the church singing was accompanied by an organ, and it was so beautiful that after the service, during the moleben before the relics of the holy empress, at which many Greeks had gathered with gallant military deportment, in white sailor's uniform jackets, I went to look for a recording of the local liturgy in the church stores of Kerkyra. I couldn't find one anywhere, until I was sold the single existing—and last remaining—CD at a small shop for ten euros. It's not like I now always wanted to pray to the sound of an organ; no, I simply wanted to be able to, from time to time, occasionally, at some point, on a dark winter Moscow evening, listen to those Corfu prayers, and be carried back in my soul's flight to the churches of the holy empress and the saint.

This time, we decided to cross the island across its middle in order to reach the coast opposite to ours—the western coast. There, in Angelokastro, an impenetrable medieval fortress still overlooks a mountain, and a little further south, in Paleokastritsa, there is a monastery with a miracle-working Icon of the Inexhaustible Cup. Here and there, along the narrow winding road, we came across settlements with amazing pink houses covered with climbing ivies and vines, and welcoming travelers with the inevitable scarlet bougainvillea. Enormous palm trees, lemon trees covered in little yellow lemons, and enormous cacti with succulent orange pear-like fruits grew there. We even stopped at one such untended cactus and picked several fruits. They reminded us of both figs and kiwis. Splendor and tranquility reigned all around. The local Greeks, if we even met any, rode around on bicycles and talked in tavernas over glasses of good local wine and unassuming snacks of tzatziki, saganaki, moussaka, or even lamb kleftiko. Nowhere did it feel like there had ever been battles waged here over the harvest or crops. All that existed was the lovely September day, the high and unreachable sky, the good life; why not refresh yourself in the taverna in between jobs in the company of neighbors, or relatives, or friends, and discuss the latest news?

The monastery in Paleokastritsa was open and active. Fifteen monks lived there, so during the day, when there were no services, it was closed to the public. They only opened it before the Liturgy and the evening service. We waited for the proper time and approached the miracle-working icon of the Mother of God, hung on all sides with the traditional silver offerings.

I remembered one of our friends—a priest who served in a church outside Moscow consecrated in honor of the Icon of the Inexhaustible Cup. There were always a lot of people there, especially women who came to order a moleben for their alcoholic husbands. They would pray fervently: "Lord, help my husband to give up drinking," and cry bitter-bitter tears. One such woman—among those praying and weeping—suddenly came up to the aforementioned priest with the following claim:

"I came here last Sunday and ordered a moleben with the blessing of holy water for my Vaska to stop getting drunk. Well, he did stop—he had an epileptic seizure and is now lying completely paralyzed, he can't lift a finger. What are these methods of yours? I never agreed to that. It would be better to make everything like it was before. It would be better for him to drink than to lie around inert. Father, make it like it was before." "You do not know what you ask" (Mk 10:38).

* * *

As for my friends, Tata and Marik, the process of miraculous healing from alcoholism took place less painfully. Marik was a bohemian—emotional, a poet. He drank every day—to alleviate stress, to overcome depression, to cheer up a little. In the morning, he would drink a little beer, then on his way to work at the *Journal* he would refresh himself with a shaken cocktail in a can; during the day at lunch he would again turn to beer; on the way back, he would buy a gin and tonic at the shop; and in the evening, he would allow himself to relax a little with a bottle of wine. The most terrible thing was that this last "relaxing" bottle of wine could have some unforeseen and irrational effects on him: either he would sit down to write poetry, or he would throw a fit and yell that he was surrounded by untalented dimwits who couldn't recognize his talent, or he would enjoy mistreating Tata, and this even went as far as physical abuse: everything, including broken ribs, abrasions, bruises, concussions. Tata would run away from him into the night and find refuge somewhere and come to the firm decision to divorce him, but the next day Marik would literally crawl to her on his knees and kiss the ground that Tata's foot might have trod; he would weep, wringing his hands and swearing off alcohol, and in the end she would give him "one last chance." He would even take measures to stop drinking, but this would only throw him into despair; he would stop writing his poetry, and go back to drinking, taking beer once again in the morning, and setting everything back on its course anew. This continued for more than twenty years.

So Tata and I started to go to church together and order molebens to the Mother of God, asking the Heavenly Queen herself to intervene and have some sort of effect on Marik.

And what next? A short while later, he began to get pimples on his face. He stood in front of the mirror, examining them, and soaked them in some sort of tonic, but that didn't cure them. Then he turned to the doctors. They said: it's your liver. You can't drink any more under any circumstances, or you'll be covered in pimples. In general, Marik was a fairly attractive man, and it turned out that he treasured his looks very much, so the pimples deeply disturbed him, and he went so far as to give up drinking to preserve the beauty of his face.

"Not bad," Tata said, "such an effective instrument did the Mother of God find for him—pimples! You know, he had ischemia, too, and acute coronary syndrome, but that didn't stop him! But pimples on his face!"

My godmother Tatiana's husband was an alcoholic. He would drink every day. If he didn't drink, he would take Nembutal. If not Nembutal, then he would smoke a joint (he had it delivered). At the same time, he was a supremely talented and intelligent person, a writer, the classic author of children's literature, S.[10] His medical history stated: "Paranoid schizophrenia, alcoholism, multiple drug use, is published in *Murzilka* and broadcast on the radio." S. explained it in the following manner:

"I'm crazy myself, and my wife is the 'wife of a writer.'"

He also said:

"In order to be crazy in this country, you have to have a strong mind and nerves of steel."

And also:

"If you want to appear insane, say the truth and nothing but the truth."

If he ever left the house, he would invariably end up in some sort of story, and so it was said about him, like Gogol's Nozdrev, that he was a "man of story." "Mother Tatiana" would follow him around like a little child and eternally assign bodyguards to him from among their friends. But her husband's daily high was what worried her the most, and her worst fear was that he couldn't be saved.

"Genka," she said, "the Apostle Paul himself wrote that alcoholics will not inherit the Kingdom of God!"

She tried everything: she treated him, admitting him into the hospital, but he would chat up the attendants, the orderlies, and even the nurses there, and they would diligently bring him alcohol and pills; she prayed for him in monasteries; she even bought a house in the country for him, where he could feel the beneficial effects of his native nature, fill his lungs with the sweet and pleasant smoke of the Fatherland, and lie it out, like Emelia from the story, on a warm Russian stove, but the cottage was burned down by drunk fishermen. She tried inviting their close friends to the house, so that they, sacrificing themselves, could pour into themselves the reserves of alcohol, leaving less for him to imbibe. She herself almost became a victim of the "syndrome of Neuhaus's wife." Whenever Heinrich Neuhaus's wife saw him with vodka, she would selflessly try to consume it, pouring it into herself, in order to say to him: "There's nothing left!" So the poor thing almost drank herself to death, though he ended his days quite well, and even found the time to start an intense love affair with a young French pianist.

So did Tatiana bravely adopt the same method, in essence ". . . to lay down her life for her friends" (Jn 15:13), though she was able to quit just in time. And in general, she created an atmosphere of normal life in the house, where everything went along at its usual pace: editors would come over, to whom S. would dictate his wonderful stories about adventures and animals; their friends would gather—someone was always celebrating a birthday, a namesday, a wedding anniversary, a dissertation defense, the opening of an exhibit, the release of a new book; a neighbor would run in for a moment on one matter or another and end up staying over, enjoying watching them and listening to them; some foreign acquaintance would stop to spend the night; a traveling monk would find shelter there. It created a strange situation in which people would flock to that warm house overflowing with bread and salt, where Tatiana always fed everyone from the bottom of her heart, literally: people who were eternally much more settled and better off than their hosts, but who flocked there to receive comfort and love and to come to terms with life.

After a bout of drinking, S. would lie on the couch like a patrician in ancient times, with his guests enthroned around him—sometimes these were people who would not really be compatible together were they to find themselves together anywhere else—and he would tell them amazing stories that would later be passed down orally from person to person, slowly losing their connection to their author and becoming legends. S. was a master of the oral tale, a prodigy in the paradox.

There was a time when Tatiana would secretly dilute the vodka with water, and what's more, the proportions of the latter would increase more and more, until S.'s shot glass would contain nothing but water. He would drink it and say in amazement:

"Unbelievable, what has it come to? I drink and don't get drunk."

Then Tatiana learned that there was a wonderful Orthodox elder who lived in the village of Rakitnoe, Belgorod Region, by whose prayers miracles took place. She took S. to the elder. This was Archimandrite Seraphim (Tiapochkin). He received him with love and said:

"Why did you take so long to visit me, my dear?"

He blessed them to stay with an old local woman and invited them to lunch with him every day in his little priest's house.

During that time, my friends would live near the elder for entire weeks, if not months. S. conversed with visiting priests and monks, and himself began to look so well that people would often take him for a priest in the church house and ask for his blessing. God knows to what wonderful changes of life this could have led, but soon the elder died, and my friends forfeited their blessed haven and returned to Moscow, where they were again thrown into the midst of that mindless whirl of guests and passions.

But Tatiana believed that the Lord would heal her Genka, and constantly visited monasteries, appealing to elders with the request to pray for him. She visited Elder Kirill, Fr Ioann (Krestiankin), Fr Pavel (Gruzdev), and even the lowly Alesha from Oskol.

But she was ill herself and badly needed an operation. However, she couldn't even imagine being admitted into the hospital and leaving her "little one" without her supervision, but even that wasn't the main problem, I think. If push came to shove, she could have placed S. with a trusted friend who would have looked after him, fed him, and done his laundry. The fact of the matter is, she was so consumed with love for her husband, so occupied with the thought of his salvation, that she could not psychologically transfer her energy and attention from him to herself. That's why she kept evading that operation, delaying it, putting it off more and more, and she let the moment pass.

He survived her by two years. All that time, he was very depressed, but he hardly drank. He just lay on his couch, remembering his life. He became practically blind, but interpreted all that symbolically, as if to say: this vale of tears was coming to an end, but what images could he now behold with his spiritual eye! My husband, as a priest, often visited him, confessed and communed him, until our friend departed into eternity.

As for Mother Tatiana, I saw her immediately after the funeral in my dreams. She looked joyful and happy. We came to a magnificent dining hall together; in layman's terms, a luxurious, very high-ceilinged and vast, restaurant, and she said, laughing:

"Well, my dear, now you will treat me!"

When I woke up, I envisioned long tables set up at the church *in memoriam*, with lit candles and all sorts of food, and thought that was what she meant by "treat me" in my dream.

She knew that I loved her.

* * *

When a husband and wife have spent their lives in mutual love, how unbearable it is for them to be parted by death! How good it is to die together. As it was in the ancient times: "They had their fill of days and died on the same day." But alas!

I read in one of the lives of the New Martyrs how the Bolsheviks came to a village priest, pulled him out of the altar by the beard, and dragged him off to be shot. His *matushka* ran after them and begged them with tears to shoot her together with her husband. They pushed her away and swore at her, but the woman didn't relent. Then those gallant KGB men, to finally shut her up—so be it—placed them both against the walls of the church and aimed their rifles at them. The *matushka*, radiant, nestled close to her husband, and in an instant they were both shot dead.

* * *

It is written in the life of St Spyridon that he was married, that he and his wife lived piously and gave birth to a daughter, then the wife died. Further on, following this calmly written statement, the subsequent events of the saint's life are described in turn. So it should be in the life of a saint: the genre prevents anything unnecessary, anything psychological. But in reality, however modest and humble he was, he probably suffered, and wept, and grieved. Even Christ, learning that Lazarus had died, "groaned in the spirit" and "wept," because, as it is written, "He loved him" (Jn 11:33, 35, 36).

So did Spyridon love his wife—how could he not have loved her, when he loved everyone? It was through love that he, having taken in a hungry and exhausted stranger but not having any Lenten food with which to feed him (it was a fasting period), gave him meat. In addition, to prevent his guest from being dismayed, he even shared the meal with him. Through love, he conversed with the idol worshiper Olympus, attempting to lead him away from the deceit of idolatry. Through love, he gave the needy money and food. He healed, resurrected the dead, and quieted storms.

When his wife died, St Spyridon was left with a daughter in his arms, the orphaned Irina, and he raised her and cared for her with all his heart, as do all good parents. Then she also died, as it is said, "in the bloom of her youth."

Irina was probably also a very good and loving daughter. A rich woman gave her all her treasured items to look after—in other words, she could be trusted, and the woman knew that she wouldn't betray her or deceive her, that she wouldn't act wrongly. So the saint's earthly life was full of grief and many things that he could only have overcome through great suffering and patience. It only seems to us, looking back from afar and through the conventional language of the saint's life, that the saints were always given everything easily.

Of course, it is understood by a believer that a departed one hasn't disappeared or vanished, but that his soul is alive and his body awaits resurrection . . . Nevertheless, Christ knew that He was soon going to resurrect the departed Lazarus, but He still didn't hold back His tears when He heard that His friend had died. Therefore, we also are not forbidden from crying in our love, and suffering, and from experiencing this suffering in full.

* * *

If you drive south along the sea from Paleokastritsa, you will arrive at a steep coastline where you can climb down and then climb up again to Mirtiotissa Monastery. Only one monk lives there—a Romanian.

We got there too late—the service had finished and the monastery was closed. So we settled into a taverna not far from the monastery. Smoking jars with burning coffee inside were scattered around to ward off pesky and greedy wasps that apparently loved the meat there. As soon as they saw (or smelled) a piece of meat or sausage, they immediately and greedily attacked it, stinging anyone who tried to get in their way. We ordered everything Greek: tzatziki—yogurt with garlic and cucumber; saganaki—fried cheese; moussaka—eggplant with meat. Also, fried squash covered with a crunchy breading, calamari, enormous shrimp, small fried fish, and kleftiko—lamb stewed with all sorts of things—and some local rosé wine. What can I say, there were also days in our life when all we had was black rye bread fried in Lenten oil, or onion baked in the oven.

* * *

Back in Agios Stefanos, I put on the CD with the Liturgy and organ-accompanied singing, but it turned out to be blank—not a sound, not a rustle, nothing. Disappointed, I turned on the TV. Some American political program in Russian came on. The moderator was asking a Russian journalist about the upcoming elections, and she was branding them as obviously rigged. In general, she could hardly be considered "Russian," since she had already lived in America for many years and taught at an American university, but I remembered her from back in Moscow. Then she was married to an aging writer whom she had taken from her friend and had borne him a child, and when our country's difficult times came, she took her son and moved with him to America, leaving the old man completely alone, so he died alone. When she was luring him away from his wife and when they stealthily met in strange apartments in secret, they probably considered it love . . .

Well, as far as the election, manipulation, and the farce of it all, I agree with her. I haven't gone to vote in a long time. But she suddenly began to urge people to go out on the streets and protest. I can just imagine what would happen if they then suggested that she back her own words and lead the movement herself. Go ahead—step right out in front of the columns and under the banners with your loudspeaker in your hands right on Pushkinskaya Square.[11]

No, it doesn't cost her anything to sit in an armchair on television and call the people to protests and demonstrations and then watch the fire of a Russian revolution burn from America.

I never understood such "love": taking the husband away from his family, meeting with him "for an hour" in someone else's apartment, whose noble hostess goes somewhere else for a while and passes the time at a friend's, at the movies, or simply walk the streets, sniffling loudly with her nose, because she didn't have the strength to turn them down—what if it's true love? Then marrying the husband amid scandal, parading him about for a year or two or three, and then leaving him—sick and good for nothing by this point—to the mercy of fate. Such romances have their special mark, their gentlemanly pattern: "flowers, candlelit dinners, wine, fruit, good music . . ." In my youth, when I first began to be courted by young men, I couldn't bear that style and intonation in courtship. Anyone who approached me with a similar proposition, even if it was completely innocent and from a pure heart, inspired feelings of near-revulsion in me.

When I was still resting in winterly Gagra, where my parents had sent me for the winter break to recover from overwork—which was really lovesickness for my future husband, as yet still in the dark about it all—and when, suffering from shingles brought on by my unrequited love pangs, I rested there among the coalminers, one old artist, vacationing nearby with his granddaughter Nastia (now an artist of recent fame), introduced me to a Lithuanian fiction writer either named Vitas or Vitautas.

"He told me in confidence that he really likes you and is asking for an introduction. Is that all right with you?"

Well, we were introduced. He was a mature, stout man, intelligent, in a suit and golden glasses, in my eyes an old man of thirty-eight years as compared to my nineteen. He was staying in the room next door. What came next? "Hello." "Hello." "How beautifully the snow is lying on the mandarins!" "The winter sea has its own unique hue." Boring!

Then suddenly he said to me:

"I recently had a book published in Vilnius. I would like to celebrate. Come visit me in my room this evening. I have wine, fruit, cognac, good music."

Well, as soon as I heard about the wine and good music, something inside began to sound an alarm, like in Gaidai's movie, when Nikulin senses that an unseen evil power is approaching his diamond arm.

"Thank you very much," I said politely. "But I want to work tonight."

No matter how hard he tried to persuade me, I merely answered:

"My calling takes precedence!"

So what happened next? He went to his room and drank his fill of the wine, and perhaps the cognac after that, and in his inebriated state began to knock on my door in the middle of the night. He claimed he wanted to find something out or clear something up. My internal alarm went off again, and I said to him:

"You'd better clear it up from behind the door."

Of course, instead of clearing anything up, he began to knock on the door with his fists and try to break in, but the door was strong, and he didn't achieve his goal.

For a while, everything quieted down, but he apparently went back to his room, drank some more, and climbed over the wall separating our balconies. I had my door cracked open a little bit: I was sitting and writing poems, fanned by the sea air and the night breeze; then suddenly—boom! Something heavy fell right onto my balcony—he had clumsily fallen down, hit his knee, and cracked his glasses.

Oh, I was both angry and scared, and threw myself to my balcony door to lock it. Just as I locked it, he jumped up and started pounding on it. He was throwing his full weight on it, and the door trembled: in contrast to the strong front door, it was fairly flimsy, and had glass in it.

"Well," I thought, "if he breaks that glass, what do I have to defend myself with?" Even though I was a strong, tough, rosy-cheeked nineteen-year-old, he was still a large, solid guy. I couldn't run away from him through the other door into the night—there young Georgian guys were walking around in the dark, flashing the whites of their eyes:

"Hey, blondie! Come on, let me take you out!"

I began to rummage around the room to find a weapon or a stick, but found nothing better than a toilet plunger and a hanger. I stood in front of him behind the glass—the plunger in one hand, the hooked hanger in the other, and began to wave them at him triumphantly, with a severe expression on my face, my eyes blazing, and my teeth bared, yelling a war cry. Apparently, that made an impression on him, because he crawled back. I kept watching him through the glass to make sure that he would fall over completely to his side. But he had apparently wasted all his energy, his leg was hurt, his glasses were shattered, his sparse hair was disheveled by the subtropical breeze. He froze standing out on the balcony in his shirtsleeves in February, though we were in Gagra, and now he couldn't manage to climb back over. But I kept strict watch, and as soon as he even glanced pathetically in my direction, expressing bitter defeat with his entire figure, I would raise my plunger and turn the hook on the hanger in his direction.

In short, he didn't make a single appearance in the dining room of the writers' house the next day. And the day after that, the old artist who had introduced us said to me:

"Forgive me, but it seems to me that our Vitas (or Vitautas) has fallen in love with you. He talked about you the whole evening last night—you made quite a lasting impression on him."

I can imagine! I tried to picture myself, all severe, like a regiment with its banners, with my plunger and my hanger in either hand . . .

It was a few days after that when I heard that mysterious voice urging me to call my future husband. Later on, I found myself in Moscow.

No, of course it wasn't all perfect when I, trembling from fear, stepped over the doorstep into his home, though I really wanted to talk about something intellectual and enlightened, something that would reflect my feelings, but I was so afraid. Vosnesensky has a really wonderful line: "I didn't know, cynic and clown that I was, that love is a great fear." So I brought along my best friend from my schooldays, just to be safe.

"Tell him how wonderful and fun we all are," I asked her.

We went into the house. He had a young poet-decadent over, who was very genteel in appearance and had just finished his book of poems called *À la Pasternak*, and we all sat down in the kitchen to drink tea.

Here my lovely friend set out to arrange my fate—a strange inspiration seized her, and she began to richly narrate stories which, to put it mildly, were not necessary to tell to my future husband, especially at the first visit. For example, she recalled how in the ninth grade, we had drunk a bottle of Gamza wine on a dare in the bathroom of the Tretyakov Gallery . . . and followed it with Golden Key toffees. Then we went out to the rest of the people in the gallery, when suddenly the rest of the toffees spilled out all over the floor.

Mind you, the poet-decadent loved these stories, and he laughed loudly:

"What amusing girls you are!"

He even invited us to his literary *dacha*, left for him as an inheritance from his academic grandfather: "Dimochka Sakharov also visits me there— the son of what's-his-name"—he made a meaningful gesture with his hand. "So come, it is always a pleasure to talk to such open people."

My husband, however, was not so impressed by my friend's stories—he sat there, politely feigning a smile, and when we came out of the entryway, my friend said to me straightforwardly: "Well? Did I completely ruin it for you?"

"You've ruined my life," I said sadly, "but I still love you."

* * *

My God, why can't I think of anything appropriate for the *Journal*? All these unfitting stories keep popping into my head that have nothing to do with anything, it's all nonsense: "wine, good music."

Once I was speaking for the Ministry of Literary Propaganda in Gorky Park. It was all very dreary: an open stage, random people on the benches, mostly old retirees and lonely mothers with screaming children, and the atmosphere of a public house—people moving around and stopping at will, drinking beer, listening, yawning, talking, and moving away.

The amplification from the microphone was spotty, and the microphone itself gave out a loud ring. In theory, a situation like this is lifeless, not beneficial to anyone, and even harmful for the poet. On top of everything, I was nine months pregnant with my little boy. Only the prospect of getting seven rubles and fifty kopeks drove me to take this adventure on. In addition, Susan, the wife of American correspondent Peter Osnos, currently living in Moscow, had given me an array of maternity clothes, and things like "Enjoy your pregnancy" were written on every article of clothing in English. In theory, I was enjoying and flaunting my pregnancy—so glamorous were those loose lacy blouses, white trousers with a large elastic band for the stomach, and the freely flowing, long dresses covered in a fine floral print.

I was performing as a duo with a considerably untalented poet, though a handsome one—Slava L. After coming down from the stage and signing the sheet along with a positive report to send back to the Ministry of Propaganda, we both sighed with relief. Then Slava L., sweetly glancing over at me, said to me meaningfully:

"Why don't we go over to my place? We can sit by candlelight, I have wine, good music . . ."

I looked at him searchingly: was he making fun of me? There I stood in front of him, heavily pregnant, while my eldest, a one-year-old, sat at home with her father—which he knew, since I told him about it before our performance . . .

But his eyes burned with an inviting flame, and I understood that he was serious, that he hadn't noticed my stomach underneath the loose, embroidered blouse, and as far as the daughter at home, well, what about her?

"Naturally, I'm grateful," I said, "but I'm busy."

The next day, I gave birth to my son. Several weeks later, I went to pick up my payment for my disgraceful performance, and met Slava L. at the cashier's office.

"How are you doing?" he asked.

"Well," I replied. "I gave birth to my son since I saw you last."

"What do you mean, your son? I thought you had a one-year-old daughter."

"Yes, then I had a daughter, and now I have a son, too. He's going to be half a month old soon."

* * *

I have two lives of St Spyridon. One was compiled by a Greek called Mikhalis G. Likissa, and the other was recently published in Moscow and written by A.V. Bugaevskii. In the second life, in contrast with the first, it's claimed that in spite of the miracles performed by St Spyridon and the pagan priest Olympus's witnessing to the saint's extrasensory perception, St Spyridon was unable to convert Olympus to Christianity. The latter, though he treated the saint with respect, did not accept the Christian faith in the end. This is no less important or eloquent a fact of St Spyridon's life than if he had, after all, managed to convert the idol worshipper.

Here, in the decision of man's free will, in his individual choice, lies the cornerstone of Christianity. Nothing and no one can be saved automatically. Even among the twelve closest disciples of Christ, a betrayer was found. A man has no real guarantee of salvation until the very final moments of his life. Until his last breath, he remains with the fateful question of his willful dispensation, the chance to confess Christ or reject him. A man is not given to know until his final hour whether or not he will be accepted—such as he is, with all his merits or without any at all—by Christ. The only thing that can alleviate his fear of being turned away is his love. His love for Christ, which "never fails," which "bears all things" and believes in the loving mercy of its Beloved: ". . . believes all things, hopes all things, endures all things" (1 Cor 13:7).

In the evening, taking the advice of our hosts, we went to a taverna called At Peter's in a nearby cove. Its tables stood out on a small pier, so we were surrounded on three sides by the sea, and the ducks swam around us; they greedily snatched the bread that the diners offered them. A married English couple sat at the neighboring table. The English have favored Corfu as a vacation spot since the time that it was their colony. They come and settle everywhere here—the English language is much more noticeable here than the Greek language. They sit in the tavernas, drive on the curving roads in rented cars, inspiring the rightful aggravation of drivers from other countries because they drive too slowly—apparently because in addition to the curves and "narrowness" of the local roads, they have to get used to driving on the left side and to the cars driving in the opposite direction of where they should be.

And so, the English man looked at me with sly curiosity and suddenly exclaimed:

"Are you an actress? I saw you in a movie."

"No," I said.

"But you look like an actress. I work in the movie industry. I'm a script writer."

So we slowly began to talk and moved our tables closer together. They introduced themselves as George and Helen.

"There on the mountain is the villa of the Rothschilds, and there lives the owner of Ferrari," George enlightened us.

We talked about this and that, even English literature. After all, the famous Durrell brothers had been born here on Corfu.[12] One of them, Gerald Durrell, wrote wonderful books about animals—I had read him in my childhood. The other, who appears in these books as the vicious and considerably unpleasant brother Larry, even became a Nobel Prize laureate for his postmodern novels.[13] The house where they lived has stayed in one piece and was recently purchased by a Ukrainian woman. As a side note, she turned out to be a zealous admirer of both brothers, and freely lets inside anyone wishing to see their home.

We also touched on Shakespeare, Dickens, Thackeray, and Byron in our conversation. Then the conversation lagged a little until it unexpectedly turned to the fall in the pound that was at the time affecting all of England.

"Yes," said George, "the entire banking system is completely unreliable. Especially when you get a loan from one bank to buy an apartment, then another bank buys that loan at lower interest rates, and often ends up bankrupt. Oh, everyone over there lives in fear and mistrust: everyone is afraid of a collapse. They don't know which direction the blow will come from. That's why young people don't want to get married.

"All these draconian marriage contracts and obligations, and yet you don't know what's going to happen tomorrow: what if your job contract doesn't get renewed, or the bank raises the interest rate on your mortgage?

That's the quiet panic in people's minds right now. And yet the financial system, the exchange, it's all so interesting. We knew a broker who worked for the exchange. Once he understood the system, he got immensely rich, but this didn't bring him happiness. His wife became an alcoholic and set fire to one of their estates, which was filled to the brim with all sorts of treasures—paintings, antiques. His son crashed his own jet. In the end, still a multimillionaire, he shot himself. Nothing was interesting for him anymore. Why isn't there anything in literature about this power of money, this thrill of the chase?"

"Why do you say that?" I objected. "What about Dostoevsky, who concerned himself so much with the topic of money? What about Balzac?"

"Yes, yes, but I mean now, right now! It awakens such passions, it uncovers such deep layers in a person!"

"Well, why don't you write it yourself? You're a script writer!"

"I wrote comedies of manners for television. That kind of thing is very popular, there will always be a demand for it. As for tragedies, you know, you have to build it up, find producers. It's just not my cup of tea."

The poet-decadent and author of *À la Pasternak*, whom I met at my future husband's house when I came to visit him that first inglorious time, followed through on his promise and invited us to his literary *dacha*. Our mutual friend, Andrei Vitte, who also wrote poetry back then, borrowed his father's Volga especially for the occasion, and we, like so many golden young things, drove off to Zhukovka. I sat in front with the driver, and my future husband sat in the back. So I constantly turned around to face him, happily babbling on. I didn't even notice how, after crossing my legs, I had stuck my knee into the cigarette lighter, and when it dutifully tried to pop out to give a light, my knee blocked its way. So instead, it set fire to something inside the car with that unused heat. As soon as we turned onto Rublevka, a black smoke started to spew out of the radio slot; we smelled something burning, and Vitte, slamming on the brakes, shouted: "Get out! Get on the ground! She's going to blow!"

We jumped out, ran off, fell down onto our stomachs right into a snow-drift, and covered our heads with the palms of our hands.

A minute passed, then another, then another. The car didn't explode, but we continued to lie flat. Finally Andriusha couldn't wait any longer: he dashed off to the car, opened the hood, and, taking off his jacket, started to beat the smoking wires with it. We ran up to him, and also threw off our jackets, despite the fact that it could still explode, but he said with relief:

"It's out!"

And we kept driving, feeling closer to each other after lying together in the snow under the bush in expectation of an explosion, in the face of death itself. As a result, we drank the poet-decadent's fine red wine with special relish, and ate plums stuffed with almonds and topped with whipped cream, while the fabulous Vadim Kozin sang to us: "Meetings only happen once in life, the thread is only cut by fate once . . ." Then the promised son of the by-then-famous Sakharov, Mitenka, dropped by for a minute. I don't know, by now he is probably a solid, mature, and attractive man, but back then he was a fifteen-year-old stripling with a skinny neck and thin face covered all over with red teenage acne. He immediately decided to join the ranks of the adult nineteen-year-olds: he threw back half a glass of whisky, ignored the aesthetically pleasing plum appetizer, and, planting himself next to me, clearly expressed his desire to "make a pass" at me.

"Do you like to hunt foxes?" he asked my future husband.

The latter chuckled. And then Mitenka, rubbing his hands together and drooling slightly, nonchalantly said to me: "How I love to hunt foxes for my lovers!"

* * *

At the beginning of *perestroika*, that same Slava L. came up with a brilliant financial scheme. He called all the Moscow poets—not only the famous ones, but also the ones who were languishing in quiet failure in literary unions, and offered to publish a booklet with their poems for free; what's more, with translations of the verses in four European languages. He claimed that the translators were locked and ready, but the project had been dropped.

"Imagine what good advertising this would be for you, not only here, among our people, but in Europe, maybe even America? Poetry without boundaries! Are you in?" he would ask each one.

Of course, everyone was in, and they all rushed to submit their poems.

"But the only thing is," he would suddenly add, as if remembering an insignificant detail, "we will need your portrait for the cover. Since this is a series, it needs to be in a specific format. But don't worry, I have a special photographer who can take your picture according to the format, touch it up, and everything will be OK, but you have to pay for this. But other than that, not a penny will be taken from you."

"Why so much?" the poor poets would say in chorus.

"Simpletons! He is a professional photo artist! For an all-European publication! And you're counting pennies. Go ahead, stay in your thrifty obscurity!"

What could they do? The poets scraped together the money, borrowing it blindly and obediently bringing it to him. I would have too, if it wasn't for my husband. He worked for the journal *Ogonek* at the time, and had professional photographers around him for a dime a dozen, all excellent.

"Just call Slava," he said to me, "ask him what this portrait is supposed to look like, find out the parameters, and our photographers will do it all for you for free."

But Slava said:

"No. We have special technology here, and other people's photographs won't work, so come here and get it done. And bring the three hundred rubles."

That's when my husband sniffed him out.

"Count how many poets live in just Moscow, and multiply that by three hundred—how much money do you get? Then Slava will say: well, guys, it didn't work, it all fell through! The publishing company backed out of printing at the last minute."

And sure enough, Slava L. suddenly disappeared somewhere. He had sat and sat in the Central House of Writers café, and then he suddenly vanished without a trace.

A few years later, when I was visiting Andrei Sinyavsky, I suddenly saw on his desk a book of poems published, I think, in Munich. The name "Sviatoslav L." flashed on the cover. Inside was an inscription, something to the effect of: "To the dear martyr of conscience, Andrei Donatovich, from another martyr of conscience, Slava L."

"How do you know this martyr of conscience?" I asked Sinyavsky.

"I was in Germany, and this dear man came up to me at one of my literary evenings and gave me his book. He said that he had also suffered much at the hand of the Soviet regime, suffered from the lack of freedom, and escaped by the skin of his teeth."

I easily imagined the crowd of enraged and disillusioned poets demanding their booklets in five languages from Slava, and thought that yes, he must have experienced tremendous relief when he finally got on the plane to beautiful Munich.

* * *

There are several stories about St Spyridon and his immediate help with money. Once, after a bad flood, a ruined peasant came to him and told him of his grief: he had gone to a well-off acquaintance and had asked to borrow seeds to plant with the aim of returning them with interest after the harvest, but he demanded a security deposit, which the poor man didn't have.

Then St Spyridon gave him a marvelous ornament to use for the deposit—a golden snake. The owner of the granaries couldn't resist such a precious offer and gave the peasant some seed. The latter planted it and soon produced a tremendous harvest. Recovering good money through this harvest, the peasant happily rushed off to the rich landowner to pay back his debt, but by that point, the rich man didn't want to part ways with the precious object—so much so, that he lied to him: he had never received any such golden snake, never laid eyes on it, and so wouldn't return anything to the peasant.

The peasant related this story to St Spyridon, and the saint assured him that the rogue would soon be punished. In the meantime, the rich man decided to admire his craftily secured treasure and climbed into the chest where it was kept. Imagine his terror when instead of the golden image he discovered a live snake there! He slammed the chest shut, found the peasant, and, pretending that he had just remembered the whole story with the security deposit, offered to return the treasure in exchange for the repayment of the debt.

The peasant brought him the money, and the rich man led him to the chest and invited him to take what was kept inside. The peasant opened the chest and took out the molten gold, glistening snake.

When the peasant returned the treasured item to St Spyridon, the latter invited him to go out to the vegetable garden together, where he placed the treasure on the ground. After that, he called out to the Lord with prayers of gratitude, and the snake, having fulfilled its duty in the form of a golden object, turned into a living, slippery creature and immediately crawled away on its snaky affairs. Then, the astonished peasant understood that St Spyridon, so desiring to help him but not having anything of his own to give as a deposit, had begged the Lord to turn that reptile into a precious object. For "Whatsoever the Lord pleased, that hath He done, in heaven, and in earth, and in the seas and in all deep places" (Ps 134:6). But what boldness on the part of the saint, and what power in his prayer!

For this is also a parable about the transience of the value of earthly things. How much is a piece of bread worth in times of hunger? Or a glass of water in the desert? A gasp of air in a gas chamber? Or even mittens in a terrible frost? How much is vision worth? The ability to walk? To speak? To hear? To sleep? How much does it cost to make someone love you? Or how much to love at least one other person? What can you buy with a million pounds for a dying man? What good can money bring a multimillionaire who is so sick of living that he would rather shoot his brains out? Does he see that same snake crawling away before sticking the gun into his eye socket?

The Slavonic translation of the Gospel, in comparison to the Russian and English, uses the exceedingly specific word *"отщетить"* for "render useless": "For what will it profit a man if he gains the whole world and loses [renders useless] his own soul?" (Mk 8:36). And truly: "Or what will a man give in exchange for his soul?" (Mk 8:37).

I say this because I recently heard the following question discussed on the radio: can everything be bought? The debaters came to the conclusion that everything can be bought for the right price. Interesting—how do they plan on buying intelligence or talent for themselves? And will they have purchased friends, purchased wives, purchased mothers?

I knew of one marriage that was secured with money, but it all ended very badly. This was a marriage between the beautiful Nana, who had a mentally handicapped daughter, and a Georgian millionaire. He was old, bloated, and had a large birthmark on his face, but most importantly, he was rude and of low breeding. However, Nana settled into a luxurious apartment in the best neighborhood of Tbilisi, luckily not having to earn her keep, and instead stayed with her ill daughter, taking her to the best doctors for treatment. Thus she sacrificed herself because she loved her ill daughter so much, but her millionaire was so repulsive to her that she poisoned him by mixing acid into his liquor. Then she bribed the proper people in court and was either acquitted or the case was simply dismissed. Then the war began in Georgia. The heating wasn't working in Tbilisi, and she lit a fire in the fireplace. A spark fell onto the floor, which smoldered through the night and then set the house on fire. Nana and her daughter couldn't get out, because raging flames stood between them and the metal door, and the windows all had screens.

But as far as marriages of love are concerned, I know quite a few instances among my friends in which at least one of the future spouses received a firm internal confirmation that the other person involved would become his or her partner in life. This happened to my friend, the writer S., when he saw Tatiana and immediately understood that she would be his wife. The same with my brother's wife: they used to attend the same kindergarten and sat on potties right next to each other. She insists that even then, she knew that he was her future husband. The same also happened to my friends Petia and Sonia—they were classmates but only married when they were twenty-three years old: Petia had spent that entire time proving to her that they were destined to be together. All these are not fateful romances but marriages forged in heaven, love to the grave and beyond. Just love.

You can never guess who will fall in love with whom, and you will never achieve mutual love if it's not destined. I remember when my friend Liubanya fell passionately in love with the young and unmarried prose writer P., with whom I had a good, friendly relationship. And so she constantly asked and begged me to somehow take her to visit him, and to start a conversation between them, so that later, having been introduced to him, she could continue meeting him on her own. She pestered me with this request so much that I agreed, despite the fact that my husband scolded me for it very much and even called it "playing around with their hearts." But I understood that it was no game; it was just that when a person is in love, they are anxious. They can't put two words together to make a sentence. And anyway, they were casual acquaintances already and not through me. It was just that she honestly couldn't bring herself to make normal human contact with him. And after all, I, too, had asked a friend to accompany me in a very similar situation . . .

In short, I learned that P. was staying in Peredelkino at some writer's *dacha*: it was winter, his hosts were in Moscow, and he was more or less keeping watch over the house; and that he was sick. So I said: I want to come and visit the poor patient. He said: come on over. I said: I'm going to bring a friend. He said: OK.

We bought some aspirin, Tylenol, that same ill-fated combination of wine and fruit, and went to visit the sick man. He already had cutlets, mashed potatoes, borscht, fruit compote, and cognac.

While he set the plates on the table, Liubanya said to me suspiciously: "Someone's already been here! I can see an interested woman's touch!"

She sat down and ate everything in sight, removed all traces of that someone else; then she began to consume the cognac as well. But since she was, as a rule, a virtuous girl who didn't drink, after such an abundant dinner, and the cognac, and in the cold weather, she got very sleepy. So when the young and obliging P., whom we had from the very beginning asked to read us something from his latest work, began to recite his story with zeal, carefully intoning the words, chuckling here and there, and even wiping away a renegade tear or two, Liubanya began to nod and hold her left eye open with two fingers to prevent it from closing completely. But her heroic efforts proved in vain: all her strength had been claimed by her gastrointestinal tract. By the time P., the prose writer, had finished reading, fully convinced that his story had been a success, Liubanya, head thrown back, was sweetly snoring in her armchair.

So nothing came of it between them. You could say that all we ended up doing that night was taking a walk outside the city in the Russian winter, having a good meal, warming up, taking a nap, and coming back home.

And yet she was so lovely to look at, so attentive, with her own apartment in Moscow—cozy and nicely furnished—while P., the prose writer, didn't even have a registered home address. She also appreciated literature, and even dabbled in writing poetry herself, so she wouldn't have crushed him with any pettiness. They could have been so good together!

But it was not to be!

* * *

I know of another tragic instance when a young hierodeacon, i.e., a monk, who, by the way, led a very ascetic way of life, met a beautiful girl, a medic, in the monastery, and asked for a blessing to go to her for treatment in Moscow. Such a consuming passion sprung up between them that he abandoned his former life and married her. But not even half a year passed before this love turned into such a burning hatred that he began to fear himself, that he would suddenly kill her. So he just ran away from her. He didn't have the heart to go back to the monastery, so he settled down at his mother's in a small provincial town, where he drank himself to waste. The most amazing thing is that when he was still in the monastery, he was constantly criticizing the other monks: they didn't pray enough or correctly, they didn't read the holy fathers, they ate too much; in general, the monastery rule was much too lax for him. He even asked me to drive him somewhere deep into the forest, from where we walked on foot, or rather blazed our trail through the impassable thicket for three kilometers or so, swatting at the clouds of mosquitoes. Finally he stopped and said:

"Right here. My skete will be right here when I leave the monastery and begin my ascetic labor. I will build a little church and will pray in it day and night."

After that, I began to act more suspiciously toward monks who complained that their monastery's rule wasn't strict enough and began to share their plans to live alone in their own skete.

As for the repulsion that the unhappy hierodeacon began to feel for his chosen one, there is a similar story in the Bible. It is when Amnon blazed with such love for Tamar that he made himself sick, lured her to himself, and forced himself on her. Immediately afterwards, as it is written, "Then Amnon hated her exceedingly, so much so that the intense hatred he bore against her was greater than the love with which he had at first loved her" (2 Kgs 13:15).

After all, love and joy are gifts from God, and He gives them to whom He pleases and takes them away from those He does not wish to have them: God does everything as He pleases. If He wishes, He will harden the heart of Pharaoh, or soften it as He desires. For this reason, beware all you who wish to steal this joy or cheat in order to obtain it. To be honest, I love this reflection on the divine will.

* * *

It is surprising how love numbs all other senses. When soon after the feast with the poet-decadent my future husband came to my house for the first time, I tried to receive him as well as I could: I cleaned everything, bought some delicacies, and, when he arrived, I started frying *blini*, completely consumed by his presence—so much so that when I grabbed the hot pan I didn't even feel it and just pulled my hand away by instinct. Only after he left the house did I discover with surprise a terrible red burn on my palm and fingers.

I think I can understand how the martyrs, in undergoing inhuman torment and suffering, patiently and meekly endured them. For love numbed their senses and covered their pain: it "... bears all things ..." (1 Cor 13:7).

St Spyridon was also tortured and tried. It is written in his life that even before his episcopate, in 305, he was sent to the mines; there, he underwent torture for refusing to deny Christ; his right eye was damaged and his right hand was cut off. Then, during the persecutions of 308–313, he was again arrested. It's true that in that same life (the Greek version), it is written that his relics show no sign of damage to the eye socket, but his tormentors could have damaged the eye without damaging his eye socket.

But I'm especially amazed that just like my father, he had no right hand. My father lost his right arm at the front when he was nineteen years old. Surprisingly, I never felt that my father was an invalid. Even his friends, or people who simply interacted with him, seemed to forget—stop noticing—that his right sleeve was empty. He would tuck it into his pocket. This happened because of how he carried himself: no helplessness, no special treatment. He drove a car very well with his one left hand, and not a car for disabled people or a specially equipped car tailor-made for his needs—no, he drove a Ford with speed controls on the steering wheel, as was usual for that time. My father, holding the wheel with the palm of his hand, would control the speed with his long and immaculately beautiful fingers. Only his government-issued driver's license had to be gotten through connections.

But the traffic cops that stopped him never even noticed that the driver didn't have a right arm.

My father wrote beautifully with his left hand; his handwriting was graceful, even if the letters always leaned to the left. He could screw in a light bulb, switch out a power plug, hammer a nail, install a tire, take out a battery and put it back in, all with one hand. How? I don't know. Only God knows. When his wonderful car got so rusty that the driver's pedal rotted through, he figured out a way to support it with a dust tray, and continued to drive that way . . . what of it, it was more interesting that way. He could fight off thugs who attacked him, asking for a light. He was well built, handsome, broad shouldered, elegant, and sharp witted. His colleague at the magazine *Friendship of Nations* had his left arm amputated when gangrene set in, and he fell into a profound depression, but Papa would comfort him. "Listen," he would joke, "you don't have a left hand, I don't have a right hand—just think of the money we'll save on gloves alone!"

Even my mother was almost proud that he was not like the rest. His missing arm was his badge of valor, glory, honor. He was like Admiral Nelson and she was like Lady Hamilton![14] I think that this had a retroactive positive effect on my father: he never associated himself with the terrible word "cripple."

That's probably how St Spyridon felt, too.

My father survived during the war seemingly by accident, but in reality it was through the miraculous help of St Seraphim of Sarov.

This was near Gdansk (or Danzig), where he, a nineteen-year-old lieutenant in command of an artillery battalion, went to battle against the Nazi tanks, after having stationed his troops in the walls of a half-ruined house that covered his guns from the rear. However, these tanks covered him with such heavy fire that the entire battalion, together with their guns, was devastated and blended with the earth. Papa was killed. The last thing that he remembers was a monstrous explosion, a burst of flame, and then everything was silenced and extinguished, and he blacked out. But suddenly, exactly as it is described by patients who have come back from a clinical death in Moody's book *Life After Death*, he discovered himself in a long open wagon rushing at breakneck speed along a tunnel, and suddenly he heard the sound of bells and saw a light ahead of him. Then an old man came out to meet him, blocked the way with his body, stopped the wagon, and said:

"Stop! Where do you think you are going? It's still early for you. You must go back."

And Papa came to on the operating table.

At that same moment when the Nazi tanks were obliterating Papa's battalion, his friend from the Artillery Institute, Pavlik Agarkov, also a nineteen-year-old lieutenant, who had occupied an elevated position several kilometers from the place of battle, anxiously listened to the distant thunder of that fatal battle. As soon as the sounds quieted down and darkness fell, he decided to go there at his own risk and peril to at least bury his friend and then be able to inform his mother later of the place of his grave. When he reached the half-fallen brick wall, he pulled out Papa's breathless and bloody body and dragged him to the nearest bush in order to dig a hole and commit the remains of his young friend to the earth. And while he dragged him, clumsily and with difficulty—he was himself of small stature, 1.6 meters at most, while Papa was tall at 1.82 meters—Papa's legs suddenly bent at the knees. Pavlik leaned over him, placed a mirror to his lips—he was alive! He dragged him to the nearest Polish village, where something like a medical unit was stationed. The doctor simply glanced at Papa and turned away, allowing Pavlik to understand that he had not survived and was not worth the trouble. But Pavlik put a gun to his head and said: get to work. The doctor began to explain that there was an enormous loss of blood, gangrene, he would have to remove the right arm, the case was hopeless. But Pavlik kept holding the gun in his hand and repeated: take my blood. So the doctor put Papa on the operating table and began to clean his wounds, repeating that the injured had one type of blood and Pavlik another, that it wouldn't do any good . . . and then the young Polish nurse, looking at Papa with pity and love, said in her Polish accent:

"So young! So handsome! My blood type matches his, take mine!"

So Papa regained consciousness on the operating table next to her.

Then, many years later, Papa and I were driving to Gdansk, explored the place and its environs, and found that field, that half-ruined red brick wall, and that wonderful woman, Marta Obegla. She had become a very respectable, fine-looking older woman, the owner of a beauty salon in the best neighborhood of Gdansk.

"But who was that old man who came out to meet you and sent you back?" I asked my father.

"I also wondered at first who he was: he seemed very familiar, like family, but I just couldn't recognize him. Then I understood where I had seen him—on an icon at home in our icon corner. That same icon had cured me of blindness in my childhood."

"And who was it?"

"St Seraphim of Sarov. My mother and grandmother always prayed to him especially, and considered him to be our family's patron saint."

I will also add: my paternal great-uncle—also named Alexander—believed that St Seraphim had also saved his family during the Leningrad blockade.[15]

My great-uncle thought that they all—his wife, two sons, and he himself—would die of starvation at any moment, just like the wife and children of his brother George, who was away at the front. He sat at night grieving in the kitchen. Then suddenly—and keep in mind that my great-uncle was no mystic, a realist by any definition, even a critical realist, a skeptic—St Seraphim appeared and said to him:

"Don't despair! I will take you away from here tomorrow."

The next morning, there was an announcement to immediately evacuate the department where my great-uncle worked as an engineer, and he was allowed to take his family with him.

Papa died in a diabetic coma on October 9, on the day of the apostle of love, St John the Theologian, in the Vidnoe city hospital, where he had been taken by ambulance from his house in Peredelkino. My husband and I (who was already a priest at the time) had literally come two hours before his death to administer holy unction. He lay unconscious on the hospital bed and breathed with difficulty, moving his dry lips as if he was trying to say something. After unction we went out onto the hospital steps. There, while I was still standing on the landing, unable to leave, I suddenly felt Papa's soul. It was like love itself, and I suddenly began to weep uncontrollably: my face was covered in tears that poured and dripped down.

It was like he was standing before me and telling me—or perhaps he really was there telling me—"Why are you crying? We will always be together now. We will be even closer than before, and nothing will part us," something like that. In that moment, I understood that he had died.

And now it grieved me that I couldn't put my mother and father in one car and drive all together along the sea there, in the south, beyond Kerkyra, to the little monastery of the Vlakhernskaya Icon of the Mother of God that was situated on an island: as always, my husband would have opened a map on his lap and directed me while I drove, and my parents would have simply rejoiced and wondered, looking out the window. They had loved to travel so much! In my childhood, we drove through all of Russia, Ukraine, Belarus, the Baltics, and Crimea in my father's car. I haven't shared a tenth of what my parents gave me with my own children.

* * *

In Kerkyra, we stopped at the icon shop where I had bought the blank CD claiming to have a recording of the Liturgy. I hoped that they would exchange it, but it was closed. At least the Church of St Spyridon was open. There was no service, but you could venerate the relics of the saint. I wrote down names for commemoration of the living and the dead in Greek and asked the priest to pray for them. Apparently, I had such an imploring expression on my face that he disappeared somewhere and soon brought me back several pieces of fabric in which the holy relics had been wound not long before. I was very happy: I had previously had a similar piece of the saint's vestments, and I would always lay it to the underside of my clothing before travel, until it fell apart. My friend, who considered that this was a form of paganism, tried to make me ashamed of that "talisman" or "protective charm," as she called it, but I defended myself by saying that since I loved St Spyridon, any item connected with him was precious to me.

I treasure Papa's chess set in the same manner, though half the figures are missing and the board is worn down. They are still precious to me because he held them in his hands at one time. As for the piece of fabric from St Spyridon, it was blessed on his relics. In short, I immediately attached it with a safety pin to the inside of my blouse. Because of that I felt more confident when driving back home to Agios Stefanos in the pitch-black darkness along the serpentine road from Kanoni, where the Monastery of the Vlakhernskaya Icon of the Mother of God is located. Wherever you go in Greece, you will find a holy relic, or a miracle-working icon, as in this tiny monastery on the island, or the relics of a saint—from the holy Apostle Andrew to St George the Trophy-Bearer, the Protomartyr Stephen, the holy Martyr and Wonderworker Tryphon, St Nicholas the Wonderworker, St Anastasia the Breaker of Chains, and the holy Martyr Thekla . . . The entire ground is imbued with blessed currents, life-giving energies, and healthy air. May God grant that we get our fill of them while we're here, that we breathe them in and partake of them as a natural state of being.

* * *

Yes, St Spyridon freely gave of his money to the needy when he had it, and to those who could become rich as a result, he gave it as a loan. Thus he gave money to a certain merchant who promised to return it once he bought the merchandise and had profited from it. And he did return it—the saint asked him to put it in some sort of chest. Then he needed the money again, and again asked St Spyridon. The latter said: take it. So the merchant took it and again returned it, placing it in that same chest. Then again, he asked and came back to return it, but this time he decided to be crafty: why does the saint need money, after all—and he didn't put the money back into the chest. The saint immediately realized it, but gave no sign of it.

Later, the following befell this same merchant, who by this time had become very successful: during a storm, all of his merchant ships sank, together with the goods they were carrying. He became completely impoverished. He came in his sadness and grief to the saint and asked him for money once again. The saint did not turn him down.

"Take it," he said, "from the same place where you left it last time."

The merchant crawled into the chest, which was, of course, empty.

Then he was seized with shame, dismay, and repentance, for it turned out that in deceiving the saint, he had deceived himself.

Well, if you pay attention, you will see that things always turn out that way.

My spiritual father told me that it's very good when a person immediately gets their comeuppance for their sin: the Lord is especially looking after them.

I immediately get my comeuppance in the most unusual and often even comical ways. Once, I was sorting my closet, and evil thoughts were filling my head. Suddenly the closet doors began to move back and forth, back and forth, and since my face was situated exactly in the middle between them, they ended up slapping me across the cheeks—to the point of bruising! But what astounded me most of all was when I tried to show my husband how it happened, I understood the physical and practical impossibility of such a unique face beating.

Another time, my son and I were walking one winter when he was a teenager, and he kept falling down because of his slippery shoes. I said to him rather strictly:

"Why do you keep falling? Strange, how is it that I never fall?"

But I didn't even have a chance to finish that last phrase, because my legs shot upwards higher than my head, and comically throwing up my hands in the air, I crashed down onto the ice with all my weight. My "never" only sounded out as I sat up on the sidewalk, and my son rushed to help me up.

* * *

But greed is such a tenacious sin, it brings such harm to the soul! How do you free yourself from it? Here it seems like I've been living a blessed life for the past three weeks—living in someone else's villa, swimming in the ocean, driving around in an expensive car—when suddenly a thought entered my head: wouldn't it be wonderful—fine, perhaps not this villa, so luxurious with its swimming pool and gardens—if I had my own house, at least a small one overlooking the sea, where I could come at any time . . . for my children, my grandchildren . . . at least that one being built next door. Or that other one, all finished and ready to be bought. There was a sign hanging on the fence with "For Sale" written in large letters. Interesting, how much were they asking? How could we scrape together that money? It would be nice if I got a nice inheritance from God knows where. What of it? Some rich and lonely great-uncle would be discovered at the last, only please not in Poland, where my great-grandmother Leokadia Vishnevskaia owned an estate called Schipiorno near Warsaw and where Papa and I had even met old Filippiak, who remembered the young mistress who had married the Russian colonel: they wouldn't give us anything in Poland anyway. Let's say somewhere in Germany: my mother's grandmother was born a baroness, and her last name was von Bishop. And this relative would say: "Dear granddaughter! Let me buy you a beautiful house in Corfu!"

Oh, how difficult it was to stop that dark and consuming stream of delusion!

One night, I took a flashlight and called my husband: let's go look.

We went out beyond the enclosure and, shining into the darkness with our flimsy flashlight, began to walk down the winding path to the house under construction. It was almost done, though it still stood without windows or doors. We went inside and up the stairs.

"The bedroom is here," I guessed. "Here is the bathroom, and here is the office."

From the hole in the wall intended for the door leading out onto the balcony, a sea view opened up. The stars shone in the sky. Little lights occasionally flickered through the thick of the trees on the distant mountain—that was the road to Agios Stefanos. An unbelievable silence stood all around—not even a cicada could be heard.

We began to feel uncomfortable standing there in someone else's unfinished house, completely devoid of people, our flashlight tilted forward.

"There is the swimming pool—it's rather small," I said, just in case.

We went down and came out onto the path, intending to investigate the second house that was being displayed for sale, but it already had doors and windows: everything was locked, and our flashlight began to act up a little.

Early the next morning, we saw a hedgehog crossing the path, an enormous bird with a blue head, red wings, and a yellow breast, and a snake warming itself on a rock. That night we saw enormous stars—a multitude of stars—and walked to an open space in the mountains from which you could watch the flashes of summer lightning: it was a thunderstorm in Italy, and it looked like it was heading in our direction.

* * *

My friend, the prose writer V., led a tumultuous, bohemian life. He changed cities and countries several times, as well as wives, one of whom he beat terribly out of jealousy, while he punched out his competitor's front tooth. He was almost summoned to court, but all ended well: he hired a good lawyer with the descriptive last name of Bucks and bought his way out of it. Then finally, in the twilight of his days, he "...returns full circle" (Eccl 1:6), sat himself down, and adopted the image of the repentant sinner. He had a wonderful son called Kolenka, a remnant of his former life overseas, whom V. himself called a "gift from the heavens": he was a meek and bright-faced youth.

Since he was a boy, Kolenka had served as an altar boy in the church, and was later accepted to the Moscow Theological Academy, where he studied with great success. At the mere sight of him, your heart would burst out singing "Axios! He is worthy! Axios!" to him. In general, everything suggested that he would soon enter the priesthood and pray for us all at the altar table with a pure heart. In addition, he had a girlfriend; they were like two peas in a pod—she was joyful and pretty, just like a ruddy, ripe apple.

He called her just that: my girlfriend.

"Can I visit you with my girlfriend? Can you give a copy of your book to my girlfriend?"

He introduced her to his father, his father's friends—everybody liked her, it looked like the wedding was not far off, then the ordination would take place soon afterwards.

So a month passed, another, half a year, a year . . .

I met him walking on the street, beaming.

"Kolenka, how's life?"

"Thank God! I was accepted to the Theological Academy . . ."

"And how's your girlfriend?"

"Just wonderful! She is so lucky! She got married—very happily and successfully—to my friend, a former classmate. He is a wonderful person, very spiritual, and sings so well! He's already been ordained a deacon. They just returned from Greece, full of impressions: they were at the relics of St Spyridon, St Andrew the First-Called, St John the Russian. I've dreamed of going there my whole life, but they described everything to me in such detail and so realistically that it was like I was there myself, saw everything with my own eyes, and venerated the relics myself. I still have that blessed feeling."

My friend V., commenting on this, said with both Kolenka and himself in mind: "God is free both to grow grapes on a blackthorn tree and to grow figs on a burdock plant!"

But still I asked him:

"Maybe Kolenka didn't really love that girl?"

"What do you mean, do you really not get it?" my friend said in surprise. "Of course he loved her, he even bought an engagement ring for her and consulted with me about it: 'Papa, you know better about women's tastes'; he was scared that she wouldn't like the ring he chose. But he didn't have a chance to give it to her: he was so shocked that he just walked around repeating: 'It wasn't meant to be, wasn't meant to be!' So he just brought the ring to the Mother of God: whether he made some sort of pledge to Her or was just seeking comfort, I don't know . . ."

* * *

My mother survived my father by seven years. In the beginning she was hurt by him, just like a child: "How could he go and just leave me here?"

Sometimes she even directed a rebuke at him: "Why, why didn't you take me with you! You just left by yourself!"

She suffered very much and began to go so blind that so she couldn't read anymore and could hardly walk; she just lay in bed or sat on the couch, developed gangrene, and almost had to have her leg amputated, but—thank God!—they were able to save it.

Then, a month before her death, completely helpless, she suddenly said: "You know, I thank the Lord for everything that He allowed me to learn and undergo these past seven years."

Her face became so illumined and her expression so open that she just looked like an oversized little girl.

"If you have any love in you, hold on to it with all your strength—with all your hands, with all your fingers!" and she smiled as if she was holding on to an earth-shattering secret. By now, she has probably revealed that secret to my father.

* * *

How wonderful life is here on the island of Corfu, after all! How unin-
hibited, how lovely! The locals stay busy by offering their hospitality to for-
eigners, sharing their joy with them and the beauty that the Lord gave them.
Or they grow fruits and vegetables. Or they go fishing. The taste of that
fish and those shrimp, mussels, calamari, octopus, and langoustine, freshly
caught and taken from the nets, is different from anywhere else, from Paris
to Moscow.

Our life is complicated and often artificial, but here it is natural and
simple. This is simplicity itself, with which St Spyridon—an uneducated
person, perhaps even illiterate—vividly explained the mystery of Divine
Triunity during the First Ecumenical Council before highly educated and
wise men. They were all arguing amongst each other, trying to convey it in
philosophical terms, but the saint got a brick and crushed it in his hand until
fire burst out heavenward, water streamed downward, and clay remained in
his hand.[16]

Well, now there were only a few days left until our departure, and we
drove throughout the blessed island again and again, lengthwise, across, and
all around. Again we visited St Spyridon and the holy Empress Theodora,
and again tried to return the defective CD, but again found the shop closed,
so I never got the chance to take the sounds of the local singing with me.
Meanwhile, the thunderstorm raging in Italy threw itself onto Albania and
finally crashed onto Corfu. The wind roared with such thundering bass tones
all night that we were frightened; it seemed to us that just so did God speak
to Job out of the storm.

* * *

The day after my husband came to visit me and I burned my hand while
frying *blini*, he said as we left the institute: "Let's go take a walk."

He took my hand in his and stuck it in the pocket of his fur coat, and
so we walked . . .

* * *

There was heavy rain that morning, but we could still drive to Kassiopi, turn toward the deep of the island, and ascend into the ancient village of Perithia, where there was once a multitude of churches, and where

everything—both houses and churches—stood in half-decay, while tourists feasted in tavernas situated among the ruins and shopped for items made from olives. We bought an enormous—it came up to the knees—wooden duck with feathers made from olive tree roots. The duck stood on its webbed feet, lifting up its polished beak, and looked heavenward.

In the old times, people chose places that were more or less removed from the ocean to live in, because pirates ruled the seas, and the settlements closest to the shore would suffer in the event of the pirates' debarking onto dry land. Perithia had, without a doubt, been a wealthy village: it had such expansive and solid two-story stone houses, inner courtyards, almost fortress-like walls, and churches. But the voice of God thundered out from the storm, and the place became deserted, the fields emptied, the roofs began to crumble, and the houses decayed.

While we were traveling, the rain kept falling and the roads became impassable, but we didn't realize this on the highway. When we turned off from the main road to our own Agios Stefanos, however, when the asphalt came to an end and was replaced with sand and clay chippings, we felt it very much. The car would constantly skid on the potholes, the loose covering of the road would crawl under the wheel, and I had to hold on to the steering wheel with all my strength because it was suddenly trying its best to wrench itself free and swerve off to the side.

I began to have dark misgivings: if the rain continued all night, then it could happen that in the morning, when we would have to drive on this same road to the airport and go up the steep hill, we could get stuck, or, losing traction, could slide all the way down. And in general, I thought, how frivolous it was of us to plan to leave for the airport early in the morning without a backup plan in case, for example, we got a flat tire, or we got stuck in this heavy clay, or our engine died, or if a snail of an Englishman was driving along at his ten kilometers per hour in front of us and we wouldn't be able to pass him. What would we do if our delay on the road would cause us to miss our flight? In any case, it was too late to think of a backup plan now. It was late at night.

That morning, at the crack of dawn, we loaded the car, and again the thought of all the possible accidents that could disrupt the easy drive in our car gnawed at me. I even examined the tires just in case. Well, OK: let's say that I would have seen something wrong, what then? There was no wrench in the trunk, no screwdriver, no spare tire. We packed the suitcases into the trunk, the olive tree duck into the car, and were off. I simply called upon St Spyridon in my mind to help us and touched the fabric from his vestments pinned to the inside of my clothing near my shoulder.

So, we made the first sharp turn, and now, pressing hard on the gas pedal, began the ascent, when hop!—another sharp turn, we slowed down, up again, upped the speed, careful not to press too hard and bury the tires in the clay. The car swerved but climbed on. Now we had to carefully pass over an enormous rock that threatened to pierce through the bottom of our car: "Holy Father Spyridon . . ." And . . . one, two! We jumped over it, and now the descent, and farther down—asphalt. Suddenly—an oncoming car: there was no room to pass each other, so we were forced to back up and press up to a fence on the right. I stopped, thinking it through. A young Greek looked out of the driver's window. I backed up and paused, allowing him to pass. The oncoming car moved and carefully, almost touching, passed us by—the Greek looked out of the window again and said something to us. I thought that he was thanking us. He was probably a construction worker from that house next to us where we had gone at night with the flashlight.

Well, the most important part was done. We drove onto the main road. In front of us was Kerkyra and not an Englishman in sight, no one at all. We drove and drove, throwing a parting glance over that already-familiar road—Sinies, Nissaki, Barbati. Suddenly, a man stood on the road waving his hands at us: stop! Stop!

"What does he want?" I grumbled, displeased. "I'm not going to stop, maybe he's a criminal."

"Have you seen any criminals around here? Stop. Anyway, I think it's the same Greek we rented the car from," said my husband.

I stopped. The Greek ran up to us, deeply worried. "You have a flat tire. This morning my brother saw you—you drove past him. He called me. You won't reach the airport like this."

I got out of the car—it was true, the left front tire was very flat. A little more, and the car would have thrown itself to the side. "What do we do?" I said, scared.

"I'll give you another car. Just leave it in the same place at the airport."

So we sat down and drove on. How amazing that the only Greek that we came across on that narrow road was the brother of the man who had rented us the car; amazing that he was able to notice the tire, amazing that he even recognized his brother's rental car, and that he wasn't too lazy to call and warn his brother. That the latter came out onto the road and blocked our way. There it was, my smothering night-terror, that dreaded flat tire! And how carefully and nicely St Spyridon arranged everything for us, how he counted everything to the minute, while I directed my prayers to him to prevent not only something terrible from happening to us, but even any difficult temptations.

So we returned home. In the end, I didn't do anything on Corfu, didn't write any short stories on love for the *Journal*, didn't bring back any keepsakes except icons of St Spyridon and the enormous clumsy duck carved out of olive wood with its head looking heavenward. I put it on the floor and saw how simple it was, how joyful, how happy. Its feathers, made of olive tree roots, boldly stuck out. I regretted not buying a second one: they could have stood together as a couple, next to each other.

The only treasure that I amassed there was a childish sense of the mystery of life, an amazed and wondering perspective . . .

And yet how I wanted to put something back into that sacred chest of St Spyridon from which I had taken so much. Just to open the creaking lid and put a treasure inside—let it stay there until that time when the heart would go begging and love would run dry. Then the saint would say:

"Child, go and find your treasure where you placed it."

A Short Reflection on Miracles

The philosopher Alexei Losev[1] examined miracles as the concurrence of two planes of existence that materialize in the plan for a single individual. This plan is the combination of the individual's predetermined outcome—i.e., God's plan for that individual, His creative idea—and the historical plan that unfolds with time and with the individual's evolution, which is the plan of destiny. These two plans suddenly combine in one inseparable image: The individual suddenly and for at least a moment—expresses and fulfills his prototypal image in full, he becomes that which immediately proves to be both the material substance and the ideal prototype. This is the true place for a miracle. A miracle is the dialectic synthesis of the two planes of the individual when he completely and thoroughly implements within himself the goal of the prototype that lies in the depths of his development.

Notes

In Lieu of an Introduction

1. This is a reference to the Trinity-St Sergius Monastery, north of Moscow, that has within its grounds the largest seminary of the Russian Orthodox Church.

2. This is a story told about St Anthony the Great of Egypt in the *Lives of the Desert Fathers*.

The New Nicodemus

1. A *matushka* is the wife of a priest or deacon in the Russian Orthodox Church.

Confusion

1. An *epitrachelion* is a liturgical garment worn by Orthodox priests and bishops around the neck and trailing down the front from the neck to the hem.

Monk Leonid

1. This is taken from the kontakion of *The Great Canon the Work of St Andrew of Crete* (Jordanville, N.Y.: Holy Trinity Publications, 2016), 11.

2. These are Russian and French writers and poets from the nineteenth and early twentieth centuries.

Another Source

1. *Samizdat* was literature produced and distributed without official sanction as its contents would not have been approved by the regime.

How I Battled the Gypsies

1. The prayer "Let God Arise" (Ps 67:1) introduces the Paschal stichera and is found in the section of "Prayers before Sleep" from *Prayer Book*, Fourth Edition–Revised (Jordanville, N.Y.: Holy Trinity Publications, 2003), 59.

2. From the Paschal stichera: *Prayer Book*, Fourth Edition–Revised (Jordanville, N.Y.: Holy Trinity Publications, 2003).

3. Zemfira is the main female character in Pushkin's narrative poem "The Gypsies."

Non-Komsomol Gingerbread

1. The Komsomol was the communist youth organization. Komsomol gingerbread is analogous to Girl Scout cookies.

2. The priest is referring to Mt 23:24.

3. This is said by the priest, during the Prayer behind the Ambo, at the end of the Divine Liturgy of St John Chrysostom.

At Blessed Xenia's

1. This refers to Lk 23:34, where Christ says of those who crucified Him: "Father, forgive them, for they do not know what they do."

The Hunger Striker

1. *Pirozhok* is a baked or fried bun typically stuffed with meat or cabbage.

Martyr Tryphon

1. An akathist is a devotional hymn that is sung in the Eastern Christian tradition. They are often dedicated to a saint or a miraculous event.

2. The Orthodox Church commonly refers to the sacraments, and in particular holy communion, as mysteries.

Criss-Cross

1. A *ryassa* is an outer cassock or cloak worn by a priest over his cassock.

2. Vladyka is a respectful, but informal, way to address a Russian Orthodox bishop.

The Queen's Pendants

1. His Holiness Patriarch Pimen was patriarch of Moscow and all Russia between 1970 and 1990.

Embrace

1. The root of each of these last names is a title of a church feast day in the Russian language.

About Love

1. A *Panagia* is a medallion bearing the icon of the Mother of God that is worn by a bishop. *Panagia* is a Greek word meaning *all holy*.

2. NKVD is an early name for the Soviet secret police.

3. *Vladychenka* is an affectionate diminutive of *Vladyka*.

4. *Oprichnik* was the term given to a member of the Oprichnina, an organization of loyal followers of Tsar Ivan the Terrible.

5. An "angel in the flesh" and a "man of heaven" are two different descriptive phrases widely used in Orthodox hymnology for ascetics and righteous ones.

Wishes Come True

1. Peredelkino was a writer's colony in the forest outside of Moscow.

2. This is a troparion from *The Great Canon the Work of St Andrew of Crete* (Jordanville, N.Y.: Holy Trinity Publications, 2016), 36.

More Than Enough or Nothing Extra

1. Pechory is another name for the Pskov Caves Monastery.

Come and See

1. The title refers to the scripture verse: "He said to them, 'Come and see.' They came and saw where He was staying, and remained with Him that day (now it was about the tenth hour)" (Jn 1:39).

2. Father Frost is a character from Russian mythology who is prominent in contemporary New Year festivities.

3. This is a reference to the retreat of the Napoleonic armies from Moscow in 1812.

4. This is a reference to the escape of the people of Israel from Egypt as recounted in Exod 14–15.

5. This is taken from a troparion to St Nicholas the Wonderworker.

6. This is a reference to a Russian folk song.

7. This is a liturgical text from the Blessing of the Waters.

Bring Back My Husband

1. *Perestroika* literally means restructuring. This term denotes the period from the mid-1980s when an attempt was made to reform the Soviet Union politically and economically, presaging its eventual downfall less than a decade later.

The Apple of My Eye

1. "Pops" is a slang and derogatory nickname for a priest.

2. An epaulent is a shoulder piece often indicating military rank. This saying implies that priests were secretly military or secret police officers.

3. The title of the journal *Nadezhda* means "hope."

4. Bulat Shalvovich Okudzhava was a singer-songwriter and sometime dissident of the Soviet era.

The Thrill-Seeker

1. Mt Elbrus is the highest mountain in Russia and Europe.

2. Communism Peak, now known as Ismoil Somoni, is the highest mountain in Tajikistan.

3. General Dmitry Karbyshev was a lieutenant general in the Soviet Red Army. He was captured by the Nazis and held in various concentration camps. He was executed in 1945, after he had cold water poured over him and was left outside to freeze on a winter night.

The Sound of Trumpets

1. This refers to "Impossible" by I.F. Annenskii.
2. Papa Carlo is the Russian version of Geppetto from the story of Pinocchio, *The Adventures of Buratino*.
3. From the proskomedia: *The Divine Liturgy of Our Father Among the Saints John Chrysostom: Slavonic-English Parallel Text* (Jordanville, N.Y.: Holy Trinity Publications, 2015), 31.
4. Ibid., 103.

"Our Boys" and "the Germans"

1. The NTS was a group of anti-communist Russian emigrees founded in Serbia in 1930.
2. Yuri Andropov became chairman of the KGB in 1967.
3. Those who are "sprinkled" with holy water in baptism are called "*oblivantsy*," while those baptized by full immersion, or "immersed," are called "*pogruzhentsy*"—Trans.

Five Months of Love

1. Anna Akhmatova was a twentieth-century Russian poet who remained in the Soviet Union.

Mysteries beyond the Grave

1. Panteleimon (Nizhnik), *Eternal Mysteries Beyond the Grave* (Jordanville, N.Y.: Holy Trinity Publications, 2012).
2. From the rite chanted following the departure of the soul: *A Psalter for Prayer*, trans. David James (Jordanville, N.Y.: Holy Trinity Publications, 2011), 328.

Augustine

1. Mowgli is the feral child from Rudyard Kipling's *Jungle Book* stories.

The Lord Gave and the Lord Took Away

1. "The Lord Gave and the Lord Took Away" is an allusion to Job 1:21.
2. Birch and other twigs are used in the *banya* (sauna or steam bath) to massage the skin and open the pores for cleansing.

Halvah

1. In the Russian language, the word "*khalva*," or "halvah," is very similar to the word for "glory," "*khvala*."

How I Lost My Voice

1. Dante Alighieri, *The Divine Comedy*, Rev. H.F. Cary, trans., Cassel and Company, Ltd., London: 1892.

Money for Sabaoth

1. "Protopope" is a Russian way of writing Protopresbytr, the title given to a senior priest in the Orthodox Church.

2. "The Beslan terrorists" refers to a school siege perpetrated by Chechen Islamists in September 2004 in the town of Beslan in North Ossetia in southern Russia that resulted in hundreds of deaths.

Kalliping

1. The quote refers to a Russian counting rhyme.

Good Material for a Television Series

1. This is a famous quote from the Russian movie *The Twelve Chairs*.

A Blessing to Smuggle

1. Sainte-Genevieve-des-Bois is a southern suburb of Paris, France. It became a major center of the Russian emigration after the Bolshevik seizure of power in 1917. The Russian House served as both a retirement home and a center of Russian culture.

2. Sheremetevo was at that time the major Moscow airport for international flights.

3. "Joyful steps" refers to the 5th Ode of the Paschal Canon by St John of Damascus.

4. This is a quote from the epic poem *Ruslan and Liudmilla* by A.S. Pushkin.

Payback

1. EMERCOM is the Ministry of the Russian Federation for Affairs for Civil Defense, Emergencies and Elimination of Consequences of Natural Disasters.

2. The "horn of Jericho" refers to Joshua 6 when, after the blowing of horns, God caused the walls of the city of Jericho to fall, allowing the Israelites to enter.

The Delusional One

1. "Overcome the order of nature" refers to the Dogmatic Theotokion in the 7th tone.

2. This is a quote from Friedrich Nietzsche translated from the Russian.

3. Renouncing Satan is part of the baptismal service in the Orthodox Church.

4. This refers to Mt 5:37: "But let your 'Yes' be 'Yes,' and your 'No,' 'No.' For whatever is more than these is from the evil one."

The Little Cloud

1. *Chakra* is a Sanskrit name used in the Hindu religion to refer to the centers of spiritual energy in the body.

The Late Husband of Mother Seraphima

1. The Babylonian captivity is a way of referring to the Soviet period where the situation of the Church was comparable to ancient Israel in the pagan Babylonian empire.

2. The Russian PEN Center is the Russian branch of an international organization that promotes literature and freedom of expression.

3. Grand Duchess Elizabeth Fyodorovna is better know as St Elizabeth the New Martyr, sister-in-law of the last Tsar.

4. A.S. Pushkin, "To . . . (Kern)." This translation was obtained from *From the Ends to the Beginning: A Bilingual Anthology of Russian Poetry:* russianpoetry.net—Trans.

5. Ibid.

6. Nuns are referred to as "the brides of Christ," as they have no earthly husbands and are considered to be wedded to Christ.

7. A *metochion* is a dependency of a main monastery.

8. A *kolobok* is an imaginary being from a Russian fairy tale.

9. Peter and Fevronia were a thirteenth-century couple seen as patrons of love and marriage. In their last days, they entered monastic life but asked God to take them to eternity on the same day.

Heavenly Fire

1. This refers to the prayer that is said before the distribution of holy communion. It can be found in *The Divine Liturgy of Our Father Among the Saints John Chrysostom: Slavonic-English Parallel Text* (Jordanville, N.Y.: Holy Trinity Publications, 2015), 213.

Corfu

1. This is a reference to Homer's *Odyssey.*

2. The Manege is the Moscow Central Exhibition Hall close to Red Square.

3. The Aleksandrovsky Garden is a public park between the Manege and the Kremlin.

4. Corfu is off the coast of Albania. Under the rule of Hoxha (1944–1985), Albania was a military, atheistic, communist state.

5. Illyria is the ancient Greco-Roman name for the area of the west Balkans that broadly corresponds to the territory of the former Yugoslavia and Albania.

6. Boris Pasternak is a twentieth-century Russian author famous for such works as *Dr Zhivago.*

7. A *panikhida* is a memorial service for the departed.

8. A bast house is one made from tree bark or other fiber of certain plants.

9. The evacuation referenced here is most likely in the face of the advancing German army.

10. Earlier in the book, the author refers to her godmother's husband as Gennadii Snegirev, a famed children's author.

11. Pushkinskaya Square is a very busy central Moscow meeting point.

12. Lawrence Durrell was a famous novelist, and Gerald Durrell was a naturalist, author, and TV presenter. They were not born in Corfu but in India and lived on Corfu at a later age.

13. Though the author states that Lawrence Durrell received the Nobel Prize in Litera-

ture, he was only a candidate, along with John Steinbeck, the actual winner.

14. Admiral Lord Horatio Nelson is best known for his service in the British navy during the Napoleonic Wars, losing his life at the battle of Trafalgar. Earlier in his career, he had lost sight in one eye. Lady Hamilton and he were lovers, and they had a child together.

15. The Leningrad blockade was the period between September 1941 and January 1944 when St Petersburg was besieged by the German army.

16. This is the way St Spyridon conveyed that the Holy Trinity is One God in three persons.

Appendix: A Short Reflection on Miracles

1. Alexei Losev, 1893–1988, was a prominent twentieth-century Russian philosopher.